T5-AFS-711

COMPLIMENTS OF EUGENE'S FRIENDS,
DON GOODMAN AND MARY BETH LAKIN

Moments With Eugene

...a collection of memories

MOMENTS WITH EUGENE

...a collection of memories

Edited by Rebecca Barrett and
Carolyn Haines

KaliOka Press
Semmes, Alabama

Moments With Eugene Walter

Library of Congress Cataloging-in Publication Data

Moments with Eugene: a collection of memories / edited by Rebecca Barrett and Carolyn Haines—1st ed.
    p. cm.
   ISBN 0-9663954-1-7
    1. Walter, Eugene, 1921-2. Authors, American—20th century—Biography. 3. Walter, Eugene, 1921- --Friends and associates. 4. Mobile (Ala.)—Biography. I Barrett, Rebecca, 1949 – II Haines, Carolyn.

PS3573.A47228 Z78 2000
818'.5409—dc21
[B]

                                                        00-035711

FIRST EDITION First Printing, 2000

Front cover artwork by Eugene Walter
Back cover photo by Renée Paul
Cover Design by Aleta Boudreaux, LOP Design

KaliOka Press, Inc.
2486 Ellen Drive
Semmes, Alabama 36575

www.kaliokapress.com

KaliOka Press would like to thank the Alabama State Council on the Arts for their generous grant, which helped in producing this book.

The kind words and encouragement of the Council members and Jeannie Thompson, director of the Alabama Writers Forum, were invaluable in this two-year project.

We also thank the contributors, who gave of their time, talent, and memories with no remuneration to help create this volume. They joined in with great spirit and generosity.

The book could never have been started—much less completed—without the guiding hand of Nell Burks, Eugene's lifelong friend, and the executor of his estate, Don Goodman, and his wife Mary Beth.

Thanks are also due to photographers Stephen Savage, Jason Thompson, Renée Paul, and many others whose names have been lost over the years.

The Squiggles are, of course, by Eugene Walter, many from the collection of Joseph Sackett.

The unpublished short stories by Eugene Walter were generously shared by Ted Dial.

Book design (and yeoman attention to detail) is by Hamilton Boudreaux of LOP Design. Thanks, Hamilton.

Michelle Roberts and Cammie East read the galleys fast and furious and did their best to correct our errors.

And a special thanks to literary agent Marian Young for advice and encouragement.

for Jim
who always takes me seriously

B.

Like so many good ideas, the seed for this book came several years too late—if only we had thought of this when Eugene was alive, when we could have asked him whom to contact. But it wasn't until after his funeral that we sat down and talked about collecting some of the wonderful memories that Eugene gave so freely.

That was two years ago. It hardly seems possible that Eugene has been gone that long.

The idea for the book was that it would be a double mirror. Through each story, the reader would be given an image of Eugene. Then that image would be illuminated by the knowledge of how that person knew Eugene. By looking beyond the reflection cast by each writer, Eugene, through the alchemy of his own personal magic, would be found. In reading over the pieces, we're amazed at how close Eugene feels, at how he ultimately allowed himself to be revealed.

This book has given us intense pleasure, and we can only hope it works as effectively on each reader. Those who knew Eugene will certainly recognize him in many different lights. Those who didn't have the pleasure of knowing him will, we hope, share a glimmer of his magic.

He was a gifted and generous man, and everyone who contributed to this book has been touched by him in a special way. We count ourselves extremely lucky.

Eugene Walter at the Haunted Book Shop, Mobile, Alabama
(Photo courtesy of Renée Paul)

For Those Who Will Never Know Eugene
April 3, 1998
Trendy Questions

What will you do with the time at hand
Sail a ship
Speak a quip
Till the land
Kill a man

What do you see in the flower, there
Something to cut and wear in your hair
Something to bind and take to your lair
Something of beauty, something that's fair
Or cut it back and fertilize
Strip its leaves or memorize
Whine because the work is there

When have you really used your eyes
Looked at another, answered cries
of those who specialize in dreary
complaining they are weak and weary
drag their feet and sigh and moan
Hold their heads and cry and groan
when you're up they drag you down
Come, let's make a paper crown
Head erect! Let's plan a fête!
Merrily, merrily buy the food
Choose the music, set the mood
Who shall we be, what will we do
It's all at hand for me and you
Light the candles, build a fire
Within yourselves and bring the lyre
to pluck with Puck, the clown as we
dance through the sky and stars and flee
from hopeless, helpless who must learn
the secret! Resurrection Fern
on oak trees ancient in Mobile
Just send the rain and turn the wheel
Behold the brown that looks so dead
When watered quickly lifts its head
And greens the limbs of mighty trees
as laughter grows whenever squeezed
and we'll burst forth in mighty roar
Each moment we create new joy.

Nell Echols Burks

Virginia Adair

When my husband was head of foreign operations for an American company, we lived in Rome for ten wonderful years. There I could pursue my career as a portraitist, inspired by the beauty of the "Eternal City,"—and there I had the opportunity to know "Eugene the Unique."

I am the author of *Eighteenth Century Pastel Portraits* (1972), and *Women of a Higher Nature* (1998)—both published in England. Blessed Eugene was always so supportive, though I'm not sure the subject matter of either particularly interested him. What a friend!

I first met Eugene Walter in Rome in the '60s at a party on the Appia Antica. It was an *instant friendship,* and a week later he called to invite my husband and me to dinner in his apartment on the Corso, adding ever so casually, "Oh, by the way, afterward I'll be presenting my cats in ballet." I hung up, wondering if I'd heard correctly.

Along with several other guests we arrived on the appointed evening to be greeted by a slightly distracted Eugene who announced, "Oh, my dears, the stove is broken—-you *do* know how things break down in Rome—but we'll work something out—"

And "work something out," he did!—for a half hour later he emerged from the kitchen and placed before us a flawlessly cooked, delicious meal. We all caught eyes in wonder.

"Bunsen burner?" someone suggested.

"No-o, I just rubbed two sticks together like any good Boy Scout," was Eugene's unruffled reply. (It was only later that I learned our host had been commissioned to write *American Cooking Southern Style* by Time-Life, and was, along with his myriad other talents, a world-renowned chef.)

Soon surfeited with the impeccably prepared food and a series of accompanying wines, we were nonetheless admonished, "Now, no getting drowsy, dears, we're all descending to the cats' quarters for coffee. They're waiting for us."

"Is he *serious*?" my husband whispered.

Joining two apartments together, Eugene had added a circular stairway down to the rooms below. Soon we were all seated on low, comfortable sofas awaiting the performance we'd been promised. Plaintive strains of *Swan Lake* emanated from an unseen source—-I looked questioningly at Eugene. "Oh, yes, *classical* ballet—always," was his solemn reply. With that, he flung open a door and out came an assortment of undistinguished-looking cats who scampered about the room in no particular order while Eugene shouted hyperbolic flatteries above the din of *Swan Lake* as they passed before him—"Beautiful, beautiful, sheer perfection—now, all together, 'Glissade,' 'Glissade'—"

To the unbiased observer they were just a group of undisciplined cats, chasing themselves around a crowded room after being cooped up all day, but by now Eugene had us so completely mesmerized we began to imagine we were actually witnessing a *spectacular* performance of feline virtuosity!

We left the two-storied condominium on the Corso well after midnight and reluctantly stepped back into the real world, quietly aware that, for an evening, we'd surely been touched by magic.

Jan Zimlich

Jan Zimlich's interest in books and writing began early, about the time she graduated from reading Nancy Drew mysteries to *Lord of the Flies* and *The Adventurers*. Life just wasn't the same after that, and she soon developed the urge to write commercial fiction.

She began her career writing science fiction stories but soon began crafting romance novels which contained elements of both science fiction and fantasy. Her first book, *Not Quite Paradise*, was published in 1995 by Leisure Books, followed by *Heart's Prey* in 1998. Her third, *The Black Rose*, will be released by Leisure in June 2000. Presently, she is working on a mainstream science fiction novel, as well as another fantasy-romance for Leisure.

Ms. Zimlich lives in Mobile, Alabama, with her husband, teen-age son, and a very large mutt named Nathan. She is also a member of the increasingly notorious Deep South Writers' Salon.

Monkeys, Mayhem, and Spanish Moss

I'd heard the stories long before I met him, all those outrageous "Eugene tales" that had drifted around Mobile for as long as I could remember, anecdotes told and re-told so many times that a curious gumbo of fact and fiction had long since merged into local lore.

I didn't believe a word of those tales. Of course, at the time, I hadn't met Eugene, either.

But all that changed some years back when local writer Carolyn Haines invited me to join her and Eugene for an early lunch. The prospect both thrilled and terrified me. I'd never eaten with a legend before. How should I act in such rarified company? What could I say to him that wouldn't sound inane or downright silly? Especially from me, a neophyte writer still struggling to find my way?

On the appointed day, Mobile's very own "legend" shuffled through the door to Hemingway's restaurant wearing a pseudo-Nehru shirt, rumpled khakis, a pair of well-worn house slippers, and an overlong jacket that looked suspiciously like a man's bathrobe. His faded hair was parted on the side with crisp, military precision, the wind-tousled bang created by that part dangling over the top of heavy, horn-rimmed glasses. Even from a distance I could see that an arm of his glasses had been re-attached to the frame with a scrap of adhesive tape.

I must admit, I was a bit startled. This was the internationally acclaimed Eugene Walter? He didn't quite fit the role of living legend that I had conjured for him in my mind.

As he sauntered toward our table, I noticed an unopened bottle of wine tucked securely beneath his arm, a definite uh-oh in most restaurants. To my knowledge Hemingway's wasn't a bring-your-own-bottle type of establishment, and I doubted very much if the State of Alabama would look kindly on a patron deciding to make it one.

Eugene called out to several acquaintances in a sing-song voice as he passed their tables, flourishing the forbidden wine bottle for dramatic effect. By then, everyone in the restaurant was aware of Eugene and his bottle, including a stiff-faced waitress who tried to head him off at the pass. The expression she wore was chilly, to say the least. For a timeless moment, the Hemingway's lunch crowd lost interest in their food and watched the scene unfolding before them, waiting somewhat gleefully for the waitress to kick the eccentric old man and his bootleg wine out the door.

I realized then that my first face-to-face meeting with Mobile's literary icon was about to come to a swift and ignoble end. I also realized, without a shred of doubt, that every outrageous tale, every outlandish story that I'd ever heard about Eugene Walter, was probably true.

But somehow, some way, Eugene managed to cajole, wheedle, and browbeat that poor waitress into bringing a silver bucket of ice to our table to chill his bottle. She then supplied us with wine glasses, did the honors of popping the cork, and poured. All very professionally. Even eagerly. She even seemed to flirt with him on occasion.

I was dumbfounded—and more than a little intrigued. How had this outrageous old man with the impish smile and manic eyes managed such an incredible feat?

Not long after that lunch, I was called upon to transport Eugene to a dinner party being hosted by Carolyn Haines at her farm. The evening started pleasantly enough. On the long ride out to the hinterlands of west Mobile County, Eugene entertained and amused me with tales of his life, of street vendors hawking fish and shrimp in old Mobile, the monkey which took up residence at his boyhood home, the streetscapes of Paris and Rome. He talked, and I listened, enthralled by the vivid imagery he managed to create from thin air.

Eugene also gave me my "name" on that ride, which I've always considered a rather dubious badge of honor. He dubbed me "Miss Spanish Moss," immortalizing the corkscrew curls that spiraled down to my shoulders, a hairstyle that appeared to amuse him endlessly. But once Eugene bestowed a "name," one could never be un-named. Eugene informed me as well that he was an expert at deducing people's ancestry, and that at some point in time one of my relatives had obviously dallied with a Romanian, which accounted for my physical appearance. (My Irish-Scots parents were very surprised by that bit of wisdom.)

The guests at Ms. Haines's farm that evening were a quirky assortment of local writers, Mississippians, and two New Orleans authors who were, ostensibly, the guests of honor. One was writer O'Neil de Noux, a very dignified former police detective who now writes crime novels. The other writer shall forever remain anonymous, though if Eugene were alive today, I'm certain he would happily divulge his identity.

Within minutes of our arrival it became painfully apparent that this nameless writer was, quite frankly, hideously drunk, and had been in that condition since departing New Orleans earlier in the day. As the evening progressed, the fellow regressed, de-evolving to a state only a small notch or so above Neanderthal on the evolutionary scale. He was obnoxious, insulting, and in general a very large pain in the derriere.

During dinner his behavior deteriorated even further, to the point that he began hammering the wooden tabletop with his fists, demanding what any red-blooded Neanderthal considered his due. Of course such behavior did little to endear him to anyone there—especially the women, who would have collectively given the man his "due" with sticks and knives if his friend hadn't once been a homicide detective.

But Eugene was positively gleeful that a total stranger had done such a remarkable job of turning himself into a social pariah, and spent the rest of the evening shamelessly egging the poor fellow on.

Eugene even went so far as to teach him the dubious merits of baying at the moon. An hour-long duet followed, a beastly serenade that's emblazoned on my memory forever. Renée Paul, another local writer, received her "name" that night as well. Eugene dubbed her "Gazelle," immortalizing what he called the "gazelle-like grace" exhibited as Renée darted from room to room, fleeing the drunken caveman's unwanted attentions.

Mercifully, the party finally ended, and I was able to hustle my charge into the car for the long drive back to midtown Mobile. Eugene sat beside me in the dark and cackled all the way home like some evil imp, gleefully recounting the evening's misadventures as well as the sly hand he'd played in setting the stage.

He *was* an imp, I decided that night. Cunning, lovable, and very, very naughty. But he was also kind, compassionate, and far too generous for his own good, freely giving his time and talent to the incredible hodgepodge of two- and four-legged strays who wandered in and out of his life. I feel privileged to have been a part of that hodgepodge, and to have had the opportunity to share in a few of Eugene's misadventures. And I'm very honored to have been able to call such a naughty imp my friend.

Francis X. Walter

Francis Xavier Walter, III was born in Mobile, Alabama, December 22, 1932, the child of F. X. Walter, Jr. and Martha Marsh Walter. He is the first cousin of Eugene Walter, Jr. He graduated from Murphy High School in 1950, Spring Hill College in 1954, and earned a Master's of divinity from the School of Theology at Sewanee, Tennessee. He was a tutor and fellow at the General Theological Seminary in New York City, 1957-1959.

Ordained to the priesthood by the Episcopal Church, Francis Walter has served parishes in Alabama, Georgia, and New Jersey. He worked in the area of racial justice and community organization in Alabama from 1965 to 1972. He developed and operated residences for mentally retarded adults for St. Andrew's Church in Birmingham from 1973 to 1985 when he became rector of that parish, retiring in 1999.

He enjoys collecting antique electric fans, writing, gardening, and salvaging things no one else wants. He aspires to ride in a blimp or, much better, one of the NT design airships being developed by the long-dormant Zeppelin Company in Friedrichshafen.

Perhaps my first memory, not just of Eugene, is a dreamy recollection of Little Gene and our grandfather Franz holding me up to the windows of a second floor gallery. It was night. Around Christmas. The house was the one my parents and grandfather were renting on Park Avenue in Mobile. The excitement Eugene and Pop radiated made me remember.

"Look!" Little Gene said. "Snow!"

I saw nothing but night beyond the panes, but then I didn't know what snow looked like. Only a few flakes fell, I guess. There is no memory of anything unusual outside the next day. My recollection has to do with how intensely they wanted me to experience something. "Look!"

Look, see, open your eyes. That was Eugene. That was a gift. For me he was a revealer, a door opener. Well—door cracker is better. He pushed his hearer's imagination to join in the revelation.

In 1960 I visited him in Rome. My mother, Martha, had been dead for six years.

"Tell me about her before she married Daddy, Gene," I asked, for he had known her then.

"Martha," he said. "Red silk stockings, long cigarette holder, elegant."

Then he drew me a little picture of my mother and Richebourg Gaillard smoking marijuana, staring at a bare light bulb to attain enlightenment. That was a vision! Even though I'd known from newspaper clippings and family talk that Martha had raced outboards in a Gulf Coast women's division— that's how she met Daddy, on a wharf, he helping her out of her boat, Golliwog—even so, dull convention was making me forget that and only know her as family cook, organist, and altar guild member at St. Paul's Church in Spring Hill.

That was all he said about her; said we'd have a real talk some day. We never did. Thank you, Gene. That was enough. During that visit to Rome, Gene went rummaging through one of his many file cabinets to show me something. I saw a file, "Little Francis." In the family he and I were both "Little" because we'd been named after our fathers.

"Lemme see that," I said.

"Ooooh no!"

He wouldn't show it. Revelation, but just enough.

The earliest photograph I have of Little Gene is a snapshot from 1937. He was fifteen. He was staying with us for a few days at our place on Mon Louis Island, which we'd named "The Camp." Our grandfather Franz, my parents and I had moved there from Park Avenue shortly before. There had been upheavals aplenty for the Walters in the '30s. Before the Depression my grandfather, whom I called "Pop" and Little Gene called "Pa-pa," operated Walter Produce Company. It had been located near Government and Broad, but at this time it was on Commerce Street where Pop, Big Gene, and my teenage father worked. Little Gene and his parents lived across the street from our grandparents' house on Bayou Street. Our grandparents' side yard abutted the back fence of the Semmes house on Government Street, over which fence the Admiral's two daughters and my grandmother, Annie, would visit. Gene's remark, "I learned to walk to run away from home," refers to his crossing Bayou to visit his "Ma-ma" and Rebecca, the cook, and their kitchen—visits vividly depicted by him in the preface to *American Cooking: Southern Style* in the Time-Life *Foods of the World* series.

But there was a darker reason to cross Bayou Street. There was trouble in Little Gene's house. I'll return to that later. To talk of pain in Eugene's life is difficult, almost a betrayal of his own absolute refusal to do so.

After the crash, Franz Walter lost his company, Walter Produce. That put Big Gene out of a job. My parents married early in 1932, and having no money, they moved into the Bayou Street house with Pop. There was room; Annie Walter had just died.

I was brought to Bayou Street from the hospital in December 1932. Within months of my birth the house was sold; my grandfather and parents moved to their rental quarters on Park Avenue. Eugene's world on Bayou disappeared.

My speculation is, that at ten years of age, his moving from place to place began. Or perhaps he lived with us a year or two on Park Avenue, where he told me to look for snow. But Park Avenue did not last long for any of us. There was just no money. Once the water was shut off. Martha called my father at work. She didn't have water to fix my formula. Daddy, the machinist, told her how to take a wrench to the meter. She began to cry. She was crying because she was ashamed. Daddy told her not to be ashamed, that half the people in Mobile had their water turned off today and the Water Works wasn't paying any attention to people turning it back on themselves.

It's said my mother suggested our move to Mon Louis Island. She figured we'd at least have enough to eat at the place on the Bay where people fished for a living. Daddy could barter engine repairs for fish. Pop could have chickens and a garden again. We could crab, fish, shoot ducks and *poule d'eaux*. Daddy could drive the twelve miles into Mobile every day to Mobile Cylinder Grinding. We could survive.

They did this by trading grandmother Annie's "cut flower garden" out near Crichton for "the Camp" on the Bay. The place was just down from the mouth of Fowl River. I own a snapshot of the cut flower garden, heavy with rows of flowers, and I have Little Gene's memory of Annie and Rebecca returning to Bayou Street on the trolley, arms loaded with blooms.

As I sit writing, I can look up at a color Xerox copy of a watercolor Gene sent me shortly before he died. It is titled *View of Mobile Bay from Front porch of Franz Walter's Fishing Camp on Mon Luis Isle* (watercolor c. 1936 by Eugene Walter). The Bay is flat, calm, blue-gray; a fuzzy line of green indicates Montrose to the east. Between the beach and the front gallery, where the painter sat, are shade-dappled patches of sand and grass below and a heavy arch of tree leaves above. Not a bad trade for the cut flower garden. Years later I heard my mother say, "Little Gene wanted to move down to Mon Louis Island with us."

"Why didn't he?"

"Your father didn't want him to."

I still don't know why, and there is now no one to ask. Eugene did not share in all that the cut flower garden provided.

So the snapshot of 1937 shows a visitor to Mon Louis Island. He is crouching behind a rimless wagon wheel, hiding half his smiling face behind a spoke. In another picture I keep framed, he is in his *8 1/2* linen suit standing in a passageway in Rome, face half concealed by a crumbling wall. The fifteen-year-old—it was surely the day of the rimless wheel—took me, a five-year-old, up the log-and-water, hyacinth-strewn beach to the Cut Off, the "new" mouth of the Fowl River designed by the Storm of 1906. At this point the land rose so that the Bay was undercutting a small bluff, making caves beneath the roots of pines and live oaks until they toppled into the water. Under one of these grottoes we sat on sand and I heard stories. The stories I do not remember, but the love expressed through imagination I do remember.

Gene lived here and there but not with his parents. His mother, Muriel, had her interior demons. We saw this slight, quiet woman on Christmases, but only after Big Gene died, never before. Then only cards came on Christmas, no return address, postmarked New Orleans. Then, nothing. My father made inquires in New Orleans with no results. Little Gene never asked us about her. I don't know how many people took him in. The Gayfers, I know. Charlotte Robinson cared for him. The Plummers gave him a back room in The Haunted Book Shop, which he decorated with blood red handprints.

When I attended Spring Hill College (1950-1954) my advisor, J. Franklin Murray, S.J., asked me to edit the literary quarterly, *The Motley*. I read back issues to figure out what it was. There was Gene's name as an editor. "Father Murray, I didn't know my cousin went to Spring Hill."

"He didn't."

"But look, he edited *The Motley*."

"Well, the Jesuits let him live out here for a while. He was talented, so he edited *The Motley*."

How Gene must have appreciated this now extinct academic laxity; he who hated comma counters, rule makers, fact collectors.

It should be apparent now that the brothers Francis and Eugene were estranged. I sensed it quite early, but the emotions around the subject were so charged, so buried, that I never asked why while living with my parents. Then at age fifty I got up the courage. It's now or never, I thought. My father was losing out to the one Gene called "Baron von Alzheim." On a visit to Mobile I managed to get out, "Daddy, was Big Gene an alcoholic? Is that why you all didn't get along?"

"Gene an alcoholic? No. Where'd you get an idea like that?"

The answer to that was most likely the conditions surrounding the only time I ever saw my uncle, though the facts didn't warrant such a conclusion.

By 1939 we'd moved from Mon Louis Island to Spring Hill so I could begin first grade. Mon Louis Island had a one-room schoolhouse for Creoles. Mobile went just a little beyond simple segregation. It had exclusive schools for Blacks, Whites, and Creoles. So we moved. One day Pop took me downtown from the Spring Hill house on his rounds as a drummer for Arata Produce. Daddy said Pop had the distinction of being Mobile's last downtown, on foot, produce drummer. He was around eighty at this time. Some said Arata didn't need him but kept him out of respect for an old competitor. This was the only time he asked me along. Goodness, what did he tell my mother?

We went to a saloon where we met Big Gene. I was introduced. Big Gene and Pop had mugs of beer. I had a soda pop. I was dimly aware that my grandfather was doing something that was important to him. I felt included and secure. A year later Big Gene died. The year 1940 is clear because of a question of propriety that was discussed and settled. My parents would both go to the funeral, but not me. But would it be proper for my mother to take me to the Roxy Theater to see *Fantasia*? It was decided that would be allowable. An unknown rite called a funeral I couldn't attend, the memory of an uncle I'd only just seen in a saloon, images of *Fantasia,* and the news that only the Roxy had the sound equipment necessary to show it, are all filed into one memory. I was told Big Gene died of blood poisoning brought on by opening a pimple on his nose. Was that true? I don't recall hearing whether Little Gene attended the funeral.

"I thought maybe he drank a lot," I replied.

My father, always an inoffensively uncommunicative person, became animated. "Big Gene was a gambler. Pop covered his debts. All the time; 'til it broke him. That's why he lost Walter Produce."

"I thought it was the Depression."

"Naw. It was gambling. Pop gave him everything. Never said no. He was going to inherit the business. One day when I was working down there I figured it out. So I just walked out the door, went on down Commerce, walking. I saw a man in a shop working a metal lathe. That was Al Payne. I went in and watched, didn't say anything. I can do that, I thought. I got real interested in the piece he was cutting. Al said, 'Could you operate it a minute? I've got to go to the bathroom.' I finished the cut, then cleaned it up real nice. He came back. 'I was trying you out,' he said. 'You're good. Would you like a job?'"

Daddy and Al Payne formed a partnership, and the Mobile Cylinder Grinding Company lasted long on Commerce Street, years after Walter Produce folded. I do know Daddy had been sent to Birmingham-Southern College but returned after one semester when there was no more money. It must have been soon after that he took his walk and presumably left his brother out of his life.

These are only hints. My father and Little Gene would have been the best sources of information about Big Gene, Muriel, and my grandfather. I waited too long and Daddy was reluctant. As to Eugene, I never once heard him mention his mother and father, but he had many expressive ways of communicating: don't go there.

After Big Gene's death in 1940 I don't recall seeing Eugene until my mother and I, alerted by the newspaper, attended a reception at the Haunted Book Shop on the occasion of the release of *The Untidy Pilgrim* in 1954. We did receive a copy of *Monkey Poems*, the 1953 Édition's Finisterre printing. It is inscribed: "For the Walters, To Spring Hill from Paris and all good wishes from Eugene Feb., 1954."

I had no idea until years later that Eugene had joined the Civilian Conservation Corps before the Second World War. Did he later tell me, or did I see in something he wrote that he joined "to eat?"

Out of his CCC experience came the unusually poignant story of him as coffin lid painter for rural Mississippi families. That story came to mind while my brother, David, Don Goodman, and I were negotiating the price of

Gene's coffin at a funeral home—a bizarre thing itself deserving of its own story.

So it came about that David transported Eugene's coffin to the Masonic Hall in his pickup truck. Paints and chalk were provided, and we invited mourners to decorate the coffin. Unexpectedly, it came to resemble a Mardi Gras float. I recommend this custom to Mobilians, if not others.

One of Gene's prescient friends at the wake pulled me aside and said, "He's not in there, is he?"

This was a practical, non-theological, question. It's not easy to lie at a wake. "No," I said, "he isn't." Time had not allowed the funeral home to put the body in the coffin before David arrived; surely, Gene would have approved.

A mourner he would also have enjoyed deserves a mention. I saw him veer toward the entrance of the Masonic Hall. The sort of opportunistic veer I am, as a downtown parish priest, familiar with. I had on my collar, and after my invitation to start painting, Ramon asked to speak to me. He identified himself as a person of such extraordinary lineage that I've forgotten it exactly, something like "Dominican on my mother's side, Hungarian Jew on my father's side." Tearing up Ramon said, "I loved your brother."

"Cousin."

"Cousin—he always had time for me. I could tell him my troubles. Never turned me away."

Ramon expatiated on this theme at length, then he slipped. "Often, I would go to his office to tell him my troubles. He never turned me away."

Office! I thought. Ramon, you scoundrel! You almost had me. Eugene, in an office! I thanked Ramon for the family. I just had to tell David about Ramon, who was still looking tearful among all the other rather upbeat mourners.

"Oh, him," said David, "he's been hitting people up for five dollars. One guy told him he didn't have any money and Ramon said he'd take a check."

So I told Ramon he could eat all the food he wanted, but if he panhandled any more people I was going to kick his butt out of there.

But back to earlier, happier memories. During World War II a carefully tied parcel arrived at 3804 Austill Lane, addressed to me. It was from the Aleutian Islands and from Little Gene. In it were rounded rocks and a variety of grey-green lichens. Each rock had been carefully selected to capture a facet of the beauty available to rockness. Each fit the hand and begged to be handled. Included was a *Survival Manual* booklet for air pilots shot down anywhere from the Arctic to the South Pacific. A more un-

Eugene book could not exist. I could not imagine my cousin planting a sharpened stick in the sand for wrenching the husk off a coconut, constructing traps to garrotte small animals or boiling lichens for soup. It was a box from a sorcerer, who it seemed, would not forget me.

I visited Gene a second time in Rome in the late '60s. I was itching to tell him about meals I'd had in Gees Bend and Alberta in Wilcox County, Alabama. During the Civil Rights Movement I helped start a black women's quilting cooperative called The Freedom Quilting Bee. Eugene, through the amazing oddball telegraph system oddballs subscribe to, heard about it in Rome. He wrote and enclosed a logo for The Freedom Quilting Bee, a drawing of a honey bee with quilt block wings.

I told him my Wilcox County eating stories over drinks in the apartment. My favorite was how to prepare a skunk to eat if you really had to. A few years later I found on page one hundred twenty-one of *American Cooking: Southern Style*, my account gloriously augmented, true to the characters and the cooking, but a little left of the facts. Eugene had placed himself in Gees Bend, though the facts say no, and even created what my friends certainly would have said to him and what some minor players would have said, had they existed. This is an insight into the truth Eugene lived for, the truth that religion, art, song, sensual delight, and deep respect for human beings manifest.

Time to wind up. When Little Gene returned—cats and boxes—to Mobile, we were able to entrust to him his dear Ma-Ma's worn cookbook and one fork imprinted "Frohsinn," the Frohsinn being our grandfather's German-American singing, drinking, and eating society. I can recall, as I know Gene could, sawhorses, planks, and tablecloths set up outside the kitchen steps of our Mon Louis Island home, covered with boiled shrimp, oyster loaf makings, potato salad, French bread, and beer, and around this a bunch of old Germans in wool suits, singing.

Eugene was dealt some bad cards in the family game. I have touched on that, but insofar as this recollection treats Eugene's adversities, it is a piddling thing. Because Eugene's soul-gifts dwarfed negative family circumstances. He would not hear or speak of them. I concluded my eulogy for Eugene at the Cathedral by quoting part of a prayer from the baptismal liturgy of the Episcopal Church. It is a prayer for God, in the person of the Holy Spirit, to give the one baptized "the gift of joy and wonder in all your works." Gene had that gift in superabundance, and he shared it generously with me and all who allowed themselves into the circle of his enchantment.

Doris (Mrs. Hal S.) Wheeler

After years of heading the Timbes & Yeager Advertising Agency, Doris Wheeler recently retired. She has known Eugene almost all of her life and has been a great admirer and supporter of his work. She was instrumental in helping to put together the Renaissance Man celebration, which honored Eugene for his many talents.

She is the former Doris Smothers.

Moments With Eugene

My friendship with Eugene began over sixty-five years ago when we were children. It's difficult to think in terms of "moments" with him—our moments were full-blown adventures, productions, excursions, and celebrations!

How does one pluck a moment from remembrances of plays, puppets, props, poetry, painting, pirouettes, pomegranates, and parties?

Perhaps with the very first peck ...

We must have been about ten years old, and he was maybe two years older when my best friend, Mary Lee Tibor, and I met "Gene." Mary Lee and I were upstairs at "Miss Aimee" McCormick King's Three Arts Studio, a dark and musty place way down on St. Francis Street, I think. (Because of Gene, I learned to love those old buildings in downtown Mobile.) We had come for costumes for a play, *The Yankee Dime*, in which we had little skip-on, non-speaking parts. It was to be held at The Little Theatre.

"Miss Aimee," an imposing little figure in high heels with raised eyebrows, called for *"Eugene!"* with fine projection, pointed to a room across the hall, and shoved us that way, all at one time. On our own, we peeked into a darkish room filled with stuff, and as we stood wondering what to do, out from under a pile of material popped a wickedly impish smile wearing a plumed hat, announcing, "I'm Gene."

When we told him we were "going to be in the play," he started humming and tossing through the pile—a "lilac" sateen dress for me and "daffodil" yellow for Mary Lee, all the while giving a running commentary on the meaning of flowers and colors. (The dresses, of course, were only shiny purple and plain old yellow costume material, but Gene, with his magic, made us see them as he did.) I knew I didn't understand half of what he was saying, but it was fun to be completely under his spell, joining him in a different kind of silliness.

At some point, one of us must have asked him what "Yankee Dime" meant, and without a word he popped up and kissed each of us lightly on the cheek. When asked if *that* was a Yankee Dime, he replied gleefully, "No, that was only a nickel—but two of them make a dime!"

Lee Weatherby Partridge

Ms. Partridge was one of the co-founders of the Mobile Civic Ballet, which made its home in Mobile from 1955 to 1967. She currently lives in Natchez, Mississippi, where she teaches ballet, is involved with the opera, helps with tours of historic Natchez during various annual events, and is active in other civic and artistic functions in that city.

Although I didn't know Eugene that well, I felt I did through his close friend Nell Burks, and my high school French teacher, Annie Lou White.

In the early '50s I was a ballet student at the School of American Ballet in New York. One evening I was returning home from class feeling just a bit homesick, when there in a bookstore window was featured *The Untidy Pilgrim* by Eugene Walter. Using money I really couldn't spare, I rushed in and bought the book. I stayed up half the night reading and loving that book. I realized then that besides the people I missed, it was all that "craziness" that is Mobile that I couldn't wait to return to!

Lewis Bushnell

All my professional life I've written, photographed, and produced training and educational movies, videos and slide shows. In 1967 I moved to Rome and founded Rena Productions specifically to create audio-visual educational programs. Eugene Walter collaborated with me on several of those projects, including *The Cities of Europe* and *The Poetry of Homer*. Back in New York, I continued to produce industrial and educational films, including the 1979 CINE Golden Eagle winner, *Gold: the Sacred Metal*, filmed entirely in Colombia, South America. A few years later I returned to Boston and worked as instructional designer, photographer, and writer for Digital Equipment Corporation. Now retired, I had my first gallery exhibit of photographs (some from the European years) last summer (1999) at the Once and Only Gallery in Wellfleet, Massachusetts.

Here's to you, Eugene

One day, while working our way through a traffic jam in Rome, Eugene said to me, "My idea of perfect love is to be locked in the honeymoon suite of a luxurious Paris hotel with a human-sized cat." It was vintage Eugene—giving the same emphasis to fleeting thoughts of fancy as to the noise and clamor at hand.

I met Eugene Walter in Rome in 1966. I was from Boston. He was from Mobile. He understood life in the Eternal City much better than I did, and he served as my mentor. His Southern roots and poet's imagination instantly related to the rhythm, myth, and magic of Mediterranean life.

Eugene was also a host and collaborator. And no one hosted like Eugene. I spent years of evenings on his terrace where celebrities and corporate minions mixed comfortably at his legendary salon dinners. Those nights were magical and we all felt like they would go on forever.

As a mentor and collaborator, Eugene was pure creativity. He believed I would make fine photographs before I knew I could. Working with him— as I did on several educational film programs—was at once exhilarating and frustrating. He lived in the present. He had no feelings for deadlines. Life was definitely the journey, not the destination. Once, when he promised to bring me a long-overdue script, he infuriated me by arriving instead with an eggplant. Without batting an eye, he told me how important a photograph of that vegetable would be for our project. He was right.

We took a driving trip through Italy to research and photograph locations for a film series on Homer. He saw magical images everywhere. He was as at home talking to Umbrian shepherds as he was to local artisans. At lunchtime he could enter any restaurant, befriend the host, discover the chef's specialties, and order the best wine—all before I had parked the car.

"Here's to the voyage of Odysseus' tall ship and to the wine-dark sea," he said as he raised his glass. And with that he led me on a journey through the poetry of Homer that still sparkles in my imagination. When we finished that difficult project, I felt relief and loss at the same time. And I feel a loss now.

So here's to you, Eugene. Surely you're still journeying somewhere. I hope you know that your fanciful brand of magic touched us and changed us, and even now, after your passing, helps light our way.

Mary Donald Sheldon

I was born in Mobile and have lived here most of my life, but I was raised in Africa. For nearly two years I thumbed my way across "the Dark Continent." When I got home—enter E.W. into my life in a big way.

I remember E.W. kissing my hand during intermission at the opera one night. I must have been thirteen or fourteen. He said, "Dahling, what is your name? I can't remember—you've done something different with your hair. You women are always out-foxing me, changing your hair all the time." That was the first time anybody ever called me a woman.

Eugene had given a puppet show for my Aunt Marie and Uncle John's fifth and sixth birthday party. He had made the puppets, set, and written the script. He was a high school student at the time, and my family adored him. In that way we were kissin' cousins, Mobile style.

I like to think of him as Santa and I was an elf. I would drive him to the bank, post office, to Adelaide's to deliver a turkey carcass to her cats, and all around town to inspect junk piles, or to the Dew Drop Inn for an afternoon Heineken, all the while telling African tales.

I can still hear Big E's voice..."Dahling, you have got to write this stuff down. Get a stock of good paper and just start. Write in the mornings when the brain is fresh and do it. You are like a sponge, and it has got to be squeezed out."

I am still not a writer, but I do tell stories and, honestly, that is how Eugene and I found each other's souls.

On Eugene

One night Eugene and I went out to see a movie and have a late supper. He and I never spoke about our understanding—I always paid his way. This, I think, was the case with most of Eugene's friends. Any "Grant" to the E. W. Foundation was graciously accepted, because as rich as Eugene was, he had very little cash tender.

Making our way home that night I was taking us up Old Shell Road, headed toward Grand Boulevard. Just as we passed the entrance to Blacklawn the treetops parted. Eugene sighed and said, "Ah, look at that boat ... stalled in the sky."

I looked up to see the bottom half of a moonlit gondola. I soaked up those wonderful words and knew this was one of those precious moments with my genius friend that I would remember forever—his way of paying me back for our evening.

Tom Perez

When I first met Eugene I was thirty-five, already finished with my first ten-year career teaching college English and just beginning a seven-year career as a stockbroker.

Six years after meeting EW, I took his advice, long before Nike stole it, "Just do it!" So I chucked the brokerage business and started "The South of the Saltline Theatre…of Comedy, Satire, and Deeper Meaning."

After giving away too many box-office proceeds to Mobile charities, and after sliding into bankruptcy, I should have taken some other EW advice, but it wasn't relayed to me 'til six years later via Frank D. [Daugherty] (EW often gave advice through a third party). Eugene had said to Frank, "After the Saltline went under, Tommy shouldn't have hung around Mobile trying to eke out a living. He should have left immediately for Paris, stayed eighteen months, and then returned home triumphant."

By the time I received the advice via Frank, I had been living in Saudi Arabia two years earning tax-free petrodollars teaching English. After nine years total, I'm still in Arabia—content to live abroad, relishing my solitude, grateful for income tax exemptions.

The second year I was here, I called Eugene on his birthday, November 30, at ten p.m. Having just returned from a birthday dinner at the Ivory Chopsticks with his hostesses, Becky and Joanne, he answered the phone breathlessly. When he recognized my "Eugene!…It's Leopold!", he put his hand over the receiver and gave a stage whisper to Joanne and Becky: "It's Saudi Arabia!"

Not "It's Tommy calling from Saudi Arabia" because it wasn't so much Tommy calling but rather another exotic location calling to send EW birthday greetings.

And so once again, dear Eugene, on the occasion of this tribute you so richly deserve, feel free to tell everyone in earshot: "It's Saudi Arabia."

Eugene Walter: Life Intervened

When I first met Eugene Walter at Termite Hall in April 1979, only a month after he had returned to Mobile from thirty years in Europe, he stared a hole through me. It was unsettling, but later I considered it a compliment when I realized that was his way of sizing up folks he thought he might like to know and with whom, eventually, develop a friendship.

We became friends. More than friends, we were colleagues in the arts and intimates, as intimate as Eugene would allow anyone to become with him. But I had the edge over his other friends in that I was his favorite drinking buddy. And he mine.

When I was a stockbroker in the early '80s, once a week I'd take a long lunch hour to take Eugene around on his weekly errands, the ones he hadn't finished on Saturday after shopping for groceries with another chauffeur, Eleanor Benz. Before Setting Out, we'd have the ritualistic glass of port, and then off to Waite's Dry Cleaners, the ABC store at Upham and Old Shell, and usually to drop off a column at a staff member's house from the *Azalea City News and Review*, which meant Eugene sat in the car while I ran up and dropped the manila envelope behind the screen door.

Our final stop, the most important, was the K&B drugstore at the Loop to pick up The Baby, a half-gallon of Paul Masson Burgundy. "Red wine is essential for proper digestion, you know!"

Our lunch was usually at the Ivory Chopsticks, that superb but now defunct restaurant across from Little Flower School on Government Boulevard. Not only was the Vietnamese food superior, but due to a petition from a Baptist church across the street, the restaurant couldn't get a liquor license, and Monsieur Casanova welcomed any customer bringing his own brown bag. In our case the bag from the K&B was purple.

After M. Casanova greeted us and took our purple bag as nonchalantly yet as carefully as if he were relieving Madame of her sable stole, he disappeared into his tiny bar and filled a liter-sized carafe with the burgundy. As Monsieur filled our goblets, Eugene would always remind him to be sure to "leave The Baby uncorked so she can breathe properly." The fact that The Baby had a screwcap instead of a proper cork didn't seem to faze the Corsican Casanova, since he had learned months earlier that if he kowtowed to Eugene the Ivory Chopsticks would get a glowing review in the *ACNR* at least six times a year. Madame Casanova (Bernadette) deserved it. I can still taste her shrimp and pork in caramel sauce.

Casanova learned exactly when to return to refill the carafe. He never brought The Baby to our table—*gauche!*—but whisked away the empty carafe while we were still nursing a half glass of wine until he returned with the filled carafe.

After a hot lunch and a quart of wine in my belly, I would drive Eugene home for his obligatory nap and then arrive at my brokerage office at three p.m. to return phone calls just as the markets had stopped trading. Although my secretary had been trained to tell clients on the phone that I was "entertaining a Very Important Client," I'd always have to deal with some nervous Nelly slighted that I hadn't been there keeping an eye on the ticker tape, usually a small investor who provided me with meager commissions but expected me to call Citibank in New York to find out why his twenty-five-dollar dividend check for his one hundred shares of Alabama Power arrived a day late in the mail.

Eugene had a money market fund with my brokerage house into which he deposited small checks from ASCAP royalties—usually from songs he had written for Fellini films. When I explained to him that *he* was the Very Important Client whom I entertained once weekly (although I never put him on my expense account), he was amused and flattered: "Well, I doubt that any of your clients receive royalties of any kind, so I guess I really am a Very Important Client ...I like *that*!"

When the Riverview Hotel took on a new chef who revamped their dinner menu, they invited nine food reviewers for a taste dinner. To find nine food reviewers in Mobile, they had to invite someone from every rag that ran a Recipe-of-the-Month, and they did. Since Eugene needed a chauffeur, he informed the Riverview that he was bringing along his Editorial Assistant, our private joke since at that time he nearly quit the *ACNR* when Mignon Kilday tried to edit his columns. We sat at a round and spacious table in a gleaming, spotless kitchen surrounded by stainless steel everything.

We tasted nine entrees over a three-hour lunch. The chef had defined "sample entrees" as two lamb chops, a whole quail, a medium-sized rainbow trout, a quarter of a chicken smothered in some deadly white sauce, and five other sample entrees of equal size. Obviously it was too much food for one person, or *would* have been too much had they not also served lubricants.

The wine list had also been revamped and, to Eugene's delight, needed tasting. We were served seven wines, each one complementing a certain entree, and a champagne with dessert. Most reviewers had one or two glasses of wine and then simply took a sip of the others so they could review them. Since Eugene had suspected we'd be "tasting" wines, we didn't bring

The Baby and felt obligated to drink a full goblet of all seven wines plus the Rather Fine champagne.

On Eugene's right sat Tommye Dunigan Miller who reviewed restaurants for the *Mobile Press Register.* As Eugene tasted each wine, she waited with notepad and pencil in hand for his opinion, herself not tasting any of the wines, explaining that her paper had a policy that if an employee had even a single drink at lunch, he wouldn't be allowed to return to work but must take the afternoon off. "What a civilized policy!" Eugene bellowed as he threw back the last of a Rather Superior Chardonnay. "In that case, *dahling*, you must drink up!"

Before the Alabama Shakespeare Festival moved to Montgomery, they operated out of Anniston where they mounted their superb productions on a high-school thrust stage. Since Eugene had given them glowing reviews as well as feature articles promoting them in the *ACNR*, Anniston's Movers and Shakers behind the theater decided to honor him with a cocktail party before a Saturday night performance. I was chosen to chauffeur him the seven hours to Anniston.

We arrived in Anniston on Friday night so we could rest up on Saturday and be fresh for the party and the performance. Saturday we slept in at the motel and found a Baby to lubricate lunch. After a long and leisurely lunch, we returned to our separate motel rooms for a Nap. Neither of us thought to set an alarm nor ask for a wake-up call. We were due at the cocktail party at six-thirty.

I awoke from my nap a bit groggy in a strange bed. When I realized where I was, I called Eugene's room and woke him up. Simultaneously we checked our watches and hung up quickly. It was six forty-five. Neither of us shaved nor showered, but both remembered to brush teeth and gargle. We met at the car in almost identical white summer suits, his seersucker, mine linen, Eugene wearing an ascot, and I sporting a wide-brimmed Panama hat. We looked stylish yet stubbly decadent.

In the car trying to speed to a leafy subdivision while reading a hand-drawn map, I asked Eugene how he would explain our being forty-five minutes late. "I'll think of something," he mused. "But don't ask me to fool with that map. I need to concentrate."

When we arrived at the party, still daylight, several thirty-ish lawyer-types and their wives were standing in the front door scanning the street for an unfamiliar car. I followed Eugene up the walk, trying to emulate his nonchalance. What would he say? What *could* he say? We had delayed these people forty-five minutes and all of us had only thirty minutes to make it to our theater seats in time for the curtain to go up.

The hostess, whom Eugene had never met, rushed forth, champagne glass in hand, and gushed quite sincerely, "Where *were* you? We were so afraid something had happened!"

"Oh, *dahling,*" he shook his head in bewilderment as he reached for her champagne glass, "Life intervened."

She let out a great sigh of understanding, swept us both through the front door and began introducing us to sixty adoring guests, all of whom claimed the *Azalea City News and Review* was their favorite newspaper in the whole state of Alabama.

After the Shakespeare Festival moved to its palatial site in Montgomery, four hours closer to Mobile than Anniston, Eugene was able to review more productions. On one of our trips up there, I picked him up at seven a.m. so we could get there in time for the two p.m. Saturday matinee. He was waiting on his curb at 161 Grand Boulevard holding several shopping bags of exotic picnic food and standing next to a small ice chest. As soon as we Set Out, he instructed me to remind him when we were *exactly* halfway to Montgomery. I didn't ask why.

He sat with hands folded in his lap, patiently enjoying the ride, pointing out endangered wildflowers, yet reminding me not to forget the halfway point. Finally, when I checked the odometer and said casually, "Well, we reach halfway in one mile," he became excited. "Pull over! You must pull over immediately!" I was doing seventy miles an hour on Interstate 65.

Luckily we were half a mile from a rest stop. When the car came to a halt, I wondered what he was up to. I suspected some sort of ritual, perhaps lighting a votive candle to St. Christopher for getting us halfway there safely. Or some kind of voodoo ceremony.

He reached into the ice chest at his feet and pulled out two champagne goblets and a split of a Rather Nice California champagne from the Vine and Cheese. Sitting in the rest stop at nine a.m. surrounded by truckers and tourists, we raised our glasses to toast. "What are we toasting, Eugene?" I asked warily. "Well," he did his fey thing, "the *halfway point,* silly!"

As his close friends know only too well, Eugene wasn't always that much fun. Like most of us, he could be trying, demanding, obstinate, and irrational. My worst trial with Eugene was enduring his designing *and constructing* "scenery" for the Delchamps play.

I would never have started The South of the Salt Line Theatre... of Comedy, Satire, and Deeper Meaning, without Eugene's encouragement. I was forty-two years old working as a stockbroker (somewhat successfully), married with a thirteen-year-old daughter and a nine-year-old son. I knew that someday I *would* have a theatre to produce my own satirical plays, but I felt I had to wait until my son finished high school, nine years later, until I could try something so risky.

In 1985 I had a reading from an excerpt from *Ambushed by the Holy Majority* at the Lumberyard Cafe's "Second Saturday Series" in which Eugene played a bumbling Birmingham mayor. It received a table-thumping ovation. Later that year we read the entire play, book-in-hand, at the Mobile Theatre Guild, again to great ovation from an audience delighted to hear such outrageous attacks on Alabama politics and society. Eugene said, "You can't wait. You've got an audience. Just do it!" Three months later The South of the Salt Line Theatre opened its premiere production of *Cockroach Hall* with Eugene playing two roles, the dowager playwright and the flighty Queenie who needed her bourbon to soothe a cough caused by Gulf Coast humidity, both female roles. He was brilliant. In the program both roles were identified by female pseudonyms. Few in the audience knew that the same actress (actor?) was playing two roles.

Two years later the theatre was riding high, but Eugene was dissatisfied with our sets. He said they were too realistic, that they weren't "fun." He wanted crepe paper and squiggles. I tried to explain that in the five hundred seat theatre at St Paul's High School, squiggles would hardly be visible. But he insisted he would design and hang the scenery for *Those Debs and Dandies at Delchamps* so that the supermarket would reflect all the "fun" in the aisles and the parking lot.

When I tried to explain that we had only three days to mount a set at St. Paul's, it didn't faze him. So when I received a seven-thousand dollar corporate contribution from Delchamps, I allocated five hundred to Eugene for his services as Set Designer, and I paid for an Assistant to help him get started in a rented garage six weeks before we were to move into St. Paul's. Meanwhile the carpenter had the set mounted and painted. The scenery was nowhere to be found. Nor Eugene.

At dress rehearsal he finally arrived with an armful of cardboard cutouts. Of course, they were charming—brightly painted mackerel for the fish market, dancing radishes for the salad bar, and seductive cheeses for the deli. They were to be suspended from the lights with nylon fishing tackle, and he would supervise the hanging. But we were in the middle of dress rehearsal, so the carpenter worked patiently on a high-rise ladder way past midnight with Eugene waltzing across stage instructing him to move the parsnip over "just a smidgen, about two inches."

When the dozen pieces of cardboard were in place to his satisfaction, we turned the stage lights up full and checked them out from the rear of the theater. They looked skimpy. It was too late to remove Eugene's name from the program as "Scenery Designed and Created by Eugene Walter." He blamed me. I didn't give him enough time. The Assistant was undependable. And besides, he had been interrupted by "one of the publishing problems from New York where I had to be on Long Distance for just days!"

We opened the play the next night with these cut-outs barely visible past the third row. The *Mobile Press Register* reviewer said the scenery looked skimpy. After four performances Eugene appeared with twelve more cutouts. We hung them silently.

A year later, when I thought the Delchamps scenery fiasco was well behind us, Eugene and I were pulling up to Waite's Dry Cleaners involved in a disagreement because I wouldn't produce a French farce he had translated and I knew would lose money for the theater. Then I made the mistake of venturing, "Besides, you don't have enough time to finish the translation and you'd leave me in the same fix as the Delchamps play."

"The Delchamps play was your own fault!" he snapped. "You didn't give me enough time!"

"You had all the time in the world! You procrastinated, as always!"

"You know your problem?" he lowered his voice. "You try to control people. You're a cross between Minnie Mouse and Svengali!"

"Two of my favorite people!" I quipped. "And you know *your* problem? You don't drive! So hush up, get out, and get your laundry!"

He slammed the car door in a controlled huff, dashed into the laundry as I busied myself with my To Do list. When I looked up, he was emerging from the Rebel Queen, his laundry in one hand and a foot-long hot dog in the other.

As he got into the car, he handed me the hot dog. "Here! Eat this. You'll feel better."

Eugene never thought much of William Faulkner, referring to him disparagingly as the Great Man, a writer who believed his own press. But Faulkner said one thing that I value and used again and again when I became exasperated with Eugene: "We don't love people *because* of what they are, but *in spite* of what they are." And in spite of it all, I loved Eugene. Still do.

Eugene Walter (on floor) and Ed Davis work on the set of "Angel Street," the first play produced by the Joe Jefferson Players in 1947.
(Photo courtesy of Lucille Davis Egan)

Sue S. Hawkins

Sue Hawkins, who has been a supporter of the arts in Mobile for many years as well as an active participant in the performing arts, first met Eugene Walter when a mutual friend asked if, upon his return to Mobile, she would allow him to stay as a guest at the Holiday Inn which she and her husband owned and operated. Fortunately she was able to say yes, and Eugene and his cats were guests of the hotel for several months. (A stay not likely to be forgotten by the management and staff of the hotel.) Little did she know that this would be the beginning of a friendship which would last from the time of his return to Mobile in 1979 for almost twenty years until his death in 1998.

Travels With Eugene

One of Eugene's most endearing traits was his sense of adventure in even the smallest activities. I was always delighted to get a call announcing "Da'ling, I've just heard about a fantastic—(person, place, event—take your choice)—that we must go and see."

Once it was a woman over the bay who raised herbs. We explored the wilds of Baldwin County for ages, finally stopping in Silverhill to ask at the barber shop if anyone knew where she lived. The looks we got made it clear that the assembled cronies wondered what kind of "herbs" those crazy people were looking for. I'll admit that finding her was somewhat anti-climactic after our search. She was just an ordinary woman with herbs for sale. Although she did have as much hair in her armpits as Eugene has claimed, it wasn't braided.

Another trip was to an abandoned pottery that he'd again been told was in Baldwin County. This was not quite so difficult to find and we only drove up and down two or three roads before finding the right one. It was a delight— dirty and loaded with trash. We climbed in through a broken door and found it filled with all sorts of interesting ceramics. We loaded up with our favorites, leaving notes specifying exactly what we'd taken, our names, addresses and telephone numbers, and offering to pay if anyone would contact us. No one ever did. As we started home, we were giggling about how the law officers must be searching for the ceramics thieves. As a friend who was with us lived in a somewhat unsavory neighborhood, her husband insisted that she carry a pistol in her purse. Eugene decided that if the police caught us while looking for the ceramics burglars, we'd simply tell them that the desperado in the back seat had pulled her gun on us and forced us to take her out to the river to grab the loot. Fortunately, that wasn't necessary or other friends might have had to bail us all out.

Sometimes we went farther afield than Baldwin County. On one such occasion Eugene and I set out for Montgomery to the state archives. Of course, for that longer trip Eugene insisted that we take a picnic lunch and a "little port" to break the trip. When we reached the Perdido exit on the Interstate, we decided we'd visit the winery or at least the grape arbors. We picnicked under the grape vines and had our wine with the chicken salad sandwiches. As we were cleaning up to leave, I picked up the now-empty wine bottle, but Eugene stopped me with, "Oh, no, Da'ling, we'll leave that here as inspiration for them," as he gestured about the arbor.

I do so miss the interesting people, places, and things that Eugene was constantly finding and his wonder in little things like a flower growing in a crack in the sidewalk in front of an abandoned building. My life has been greatly enriched because of him, and I like to think that perhaps my sense of adventure and wonder has also increased because I knew him.

Margaret Ellis

Margaret Ellis is a native Mississippian with a long history in writing and journalism. Her careers range from her first job as a reporter on the Meridian, Mississippi, *Star* to teaching writing at both the high school and college level, writing a weekly newspaper column, and working in public relations. She has published many magazine articles and had a byline in the *New York Times*. A member of the Press Club of Mobile, Society of Professional Journalists, and Public Relations Council of Alabama, she brings her long and wide experience to her newest venture, Magnolia Mansions Press. One of the books published under their logo in the past year is *The Shamrock Diary*, written under Margaret's pen name, Megan O'Meara. Their latest release is *A Widow's Might* by Carolyn Ellis Lipscomb.

I Remember Eugene

He may have remembered the last time he saw Paris. I remember the last time I saw Eugene Walter. It was at Barnes & Noble's Christmas special for local authors, held on a chilly overcast afternoon in December 1997.

Eugene and I sat together as a crowd gathered and conversations developed. He was dressed in his usual comfortable slippers and casual shirt and trousers. As always with Eugene, the conversation was as soft and comfortable as his attire. Suddenly he looked at me and said, "We've known each other so long. When and where did we first meet? I can't remember."

I immediately knew exactly when and where it was, but I paused and let the old memories come back. After graduation from Ole Miss, I went to Atlanta to work for Eastern Air Lines. Later, I had been transferred to Mobile. I rented an apartment on Dauphin Street, down from Trinity Episcopal Church, and decided to attend that church. Upon joining the choir, I met Jeanne deCelle, daughter of Mobile's famous artist Edmund deCelle. The deCelles, Ed and his equally talented wife Katherine, son Ed and Jeanne, had a family friend named Eugene Walter. They often spoke of him, but I did not meet him for a while. The deCelles frequently had gatherings of local artists, writers, painters, and friends, and soon I was invited to attend them. I was an aspiring writer but mostly using my English and journalism degree producing magazine articles, news releases, and public relations pieces. My friendship with Jeanne, who later became the godmother of my son, was my ticket to the events.

This was in the early '50s and many of the get-togethers were held at a delightful place owned by Aimée McCormick, another friend of the deCelles. She had a lovely house on the wide part of Dog River called "River Home," which had previously been in the possession of the Gayfer family of department-store fame. A patron of the arts, Mr. Gayfer had the house built with a long, rectangular living room which opened off a wide screened porch across the entire front of the house. Double bedrooms with baths between were built on either side of the main room. At the far end of the living room was a raised dining room with three steps leading up to its level. It was, as intended, a natural stage, and many performances took place on those "boards."

I arrived for one of the parties a little late one Friday night, and Eugene was on stage "orating." When I asked who he was, someone said, "That's Eugene Walter. He's something else."

And, indeed, he was something else. For Eugene all the world was always his stage, and River Home was made to order for him. The deCelles' gatherings continued, and everyone had a marvelous time exhibiting various talents. (My contribution was playing the guitar and singing old English ballads.) We usually stayed the entire weekend enjoying each other's company and the peaceful surroundings. Groups of us would walk along the river bank, and sometimes we would take the canoe out on Dog River, which was clear enough at that time to see almost to the bottom.

Eugene was always ready for conversation and ever ready to take to the stage in some part of a real or created "play." Sometimes he would read a poem, or talk about his writing. He was working on his novel, *The Untidy Pilgrim*, which was published for the first time soon thereafter. He was always fun and entertaining, and just as in his later life, it was comfortable to be in his presence. He projected the idea that life was a great adventure, meant to be enjoyed. There was every indication in those, his salad days, that he was bound for glorious things. He did not disappoint us. He left such a lasting impression in those early '50s that years later, when I heard of his many accomplishments, I was not at all surprised. I had known him "when."

Eugene and I renewed our friendship when he returned to Mobile although we never again had the marvelous experiences that we had at Dog River. The elder deCelles and Miss Aimée were dead; the house, long ago passed to other owners, is still there and even lovelier.

And now he, too, is gone; but in my memory, Eugene Walter will always remain a young man, handsome and full of energy and enthusiasm, unforgettable as "The Bard of River Home."

To introduce readers to the new staff writer, Eugene Walter
interviewed himself for a September 1979 *Azalea City News and Review*.
Walter took Alan Whitman's photos and created this Eugene
interviewing Eugene image.

Francis Imbragulio

Although Francis Imbragulio has made Mobile, Alabama, his home since 1967, he considers himself a dyed-in-the-wool Mississippian. The pianist/composer spends most of his time reading, composing, and writing his monthly literary magazine and weekly *Fax Facts* for family and friends. Educated at University of Southern Mississippi in Hattiesburg, Mississippi, Michigan State University (where he received both the Master's degree and Ph.D. in music), he also attended Florida State, where he studied piano and composition with Dohnanyi. As a bridge player he has attained the rank of Master, and likes nothing better than a day at the bridge tables. A rabid USM Golden Eagles fan, he lives with his two cats, Trudy and Chipper.

MEMORIES OF EUGENE

The very first time I heard the name Eugene Walter was on a mild late winter morning when I called my good friend, Mary Jane Scruggs. She began our phone conversation by telling me that she and our mutual friend, Margaret Murphy, had spent the previous evening in a most unusual and delightful manner.

"Frank, my old buddy from high school, Eugene Walter, is back in Mobile, and he had us to dinner last night."

"Where has he been?" I asked.

She went on to tell me that he had spent the past several years in Europe. Then she began telling me about the highly original meal, first mentioning that Eugene was the author of several cook books, including a volume of the prestigious Time-Life series. "We started out with Turkey Carcass Soup!"

I gasped and she quickly added, "He swore he rescued the carcass from his neighbor's garbage can!"

"Who is his neighbor, for goodness sake?"

I must have gagged as she went on, "John Thresh." She laughed some more and then added, "Then he served Spaghetti Squash, and—"

"What on earth's that?"

"Frank, it looks and tastes just like spaghetti—only it's a squash! It was delicious! But when he first brought it out, I thought he was serving us sauerkraut. It looks exactly like that when it's cooked. Next, he served what he called 'Patent Leather Pie!'" She dissolved into peals of laughter at this, and I could almost see her wiping her eyes as she tried to go on.

"And what is that?"

"Well, a sort of tuna casserole—but he put these slices of eggplant peeling on top, as a garnish, or cover. It was really good and looked so pretty!"

Other dinner guests that evening had been a Russian actress clad in a very sheer silk gown with high-heeled, open-toed shoes, and a young photographer. There had been only a fire in the fireplace in the living room at Eugene's house, and the women especially almost froze during the meal. Margaret Murphy later told me she had on her pajamas under her pant suit and was still miserable.

After their bizarre meal, Margaret had driven them downtown, where they stood shivering on a street corner to watch a Mardi Gras parade. It had been one of the coldest nights in Mobile's history. Eugene had tied a great woolen muffler under his chin before going out and looked like he had mumps. They were all bundled up in great coats yet nearly froze solid by the time the first float rolled by. Eugene was always very much into Mardi Gras.

As Mary Jane talked on and on about Mr. Walter, I was turned off more and more.

"Frank, you've just got to meet him!" Mary Jane concluded.

"I don't think so!"

"Why not? You two have so *much* in common."

"Really!" I was highly insulted at the time.

We let the matter drop as we went on to discuss our mutual interests: piano teaching, movies, and bridge.

Months went by, and then one night Mary Jane and I were together at either a concert or a Broadway musical at the Municipal Theater, and she spotted Eugene in the lobby. I was a sitting duck.

"Frank Imbragulio," dragging me over, "I want you to meet my dear old friend, Eugene Walter." There was no escape.

Eugene's eyebrows formed a question mark.

"Frank's the piano teacher and composer friend of mine I was telling you about."

"Of course!" And I knew he had not the foggiest notion of who I was.

I did not like the way he looked, either. Nor his voice. In short, I had yet to see anything worthwhile in this rather shabbily dressed, unkempt individual, with his affected way of speaking. At least that's the way his speech struck me then. Just another inflated ego, I decided.

But curiosity soon got the better of me as I learned more and more about this eccentric but unique and quite wonderful individual. I decided to give Eugene a telephone call.

"Hello—?" his soft voice so like a musical instrument, fluted over the phone lines.

"Eugene, I'm sure you won't remember me, but I'm Frank Imbragulio—Mary Jane Scruggs introduced me to you at the theater the other night—"

"Of course I remember you, Maestro Imbraguglio!"

My name rolled off his tongue in a most musical manner. In all the years I knew him, Eugene never once addressed me as "Frank." I was either Francesco or "Maestro" to him. It was different—and I loved it. He gave my family name the proper pronunciation, spelling, and inflection.

"And how are you today?" Eugene asked now.

I said I had called because Mary Jane intimated to me that he might have an opera libretto or two that he had written, lying around.

"Oh, Lord, YES! I have a whole stack of 'em. I call 'em *Six Libretti in Search of a Composer*! I have 'em coming out my ears!"

I then explained that I had composed three little chamber operas and had recordings of their performances from the junior college where I used to teach in my home town of Ellisville, Mississippi. I said I'd love to have him out to dinner one night soon and to hear a few excerpts to see if he liked my style of composition at all.

"That would be delightful! Just let me check my dance card and see when I'm available."

This was the first of many times I would hear him make that same endearing little remark.

The evening came and I was very excited about having him hear my work for the first time. Of course, I had yet to hear or read any of his own works.

I have long forgotten what I served, but I'm sure I tried especially hard to impress him, knowing that he was, after all, an author of several cook books and was supposed to be a gourmet cook himself.

He could not have been more charming or gracious as we supped and sipped wine. Then I turned on my stereo and played a tape of my last opera, *The Taming of the Shrew*. It's a very amateurish performance, given by a group of freshmen and sophomore voice majors, helped out by a few adult choir members from the now defunct Laurel Community Chorus. The only accompaniment is a piano, played by me. All at once, I was painfully aware of these shortcomings and imperfections. But I still consider it one of my better creations and fairly representative of my work.

He listened to the opening octaves, a smile forming early on and lasting throughout the entire overture. Then, as the duet between Lucentio and Tranio, which is sung in front of the curtain, progressed, he could contain his enthusiasm no longer. "But this is wonderful! You have a true Italianate gift of melody!"

I'll admit, I almost wet my britches at that.

"But, my dear, you simply have to orchestrate it," he said at the conclusion of the first act.

"No. That's one of the biggest selling points. I wrote all three of my little operas for small casts; few, if any, set changes, and only a piano accompaniment. I was hoping to make them easily accessible for other schools and small choral groups that might want to perform them."

"Oh, but I can just HEAR the orchestration!"

"So can I. But I'll have to think about that." I had not done a lot of orchestrating, though I had taken numerous courses while in college.

He preferred to listen to this entire opera that first evening, rather than hearing any of the other two. We'd save those for later.

Thus began a long and happy association. He never gave me the libretto, though he kept promising it to me right up to his final days.

"Eugene," I'd say each time the subject came up, "we're neither of us getting any younger!"

"I know—I know. I have it all right here," tapping his forehead, "it's just a simple matter of getting it down on paper."

What he did give me was a considerable stack of his beautifully copied poems, in gorgeous calligraphy, all of which I set to music. These included an earlier version of *The Mermaid's Lament*, which I set and he said he loved, but later, I read another version he had written, considerably altered. *The Stone Guest, Hermione at Home, The Glass Harmonica, The Dolphin, The Goatherd's Song,* and many others.

In the early days of our long friendship, Eugene was art, food, and theater critic for the *Azalea City News and Review*, and, as such, had free passes to most theatrical events and all movies. As his chauffeur, I got to see some of the movies free. I even got to eat free at one of those "Taste of Mobile" dinners.

One Friday morning, Eugene called me to ask if I'd care to see the movie *Rhinestone* with Dolly Parton and Sylvester Stallone that evening.

"Eugene—don't tell me you like Dolly, too!"

"Listen, I'm positively MAD about her! I consider her a great artist!"

I was astonished at our similarity of tastes. I had first been amazed at her performance on The Hollywood Squares, years earlier, when the aria *Un bel di* was the answer to one of her questions—and she began to sing it in a quite lovely operatic voice, and in Italian, no less. A country western singer who knew any kind of opera other than the "Grand Ole" was refreshing enough!

"But the theater's bound to be packed tonight. It's supposed to be such a big hit and this is the opening night," I argued lamely.

"Yes, but it's at that new Dauphin Theater—it's the biggest and cleanest one in town."

I gave up arguing. After all—the price was right. Unfortunately, the movie was a bomb. But Dolly was delicious!

A few days later, I received another call from Eugene inviting me to supper. He said he wanted to give me a surprise he had for me. Supper at Eugene's was not something I looked forward to, having eaten there several times already. There were just so many things he could do with Vienna sausage and other scrap meat bargains. And although we were both cat fanatics (I have always kept one cat in the house, declawed and off the dining table), I found his dozen or more unneutered felines incredibly smelly. I was always exasperated at the way he let them tear up what furniture he had, and I could never quite reconcile myself to having them crawl all over the table and our food.

The meal was delayed for hours, as usual, while Eugene slowly sipped glass after glass of red wine, always at room temperature. He could never understand how I'd prefer a cold Coke to this. It's all a matter of what you grow up with, I told him. Once he got furious because I had him out to dinner and had only iced tea, water, or Coke to offer him. I had been short of cash myself and just did not feel I could afford a bottle of wine for him to drink with the meal. To make it even worse, he never drank cheap wine or whiskey. "You're not a good host!" he said menacingly. "You should always have wine for your guests!"

"Why?" I countered. "You never have Diet Coke for me." I had taken to bringing along my own cold drink when I'd eat there. And, for many years, I kept a bottle of Jim Beam just for his use at my house.

"Carbonated drinks are bad for you. Everybody knows that," was his excuse.

After we ate, he arose and went into another room, returning with the original version of his wonderful poem, *Byzantine Lady*. He read it to me and I was in stitches by the time he finished. He gave his imitation of an oboe before commencing the actual poem, and I decided then and there to do the same in the piano accompaniment. Eugene was very adept at imitating musical instruments—harp, flute, clarinet, cello, trumpet—you name it.

"I wrote it for you to set, but I'm dedicating it to Dolly Parton—the darling. She's a heavenly creature!" He did tend to overreact when he liked something or someone.

I never had so much fun setting anything in my life. The piece virtually wrote itself. After he specified that he heard it as a sort of rag tango, and with the oriental overtones, I just let myself go. I'd call and over the telephone play him stanza after stanza to see that it met with his approval. He seemed delighted with the results. He was always highly complimentary of my talent.

Shortly after this, he said he was writing his first poem entirely in French for me as a vehicle for singer Shannon Williams. The result was *Je viens de ce Pays*, which was very difficult to set, mainly because I do not have a command of the language and Eugene's French was extremely idiomatic. I kept him on the phone during the composition of most of this fairly long vocal piece, asking what he meant by such-and-such a phrase, how to pronounce it (I wanted to get the stress accents just right) keeping Williams' vocal range always in mind. My idea of scoring it for several guitars and soprano thrilled him, as did my tempo marking, *languido,* which, to my mind, perfectly suits the entire mood of the poem. I utilized a neo-impressionistic style, with just a touch of *quasi Puccini* flavoring. I was quite pleased with the finished product, and so was he. It was performed only once, by Phyllis Demetropoulos on the *Monkey Shines* concert at Bernheim Hall. It was done with piano accompaniment, and the work's reception was quite good. The basic idea is typical Eugene Walter. "We, here on the Gulf Coast, aren't like other people. We're all a little mad—with our ghosts, our demons, and our phantoms. Ah, the perfumes here on the Gulf of Mexico!"

After the reception *Byzantine Lady* received, I was all for our collaborating on a musical for Broadway. He loved the idea, too. But we could never agree on a suitable project.

I presented him with the complete musical setting of his *Pokeweed Alphabet* at his sixtieth birthday party given him by Sue and Ron Walker. He later heard the entire work, played through my synthesizer, and just sat there, laughing the whole while, and he kept uttering praises like, "You've made a whole new work out of it. Fantastic! I love it!"

I have set most of *The Pack Rat* and am now at work on *Lizard Fever.* My biggest regret is the small number of dramatic poems (like *Bird as Night Watchman* and *The Stone Guest*) he left. But then, Eugene was such a happy person that one scarcely thought of him as being a writer of tragedy

Like most of us, Eugene hated hospitals and was not a very good patient. It was a chilly late Saturday afternoon in January, and Mary Jane and I were both wearing coats for a change. We had been to a matinee at the Municipal Theater and had decided to stop by on our way back to Mary Jane's house to visit the "Sick and Afflicted."

Mary Jane and I entered his room in Mobile Infirmary and there he lay, looking very sad, dejected, and depressed.

"How do you feel, Eugene?" Mary Jane asked solicitously.

"Oh, better. I guess—but this damned place—"

"You don't look sick at all," I said, before he could attempt to garner any sympathy from me.

"How's the food?" Mary Jane made the mistake of asking.

"Well! It's absolutely ghastly. All they give me is Jello—with nothing in it! No fruit—NOTHING! I'm so sick of eating coal tar derivatives that I'm about ready to scream!"

We both found this description of Jello quite amusing. Eugene was in for the first of several bouts with kidney stones.

Then I made my crucial mistake. "Is there anything we could get for you to eat? Now, be sure you don't ask for something you're not supposed to have."

"No. I really don't feel like eating anything. But if I don't have some red wine right this red hot minute, I'm going to go into cardiac arrest!"

"Now, Eugene—you know they're not going to let us bring you wine to this hospital room!" I said.

"I don't see why you can't smuggle it in under that greatcoat you're wearing. I'm languishing here in this miserable hospital bed—" Eugene was trying mighty hard.

"I know—eating nothing but coal tar derivatives."

Mary Jane laughed and said, "I'm game if you are, Frank."

And so it was decided that we should go to a nearby store, buy a bottle of red wine small enough to smuggle in to the ever-thirsty patient without getting ourselves pitched out on our ears.

We left the hospital and went to the nearest Delchamps where we purchased a small bottle of red wine, then drove back to the Infirmary.

Before entering the lobby, we decided I would be the one to smuggle the bottle under my overcoat. Laughing like two idiots, we tried to act very sedate, prim and proper, as we re-entered the lobby.

When we reached his room, a nurse was checking his temperature so his mouth had to be shut, for once. But he managed to convey with his head that he wanted us to look at the food they had brought in our absence. It was a solitary bowl of pale green Jello, devoid of anything else.

"Mr. Walter, you should try to eat something," the nurse scolded as she removed the thermometer from his mouth and glanced at it. She made a note of his temperature.

"Can't eat that mess! You might just as well take it away. But tell me—am I normal?" he asked.

I thought at the time, "Hardly!"

"Yes," the nurse replied. "Everything looks fine."

The moment she was out of the room, Eugene fell back onto his pillow, grabbing his throat and doing his priceless imitation of a man dying of thirst. Then, he was holding out his water glass for me to fill.

I poured a goodly sized drink and he gulped it down, exactly like a man who is dying of thirst.

"Where shall I put the rest of this?" I asked.

"Let me have that bottle," he said, reaching greedily for it.

When he had it in his hands, he poured another drink and put the bottle next to him under the covers. "Oh, you don't know—you just DO NOT know, but you've saved my life!"

Before we left him, I told him that I would be praying for him each night and he said, "Oh, good! Be sure to pray to Saint Rita for me!"

He always choose that obscure saint for reasons known only to someone who professed to be "Wildly Catholic" and would invariably add, "but I don't go to Mass." He gave as his reason the fact that his grandmother, who had charge of him in his childhood, made him accompany her to Mass every day. That had done it for him, he said.

Eugene sat down and pulled the imaginary instrument to him. Then, with painstaking exactness, he began tuning each string of the harp. He'd pluck a string, and we'd get the ensuing sound—then the next (a frown, once or twice, as if an offending string were really out of tune) and on until he was ready to begin his performance. The fact that all of the strings were now in tune was signified by a pleased smile and an almost imperceptible nod of his head.

His reedy voice intoned, "Chlo-res-ter-ol." There was a beatific expression on his face—then the single word was thrice repeated. Eugene never called it Cholesterol, but always put that extra "L" and "R" at the beginning.

I glanced around at my fellow music teachers to note their reaction. Having enjoyed Eugene's delightful "musical" performances many times, I had asked him to perform at our annual banquet as our "entertainment," and he had agreed, saying the only fee he would expect was a fifth of Jim Beam. A small fee, indeed, for such delightful entertainment. Some of the younger teachers had bewildered looks on their faces, but most of the more mature members had smiles of appreciation and anticipation. Between the phrases, he "plinked" and "plunked" smiling sweetly throughout.

At the conclusion, the group went wild with applause.

Eugene was an incredible pantomimist, actor, and mimic: he could look or sound like almost anything. How many times did he embarrass me when we were attending movies together by crying—*fortissimo*—exactly like a baby, when they'd show those little signs about being considerate and taking your crying child to the lobby. Billy Helton, our mutual barber, told me recently that Eugene would often entertain children who happened to be waiting for haircuts by imitating cats and dogs!

I was first struck by his unusual gift when attending a poetry evening at the Walker's home early in our acquaintance. Eugene read a translation of a classical poem about time, and, as he read, he stroked an imaginary cat lying on his lap. It was so vivid that I could almost have sworn there really was a cat.

His good friend, the Italian filmmaker Fellini, must have recognized this gift early on because he used Eugene in any number of films. I was told that once, when Fellini needed a nun for a short bit in a film, he put Eugene in "drag" for the part. I would kill to see this movie!

But back to our Music Teachers' banquet. Next, we were treated to a rather lengthy introduction by a reed instrument (masterfully reproduced by his nasal passages) and then followed by my favorite of all Eugene's vocal offerings, *In Westchester County* (or *The Chambermaid's Lament*).

Often Eugene would perform these little parodies without too much coaxing or encouragement if he had a few drinks in him. But, sadly, he never would allow me to videotape them.

At a dinner party I had one Saturday night, Eugene was entertaining the guests with his humorous stories of some early army experiences at Camp Shelby in Mississippi. He had worked in the Reception Center while little more than a recruit himself and had to interview the incoming recruits from all the rural and faraway places in this section of the country. He was acting out all of the parts, in true "Willoughby" fashion, telling that, even though many of the men could not read or write, they could tell you where the best hunting was, and what the weather would be like at any given moment in any situation.

Suddenly he chanced to look up at me. I had been taping his narrative for some minutes without his noticing, but now he glared at me and said, "What are you doing?"

I just kept right on taping as he went on, "I consider that an invasion of privacy, and I won't say another word."

My friend, Cora Fairley, tried, in that soft, persuasive voice of hers, to have him continue his performance, saying, "Oh, Eugene! I think you ought to let him tape this for posterity."

But he was adamant. Happily, the tape is preserved, with the guests' reactions to the impersonations.

On a cold wintry Sunday, I had gone by to pick Eugene up to transport him to a meeting downtown in the early afternoon. He did not answer the doorbell when I rang, so I walked around to the fence that enclosed the back yard. The gate was always kept locked, so I called, "Eugene—are you there?"

After two or three calls, he responded with, "Oh, just a minute—I'll be right there!"

He came to let me into his backyard which, in summertime, was a real showplace, but now, like most of Mobile yards in February, was a sad and desolate place. He was in the process of carrying his many potted plants into the garage. There was a hard freeze warning issued for that night.

I looked at his herb beds. They were so forlorn looking now. He always had several varieties of basil, mint, thyme, oregano, and rosemary, along with such wonderful salad makings in that tiny back yard—all sorts of lettuces and exotic greens from all over. His knowledge of plants of all kinds was encyclopedic.

"You know, when I first got back to Mobile from Rome, I heard these local radio announcers talking about the wind chill factor and for the longest I thought they were saying, 'Wind Shield Factor! Lord!!'" And he gave that great guffaw of his.

He was always saying, "I just don't understand any of it!" in reference to present-day terms and practices in general. Such things as television commercials made him see red! But he adored good television. When I'd make him watch something I had taped, before he had his own set, he'd carry on like a spoiled brat during the commercials, even as I fast forwarded through them. I'd patiently try to explain that this was the price we must pay for our programs—good or bad. It did no good at all. And I suppose he got some perverse satisfaction out of continuing to mispronounce "Chloresterol," because he considered the whole concept ludicrous. How could anything good to eat or drink hurt you? Especially, to drink.

I helped him finish the storing of his plants and then we were off to our meeting. Afterward, he wanted to treat me to dinner at Rousso's. I knew he could ill afford this, but he assured me he had just gotten an unexpected royalty check from something he did in Italy years earlier and wanted to share his bounty with me.

And let me so say here and now that I never knew a person more generous when he did have a little money, or more honest about repaying his debts, than Eugene Walter. I had been warned early in our acquaintance never to lend him money. "He'll conveniently forget that he borrowed it," I was told. So, the very first time we were out together and he turned to me (I believe it was at a movie after he no longer got his free passes) and said, "I'm like the Royal Family. I don't carry money. You'll have to get mine!" I was just thankful I was able to pay for the two of us and never expected him, especially with that rather regal attitude, to pay me back. Imagine my surprise, then, when the very next time we went to a film together, he walked up to the box office and said, "Two for—what was the name of that picture, Maestro?" I tried to hand him my money even as I told him the name of the movie, but he shoved my hand back saying, "No, no—you got them last time." And it was always so.

Eugene and I both loved movies and enjoyed dozens of them together. Two of the last times we were together, I took him to see *The English Patient* and *Shine*. When I called and asked if he'd care to go to a matinee of *Patient* (he usually wanted to go at night because he hated to miss his nap), he said, "If we can go to an early enough one that I can get home and have time for my nap." I told him there was a showing at one o'clock.

"Good! Why don't you come about eleven fifteen and I'll take us to eat lunch at the Dew Drop Inn."

"Eleven-fifteen! Why so early? It takes only about fifteen minutes to get to the theater."

"Listen, if we don't get there before the crowd, you'll never find a parking space."

I gave in to him, as I usually did, feeling he was exaggerating. He wasn't. The place, at eleven-twenty, was already crowded, and by noon there were no tables or booths to be had.

We had pork chops and a variety of vegetables on the special for the day, and everything about the meal was memorable. It would be the last time we would share a meal. Eugene always carried his own carafe of wine when dining at restaurants which did not have liquor licenses. So he was happy.

After the movie, which I had loved, I asked him how he had liked it. I was surprised when he told me he had thought it too long and slow.

"But, that's what you usually like about English films," I reminded him.

"I know. I'll have to think about this one a bit longer." Then he added, "But it is a truly remarkable film."

When he found out that the movie *Cold Comfort Farm* was coming to town, I was given no rest until I took him on a Sunday afternoon. Now it was my turn to be disappointed. I never could see what he found so enchanting about this novel.

For the last year or more of his life, I rarely saw Eugene. I'd call periodically and invite him to dinner and he would always have an excuse.

Then I'd call when I thought some film of particular interest to him was playing. But the simple fact was, he just did not feel up to going out any more. He admitted that he was embarrassed about his teeth and the way he could not eat graciously anymore.

The last time I saw him was when our dear friend, Andrew Dakovich, lay dying. I called to ask Eugene if he would not like to go by with me to say goodbye to Andrew and he reluctantly said he would. At the appointed time, I tooted the horn outside the little cottage on Grand Boulevard but I was not at all prepared for the sight of Eugene. He was so terribly wasted away that I hardly was able to recognize him. I knew he could not last much longer.

After our melancholy visit, I returned him to his home and we made our usual comments upon parting about the fact that we'd get together again, just as soon as he felt better. But it was not to be.

Within a month, Father Hay called to tell me the sad news that he had passed away the night before. I miss him so much. A real part of me died with him.

Eugene displays his squiggles at the Haunted Book Shop

(Photo courtesy of Renée Paul)

Ann Evans Berthoff

Ann E. Berthoff is retired after forty-five years of teaching (from Bryn Mawr to the University of Massachusetts, Boston). She has published five books for writers and teachers of writing, one book of literary criticism (on Marvell), and one on the philosophy of language (*The Mysterious Barricades: Language and its Limits*). Another book on metaphor is just setting out on the long trek through the university presses. She lives in Concord, Massachusetts, with her husband; they often dream of Mobile and occasionally get there.

A Memoir of Eugene in New York, Rome, and Sicily

I knew Willoughby for three years before I met Eugene. That was because of WWII, which found EW in the Aleutians and me at college, first at Birmingham-Southern College and then at Cornell College in Iowa. It was Ann Blevins who told me about Dr. Willoughby, saying that he would probably like to hear from me since we shared so many interests—Tibet, the Brontes, islands, Isak Dinesen, and Henry Purcell. I hesitated to ask for admission to the Willoughby Institute since I was not a bona fide Southerner, but Eugene said never mind, Willoughby's aunt was born in Silly Rock, Maine, and that geography was not just a thing of maps. What was essential, I learned, was commitment to the principle that "Fun is worth no end of preparation."

Ann and I had our W. I. station at Birmingham-Southern College with several other souls, including my brother, who was offering an adjunct course, Witchcraft 101. Eugene gave us all Willoughby names: Ann Blevins was Mittie Mae Korsetkover; Ann Evans (I) became Mimadole Trippit. There was also a large, white, stuffed dog named Eustace and a housemate newly named Charlotte Ruse. Eugene wrote a commemorative poem which Mittie and I recite when we meet, *The corpuscles are waltzing, the red ones with the white.* Once when Yoga (Yoga Mae Pom Pom) was visiting, the local Willoughbites, including Genie Earle, walked to Soapstone Cave (about three miles) reciting *The Hunting of the Snark.* We named the red dirt hill in front of the cave entrance "Snark's Knoll" and there we had a memorable picnic. Fifty years ago—and still one of the great expeditions.

My letters must have been full of post-adolescent Angst. In one to W, I'd observed that I really didn't know who I was and sent some blurry photos of myself wandering around my grandmother's backyard in Newton, Iowa. Eugene responded with a huge sheet of newsprint covered with poems, "inscribed on Mimadole's mirror in soap." One was called "Mimadole Among the Appletrees," and it saw me through a rough summer. Writing Willoughby was a lifeline out of dullness. The fact that he was creating a world in the Aleutians was itself an inspiration. And there was the picture of him seated on a snowy wall with a pile of books, reading one and eating an apple— BAREFOOTED. My friends got to know him— Jan Challman, Lois Condon, Tom Tashiro. And they told their friends, including those away at war, about this magician. Thus Jan's fiancé, walking on a road in Hawaii with a fellow Lt. j.g., heard him address a stray dog as 'Willoughby.' "That's funny," said Paul. "My fiancée back in Iowa knows about a guy in Alaska who calls himself Willoughby and thinks of himself as a poodle." The j.g. turned out to be John Goetz from Mobile. When we celebrated International Willoughby Day on May 28, 1945, at Cornell, with a masque written by EW, we knew it WAS an international conspiracy to have fun, no matter what.

When at last we did meet, Eugene and I, it was a cold night in Times Square: "Mimadole, don't you feel that this town is ready to be taken over?" His vision was to establish The Alabama Embassy, to sell cotton plants, start a restaurant, to offer a home away from home to all those post-war Alabamians who were showing up in Manhattan. Like all good clubs of childhood, the true point was the vision and the planning. The best part was that I got to know Edith and Edwin Zelnicker.

Eugene worked at the Chaucer Head Bookshop, Fifth Avenue and 59th Street (he was told to take seriously only those customers who wore expensive shoes), while I worked at the Columbia University Bookstore. Later he went to the Astor, Lenox, Tilden Foundation, as he insisted on calling the New York Public Library, where his job was throwing away things. Of course much of this stuff was transferred to W. I. archives on West 10th.

I worked for Fairchild Publications (13th Street) and lived on the Lower East Side in a beat-up apartment with a glorious view and no heat—until I bought a tiny, wasp-waisted stove which Eugene christened "Mrs. Piozzi-Thrale." He was learning to play the alto recorder, so we spent a lot of time practicing innocuous duets with tricky tempos. He took me to galleries, had me listen to new music (e.g. *Facade*), supplemented my knowledge of English literature, cooked amazing things without extravagance, explained why my Schrafft's vanilla ice cream had those black specks, gently ridiculed my sobriety, amusingly encouraged any sign of wanting to be a writer. We (usually) liked one another's friends and there was a lot of visiting, but what I chiefly remember is the two of us exploring Manhattan, which he continually invented as a magical place right before my eyes. With him, I saw Martha Graham out for a walk on West Fourth, a real estate office with CHRIST & HERRICK in gold Gothic on the window, W. H. Auden reading a book by the light of a wood fire at Number Seventeen Barrow, which served the heaviest Bohemian atmosphere and the worst food in the Village.

I left New York for Cambridge and graduate school in 1947, Eugene in 1951 for Paris on the G. I. Bill. He signed up at the Sorbonne just short of the expiration of this humane legislation and thereupon began his Thirty (?) Years in 'the New World,' as he called 'Yurp.'

Ten years later (1957), we met in another magic city. Warner (my husband) had a Fulbright to Catania, Sicily, but Eugene persuaded us to stay on in Rome for the three parties he was throwing for Isak Dinesen. That was a highlight of the year—and another was Eugene's visit to Sicily. He and Warner drove down via Fiat 600, stopping for infusions every twenty miles, to our seaside villa in Acicastello. He enchanted our children (five and three), who were easily persuaded not to yell because that might awaken the mouse asleep in his ear. Life in Acicastello was not all roses, you might say, but when Eugene was there we did see roses sprouting from the lamb carcasses hung in the butcher's doorway. And when we ran into a traffic jam in Acireale, en route to Cav. Macri's marionettes, a policeman escorted us riding a pink motorcycle: "It's the only way to go!" cried Dr. Willoughby, noting that down the street from the *pupi*, towards which only men were strolling, was a movie theatre, with only women rushing for tickets to see *I Peccatori de Peyton*.

We ate seafood at Acitrezza (scene of *La Terra Trema*) where Eugene chose the fish from the ice chest and suggested how they should be prepared. The wine was "rainwater" he thought until, after the *fragole*, we found that we couldn't rise from the table. The label said that these gems of Vulcan were wines *i pie pregiati e meno conosciuti del mondo*—the most prized and the least known in the world. The logic of that is pure Sicily.

Remembering Eugene in New York, Rome, and Sicily is to know what Past Time With Good Company can be.

Samuel M. Betty

Samuel Betty is a retired professor of economics from Spring Hill College. He and his wife, Lilly, took many friends and students on their "Betty Tours" to Europe, always stopping off in Rome to visit Eugene.

Mr. Betty is currently working on his memoirs.

I knew Eugene only slightly before the war. My wife, Lilly, knew him better at that time as she had been a classmate of his at Murphy. She frequently told of sharing an ice cream cone with him during recess.

After the war, we saw Eugene in New York, where I was doing graduate work and he was working in a bookstore. He was living in a coldwater flat on the fifth floor. Upon moving in, he decorated his new home by painting the floor jet black with bright red footprints leading from the bed to the bathroom. It was at this stage of his life that he won the Lippincott award for fiction. I have often wondered if Lippincott ever realized all this award accomplished.

In the summer of 1957 Lilly and I went to Europe, spending a sweltering week in Rome. We had previously been in touch with Eugene who had furnished us with a map directing us to his lodgings. He lived in a remote part of Trastevere on the top of a small hill. One would go into any of the many shops of the neighborhood and ask of the clerk, "*Dove l'americano?*", whereupon he would take you to the door and point to the steps, all one hundred fifty-three of them. It was characteristic of Eugene that wherever he lived you had to climb a hell of a lot of steps to find him. At the top we found him. His abode was part wood, part cardboard; however, modest as it was, it was surrounded by lovely flower beds. It was also characteristic of Eugene to plant flowers wherever he could. Shortly before our arrival, he had been apprehended by Roman police for planting Four o'clocks on the banks of the Tiber River. After they learned he meant no harm, he was released.

In the following year, 1958, I took my first group of students to Europe. Eugene was living in the same place. Little had changed except for the fact that there were many more flowers and quite a few cats. I should explain that in Rome one has no difficulty in obtaining cats. They inhabit the ruins. The locals feed them because they like them and they minimize the rat problem.

By this time Eugene had developed contacts as only Eugene could. He never forgot a face or a name and he spoke fluent Italian with a Southern accent. He was busy doing a great variety of things. Eugene wrote, of course, but he was in the cinema as an actor as well as a translator doing English subtitles for Italian films. He had met Fellini and Fellini remembered him. Eugene was headed in the right direction.

He gave us a wonderful party. The next day an article about us appeared in the *Daily American*. We visited Rome at least once every summer. And at least once each summer we would go out for a grand dinner. We never ate at the same place. There are many great *trattoria* in

Rome and Eugene appeared to know them all. We invariably would polish off our dinner with a local *digestivo*. The following morning we paid dearly for it.

In the early '60s Eugene moved to his grand apartment on the Corso Vittorio Emanuele, number eighteen. Like all his previous abodes, it was at the top of the stairs. To be sure, there was an elevator, but it was rarely in use. Inhabitants of upper floors would habitually leave the door open so that it could not be summoned to other floors. Eugene lived there for the rest of his days in Rome. At one time the flat directly beneath him was occupied by Leontyne Price, a close friend of his. We met her on one occasion with a small party of contemporaries which we called the "Jet Set." It proved to be a delightful evening.

Eugene's success can, in part, be attributed to his ability to meet and make friends. When you look at the list of artists, musicians, singers, actors and actresses, and writers you are struck with awe. To name a few, Isak Dinesen, Leontyne Price, Federico Fellini, and many others. There is one young lady who, above all the others, must be mentioned. Ingeborg Bachmann was a poet who lived in Vienna. She was a close friend of Eugene's. We met her on several occasions, as she visited Rome frequently. She was a real charmer, and I have often thought that there might have been a spark there between the two. In 1965 the composer Hans Werner Henze, also a friend of Eugene's, wrote an opera called *Die Junge Lord*, translated as *The Young Milord*. The leading character in this opera is "Sir Edgar," who acts but is silent. This was written for Eugene, who appeared in this role on several occasions in the Rome Opera and, I believe, in La Scala. The libretto, incidentally, was written by Ingeborg. Would that this relationship had ended happily, but unfortunately, a few months later Ingeborg died tragically in a fire in Vienna.

There are many other things that could be remembered about Eugene. In a way he reminds me of Leonardo da Vinci. He was too busy doing so many great things to be identified with any single masterpiece.

Chances are...

Mary M. Noland

It seems like it was only yesterday when my husband discovered my car stuck in the snow in front of the garage doors and said, "Once more, and we're moving south!" The next night he found the car stuck again, so we packed up our four children and moved to Mobile in 1955. We had lived on the Gulf Coast during World War II and knew we loved it. We found Mobile to be warm, welcoming, and hospitable, and soon made many life-long friends.

I joined and served as president of the Mobile Symphony Guild, helped found the Art Patrons League, served as its third president, and was elected to the Board of the Mobile Museum of Art.

Early in the '60s, I was invited to go to Europe with friends under the guidance of Mr. Sam Betty. It was during this visit to Rome that I met Eugene Walter and was captivated by his talent and personality.

Upon returning to Mobile, I was offered the position of talk show hostess on WKRG-TV. After thirteen interesting and sometimes very exciting years, I retired in 1979. Dr. Gerald Wallace asked me to join the staff of Springhill Memorial Hospital, then in its early years, and I became Director of Volunteer Services.

Over the years, I became more and more intrigued with the work and sparkling spirit of Eugene Walter.

Eugene Walter in Rome

It was summer 1963 in Rome, Italy. Five Mobile women, Betty Bauer, Jane Burton, Margaret McLean, Betty Walker, and myself were totally captivated by the beautiful sights and glorious antiquities that are Rome. Sam and Lilly Betty were our expert and talented guides. We were all, for one magic evening, invited to dinner at the intriguing apartment of Eugene Walter on the Corso Vittorio Emanuele. Eugene's apartment proved a wonderful background for him and his friends.

We gathered recently to remember the ebullient Eugene, recalling so many memories of that wonderful evening. Betty Bauer remembered that because Eugene loved Rome so much, he wanted to share it with all of us and encouraged us to love it as he did. Jane Burton remembered that Eugene had used votive candles along the edge of the balcony of his apartment, the first time she had ever seen them used thus. Betty Walker reminded us of Eugene's love of the arts, and that Eugene had planted collard greens near the Coliseum to pluck, cook, and serve to his Roman friends unfamiliar with these Southern delicacies.

We all recalled several guests, actors in Fellini's great movie *8 ½*, however the guest we'll never forget was the great diva Leontyne Price. We all shared a delicious buffet, effortlessly prepared by Eugene, featuring a delicate rice pilaf. Following dinner, we were all invited by Ms. Price to join her in her apartment directly below Eugene's. We were totally captivated and when told Ms. Price was singing *La Traviata* in Salzburg, we immediately made plans to attend and were invited to join her backstage after the performance.

The entire evening at Eugene's was a time to savor—and to remember for a lifetime. All due to Eugene Walter and his love of, and interest in, his friends, in life, in art, and the excitement he found in living every day.

Perilla Wilson

If memory serves, my first meeting with Eugene was at a birthday party in Washington Square, an informal picnic-type affair. We, of course, saw each other over the years on various occasions and at various functions. I would go by to pick up some plants or just for a chat. He was most hospitable with the ready offer of a little drink of something, but generally it was too early in the day for me. He was taken with my name, Perilla. He would often review events for me for whatever publication he was working for at the time. When I was in charge of obtaining a speaker for the Alabama Instructional Media Association meeting, I got Eugene to address the group.

I used to think what a shame that all the creative outpourings of the students went largely unnoticed except by teachers and parents—the drawings, choral performances, dramatic skits. Together with Gwen Byrd, I organized what later became Catholic Schools Week. We started with the active arts (dance, drama, music) at McGill. The artwork and projects were displayed at Toolen. Eugene covered this event for us for the *Azalea City News and Review* during those early years. Now this event takes place at the local shopping mall.

I received my degree in journalism from the University of Alabama, obtained my master's (I am librarian emerita, now; Eugene would love that.) from the University of South Alabama, and got my Latin certificate from Troy State. I'm a librarian at Holy Family and have taught part-time at McGill-Toolen.

I tried to get in touch with Eugene that last weekend of his life. My daughter, Laura Wilson Roberts, is the drama teacher and head of the speech department at UMS-Wright. Her students were giving an especially good performance that spring and I wanted Eugene to see it. I've no doubt now that he probably was unable to get to the telephone. I still grieve for him.

I had a long and wonderful association with Eugene as we shared particularly a love of the theatre. I have a daughter who directs at UMS-Wright School and acts, as well as two sons who made television plays and series. But I enjoyed most our visits over a glass of wine when Eugene would call me up and say, "Perilla, you know it's time to plant your parilla plants so when are you coming to get them? I have a few other little goodies for you, too!" And, of course, he would indeed have several different samples of plants and bushes all ready for me so we would waste no time digging and bagging but spend it in a pleasant conversation!

He gave Eleanor Benz (a fellow librarian) and me an original drawing. The writing says:

> *First Satyr (left):*
> *My back is killing me.*
> *HOLDING UP a pediment is*
> *hard work.*
> *Second Satyr (right):*
> *You ain't just woofing,*
> *Bubba. With me it's the*
> *knees.*
> *Faun (above):*
> *Shut up, the two of you.*
> *HOLDING UP a pediment is*
> *a lot easier job than*
> *HOLDING DOWN a position*
> *as TEACHER or in an office or*
> *Bureaucracy.*
>> *For practical, poetical Perilla*
>> *Merry Merry & Happy Happy*
>> *from Eugene*

He was always a delight, always unpredictable, and always willing to help out. It was a most delightful experience to hear him read from his works. He can never be replaced, but we are certainly fortunate to have so much of his work to remember him by!

Robert E. Bell

Robert E. Bell (October 13, 1926 - November, 1999) was born in Tarrant City, Alabama. He served in the United States Army in 1945, after which he lived and worked in Mobile, Alabama, where he first met Eugene Walter.

Mr. Bell received degrees from Birmingham-Southern College, Harvard University, and Louisiana State University, as well as a Ph.D. from University of California, Berkeley. With a long and distinguished career in major city and university libraries across the country, he also owned and operated a used book shop in New Orleans, Louisiana, and was an acclaimed author. His books include: *A Bibliography of Mobile, Alabama*, 1956; *The Butterfly Tree* (novel), 1959; *A Dictionary of Classical Mythology: Symbols, Attributes, and Associations*, 1982; *Place-Names in Classical Mythology: Greece*; and, *Women of Classical Mythology: A Biographical Dictionary*, Oxford University Press, 1993. Most recently, he completed the introduction to *The Pains of April*, a novel by Frank Hollon, published by Over the Transom Books, Fairhope, Alabama.

(Shortly before his death in November, 1999, Mr. Bell submitted the following piece to KaliOka Press for this collection.)

Eugene

Eugene Walter was a kind of legend before I ever met him. Dac [Andrew Dacovich] and Ms. Julia would speak of him. They talked about a time when Eugene came to parties at their house and held everyone captive most of the evening with his conversation and wit. When we would run into Catherine Ann Middleton or Max McGill, they would be full of the latest fascinating things Eugene had done. After I became a member of the Mobile Art Association, I found that just about all the members knew Eugene, especially Ed deCelle, who was assisted by him in organizing and producing the Mardi Gras floats each year. I don't know how I managed to miss him during those first two years I lived in Fairhope, since I was in Mobile rather often apart from working there. Perhaps it was because my Mobile jobs were not the kind that invited people to drop by.

While I worked at a plastics coating establishment on Three Mile Creek, I arrived each day by car pool and got back across the Bay the same way. It was a rare occasion for me to get downtown after work, but occasionally I met my brother who worked in mid town. It was on such a day as this that I finally met Eugene. I was passing the Haunted Book Shop on Conception Street and saw a set of books on a bargain shelf outside. I went inside and knew at once that I was talking to the famous Eugene. When I asked him if the set of Waverly novels was one dollar each or ten for a dollar, he gave me an odd look. I was in my dirty work clothes and covered with fiberglass dust and various colors of plastic coating. Probably surprised that a grimy blue collar worker would be interested in the Waverly novels, he answered that the whole set came for one dollar. I then told him I knew who he was and introduced myself. He had heard of me from a few people, and we talked for half an hour or so. He told me that he would be moving to New York very soon and invited me to visit if ever I was there. I told him I would be finishing my degree at Birmingham-Southern College as soon as I could save enough money. That was the last time I saw him for about three years and, interestingly enough, one of the five times I ever saw him in Mobile.

I went back to Birmingham-Southern where I spent the next two years. At the end of that time I was preparing to study and teach at Tulane where I had received a fellowship. During the summer, however, I received a call from the General Education Board of the Rockefeller Foundation informing me that I had been awarded a fellowship to anywhere I might choose to go. I immediately applied to Harvard and was lucky enough to be accepted.

I went from Mobile to Boston by train. I stopped for a couple of days with a BSC classmate who lived in Greenwich Village at 194 West 10ᵗʰ Street. Then I went on to Cambridge where life took on a new dimension. I was surprised one day during a spring visit to this former schoolmate in New York when he said that he had meant to tell me before that a man from Mobile lived on the next floor. He really didn't know him except his first name, which was Eugene. I couldn't believe my ears. I promptly went up and renewed our acquaintance and Eugene was delighted to see me.

Not long afterward Eugene came to Cambridge and we spent a great weekend together. We went to see Hermione Gingold and Ronny Graham in the forerunner of *New Faces* at the Brattle Theatre, then on to a splendid smorgasbord at a place he knew in Boston. The next night we had dinner with some long-time friends he had known in Alabama. They caught up on things and performed on recorders. Eugene was quite good at this, good enough to convince me that I had to have one. Most of all, though, we sat and talked through the night and into the morning back at my apartment. I was fascinated with all the things he knew and had done.

His recital was mostly about Mobile where he seemed to have been into almost everything. He and several others had stolen a statue from the Saenger Theatre and dropped it into Mobile Bay at the foot of Government Street. They had hated the ugly statue and finally decided to rid Mobile of the unlovely object. He told me of writers he knew. Julian Lee Rayford, whom I admired, had a studio over the Haunted Book Shop. Famous people had dined at Mary's Place, the restaurant owned by a black woman in Coden. A German submarine had come into Mobile harbor during the war and its crew had come ashore to eat and go to a movie. He had an imaginary dog named Willoughby when he was little and had kept Willoughby for years longer. He named an exclusive society after the dog and published *Jennie, the Watercress Girl* under the society's imprint. He knew about early theatre in Mobile and mentioned books that I must read. I was sorry when the night had to end.

Rather soon after his visit to me, I went to New York at his invitation to do a few things and meet a few people. I again stayed with my friend Homer but spent all my time with Eugene, something Homer understandably wasn't happy with. I had a marvelous time. Eugene took me to the Cloisters and reveled in pointing out his favorite things and people. He loved St. Barbara, the patron saint of bathhouses and pyrotechnics. He loitered over hangings and paintings. It would certainly not have been the great experience it was without him. He also took me to the Metropolitan Museum. Even though I had been there before I hadn't seen his private favorites—like a little room you couldn't enter because it wasn't a room but a two dimensional wall in elaborate inset wood which caused it to look three-dimensional. There was a highly decorated harpsichord. There were special loves among the ancient Egyptians and Greeks. I looked at everything with new vision and I knew that I really hadn't ever seen things simply by looking at them.

This first visit also included a subway trip to Brooklyn to visit artist Marie Mencken and her poet husband Willard Maas. Another guest the same evening was Clifford Wright, an artist. Willard, one of the most foul-mouthed people I have ever met, was showing off his new acquisition, the couch on which Truman Capote had his famous photo made for the back cover of *Other Voices ,Other Rooms*.

I probably paid four visits to Eugene after that. I can't remember each one, since they tended to run together with their surfeit of people and experiences. Homer had acquired an apartment mate, Donald Ashwander, a composer, so I stayed with Eugene. Every time was great. We ate at inexpensive and charming Italian restaurants where we ran into people Eugene knew. By this time he had completed his plans to move to Paris, and the only reason we didn't talk more about that was that he didn't really know what lay ahead. Everyone was happy for him. We went to people's houses for dinner. One was the home of Edith and Edwin Zelnicker from Mobile on May fifth. Eugene had talked her into making avocado ice cream he had told me about, but it was no better than the rest of the meal. Other guests included Jean Garrigue, Marie Dunnet, John Vari, Jean Mercier (from Balanchine's stable), Sam Yuell from Jackson, Tennessee, Larry Rivers, Henry Winston (who had two red-haired mistresses), a man who preceded me at Birmingham-Southern, and Donald Ashwander, who was nicknamed Bugeye by Eugene. Marie Dunnet followed with a party on May seventh, and guests were: Edith and Edwin, Jean Garrigue, Josephine Herbst, Larry Rivers, Jean Mercier, Alan Christie, Pat Byrne, Peter Carney, Robert Gilbert, Jane Mayhall, Elenore Vernoy, Cedric Nevin, Emily Bell (from Mobile, later the mayor's wife), John Holland (from Mobile's Joe Jefferson Players), Robert DeVries, David Walker, John Vari, and Henry Winston. Actually, these two parties were going-away parties and included many more people than remembered here. When I heard from Eugene after *The Butterfly Tree* came out, he told me that Andy Warhol had been at the party.

My last two visits to New York were met with a feverish activity. Eugene was disposing of everything, and anyone familiar with him knows what that must have involved. Eugene collected things, and one could scarcely get around in the apartment. People from museums were making appointments. Bugeye got a door prize each time he popped in, which was every fifteen minutes. One museum curator came by to purchase John Barrymore's toy theatre, and only God knows where Eugene got that. Books, records, art works, on and on, had to go, since he could not transport them to France. But somehow it got done, and it was not long until he sailed on a Dutch ship to France in May 1951. Suddenly Eugene was no more in the United States and this would be so for several decades.

His address in Paris was 18 Rue de Tournon. He wrote to me fairly often during his first year or so. I had never been to Europe and it was great to experience things through his eyes. It wasn't long, of course, before he began to have adventures. I wish that he had kept some kind of record of his activities and writings (there has never been a Eugene Walter bibliography). He got over to England at one point and managed to meet Edith Sitwell, one of his idols. He wrote some kind of tribute to her that was set to music by Donald Ashwander (Bugeye). I seem to remember that the Mobile Public Library bought this. He met many famous people when he eventually had a job on the *Paris Review*. I remember that William Styron was one of these. Eugene never seemed to slow down. His first novel, *The Untidy Pilgrim*, appeared during this time, winner of the Lippincott fiction award. I believe *Monkey Poems* was published then and maybe *Singerie, Songerie*.

I worked during the first of these years at the Mobile Public Library. Eugene made a trip back to Mobile somewhere around 1953 or 1954. I was invited along with several people from his early years to Termite Hall, Eugene's name for the old mansion on Dauphin Street belonging to Adelaide Trigg. I didn't get to spend any time alone with him since he was very much in demand. I think the next night everyone met at Constantine's when it was still on Royal Street downtown. I didn't go since I knew it would be a repeat of the night before. Eugene was also taking up a collection to help pay his way back to Paris.

So the years went. I moved to Fort Worth and although I kept up with him intermittently, we tended to lose contact. My novel, *The Butterfly Tree*, came out during this time; Andy Warhol did the dust jacket. I then moved to San Francisco, and about the only connection with Eugene was his appearance in Fellini's *8 ½*, which I saw during my last year there.

I returned to the South and opened a bookshop in the French Quarter of New Orleans. I think during this time Eugene's second novel came out. It was *Love You Good, See You Later*, which he had wanted to name *You Bet Your Sweet Ass*, but not been allowed to by Scribner's, the publisher. The desired title would not have saved it from being a perfectly wretched and silly book. I might say here that I didn't care for his fiction. *The Untidy*

Pilgrim had merit but it was a little too derivative of Eudora Welty, whom Eugene adored, with all the chasing about on lawns and curious personal relationships that couldn't seem to be resolved. The second novel was ridiculous, too cutey-poo with children throwing their voices into closets and older women trying to make it with young handsome sailors who weren't sure of their sexual identity. Eugene could do a lot better as demonstrated in *Jennie, the Watercress Girl*, a charming little piece of local color. And he turned out some very nice short stories. His finest work, though, in my opinion, was his Southern cookbook in which he really could show off his splendid writing talents along with his culinary expertise. And, of course, his poetry sang across all the years I knew him.

I returned to Mobile to work in the Public Library. The New Orleans bookshop still existed but it needed financial assistance which I could provide by working in libraries. My first vacation from the library was a trip to Europe with my bookshop partner, Mark Hanrahan. Part of the trip was intended to be for book buying. We went first to London, then Amsterdam, Frankfurt, Munich, and then Venice. From there we sent a wire to Eugene that we would be arriving on such-and-such a day on the train and would get in touch with him from our hotel. He didn't meet the train as I had hoped, but I discovered later that I had given very vague information. We looked for the Rome address, 18 Corso Vittorio Emanuele but got lost when we tried to find it on foot. We did locate his building the next morning, not very far from where we were staying. He didn't answer a ring and we had to summon a doorman who didn't speak English. But he let us look at the apartment mail boxes and there Eugene's name was. So was Leontyne Price, in an apartment immediately below his. Eugene was at the grocery store but came in shortly and we had a chance to catch up on many years. He and Mark were immediately friends.

We went out with him a few times. He introduced us to *negronis*, the lethal mixture of vodka, vermouth, and campari, in Piazza Navona. He also took us to a fine restaurant in Trastevere, across the Tiber. During these times we were filled in on his work with Fellini, whom he vastly admired. He also told us of some of his adventures with famous people. He and Leontyne Price often shopped together at a five-and-dime and the grocery store where they would buy black-eyed peas and anything that resembled Southern food. He had met Isak Dinesen in Paris and she came to Rome more than once. There was no end to his stories about people from his past. One evening after we had been out, we sent a somewhat drunken Mark back to the hotel and sat up the rest of the night talking about a little of everything.

Our last day he took us to lunch at a famous little restaurant near the Spanish Steps. And that was the last time we saw him until he returned to Mobile. We did see him in Fellini's *Juliet of the Spirits,* in which he played an ancient seer.

I was back in California working at U.C. Davis when he returned. I called him when I visited Mobile just after my first mythological dictionary was issued. He insisted I come to his house on Grand Boulevard so he could get a photo of me for the review he was writing. It was 194 West 10th Street revisited— things piled all over the place, toys, objets d'art, cabinets, tables, paintings. He had summoned a young photographer friend (he always managed to create a following, no matter where he was). If I ever suspected that he was in any way jealous of my accomplishments, it was after the photo appeared in the *Mobile Press Register.* Probably the worst picture ever taken of me, old age notwithstanding. We visited a short time and he showed me a few things he was working on.

Another time I went to visit my brother and this time Edie Cohen took us to lunch as a surprise to him. Another time I was in town and decided to drop by his house since it was almost walking distance from my brother's house. After I knocked several times he came to the door looking like the wrath of God and was very upset that I had not called first so that he could tell me he was very sick. I didn't go in this time, of course. I think he subsequently thought that I held this against him. The last time I saw him was on another visit, about 1983. French Greene and Faye Rollins invited me over for dinner and Eugene came by for a couple of hours. By this time he had thrown all his pills away and said that he was in the care only of Dr. Beam.

This was the last time I saw him. I also did not hear from him except when he had some new publication to sell. So Dr. Beam kept him going another five years or so.

Eugene was very important to me in our earliest years. He was someone different from anybody I had ever known. He was equally happy in big cities and small towns alike. People seemed to gravitate toward him, including famous people, and he never seemed awed by them. In fact, there was no *poseur* about him. He was never bored and never boring. And I could go on and on.

I met Eugene ten years before *The Butterfly Tree* was written. On a conscious level it can be said that he did not appear in the book. But on a subconscious level it would be hard to say that he didn't. For one thing, the book had a certain sophisticated quality it would not have had if I had never met Eugene. I probably transferred some of his knowledge into the minds of a couple of the characters. He also had a universality that could have given rise to the mysterious stranger who impacted the lives of those searching for the butterfly tree. But the stranger was not knowingly based on Eugene. For one thing, Eugene lived in a kind of fantasy world of monkeys, clowns, curiosa, mysteriosa, eccentric people (mostly women), which he fashioned into poetry and artistic decorations. He was enamored of the middle ages and quite knowledgeable. It was Eugene, as I pointed out, who took me to the Cloisters. So there was one strong connection, at least, with the stranger. Otherwise he was in no sense the model, even though the stranger had a profound effect on the lives of four of the characters, just as Eugene had had an effect on my life.

Carolyn Daniels Clarke

Carolyn Daniels Clarke grew up in Bay Minette the daughter of high school principal and civic leader, C. B. Daniels. She graduated from the University of Alabama with a degree in microbiology. After spending time in Pennsylvania and Kansas, she and her husband, Dr. Kendall Clarke, returned to Mobile where they have been actively involved in community and arts organizations. For many years Carolyn chaired the youth concerts program for the Mobile Symphony and served two terms as President of the Symphony League. For this work she was presented the J. C. Penny Golden Rule Award in arts education.

Carolyn works with her husband in his engineering consulting company. They have one daughter, Valerie, who is a resident physician at Wake Forest in Winston-Salem, N. C. The Clarke's are active members of Dauphin Way United Methodist Church and enjoy dancing, traveling, and spending time at the beach.

"I first met Eugene Walter while I was involved with the ballet company. His wit and enthusiasm always made meetings interesting. My daughter, Valerie, danced with the company until she went to college and Eugene never failed to ask about my 'charming daughter' whenever he saw me. His note of congratulations to her at the time of her marriage are among her treasured possessions.

I was thrilled when my dear, precious, friend Nell Burks invited me to serve on the Eugene Walter Celebration Committee and it was during this time that I came to know and appreciate this very remarkable man. I feel blessed that I had the opportunity to know him as a person, an artist, and a friend."

A Gift of Life

Once when visiting with my friend Eugene Walter I mentioned that I was currently raising a baby squirrel that my Australian terrier had found and mistakenly thought she could nurse and mother. Eugene then told me the following story.

During World War II Eugene was stationed in Alaska with the assignment to intercept and decode Japanese messages, a job requiring him to spend much time alone. Late one fall after the local caribou herd had migrated from his area, an orphaned calf appeared at his door. He took her in and became her surrogate mother.

According to Eugene, there were two food products available in abundance to him—Karo syrup and powdered milk. So he fed and loved his baby, keeping her through the winter and enjoying her company.

When the herd returned the following spring, he knew he must release her. At first she returned nightly to her home but finally became accustomed to living with her own kind. She then left with the herd that fall, as she should. Eugene assumed that she would not return to his cabin again, but when the herd arrived again, he was given a wonderful surprise. She returned to his window with a new calf. Following that visit she never appeared again but he was convinced that she came back to show him her new offspring as a gift of thanks for what he had done for her.

Ben Sederowsky

Ben Sederowsky's love and talent for photography began in his native Sweden. His family fostered an affinity for art; childhood sketching and photography led to a master's degree in Italian literature, anthropology, medieval archaeology and art history from Lund University in Sweden. Since 1975, Ben has shown in exhibits worldwide. His photographs have appeared in *Advertising Age,* New York; *Vogue,* London, England; *Daily American*, Rome, Italy; *Daily Mail,* London, England; *Boutique de France,* Paris, France; *Australian Consolidated Press,* London, England; Time/Life Books; and Andy Warhol's *Interview Magazine.*

Mr. Sederowsky's photographs are in private collections all over the world. Unfortunately, all the negatives for photographs taken by Mr. Sederowsky of Eugene Walter in Rome were sent to Eugene and are somewhere in the archives of his estate, as yet to be unearthed.

Eugene F. Walter was not only an artist of living, he was an intellectual, a gourmet chef, a clown, a poet, but first of all, a great friend. We met the first time in 1972 over cocktails with the Halston fashion maestro Valentino and some of his assistants, two English lads and two from New Zealand. Richard Nolt was Valentino's right-hand design assistant and now is a well known fashion designer in London. Nicholas from New Zealand worked with interior design at "Valentino" and later on left for the Philippines and started a factory for basket weaving.

Eugene was very much a Felliniesque character in his looks, speech, and manners, so, of course, he was acting in some of Fellini's movies like *8 ½*, *ROMA*. But, perhaps foremost he was his right hand and advisor.

People like Karen Blixen (Isak Dinesen) who wrote *Out of Africa* often stopped over on her way from Africa to her family home in Denmark. Of course Federico Fellini and his wife Giulietta Masina were frequent guests for dinners at Eugene's.

Eugene preferred to cook and eat at home and, of course I never said no to a lovely lunch or dinner at his spectacular home, though the first time there I nearly choked when the smell of cat piss welcomed me. We always started with a *digestivo* of one of two types, gin and tonic or Campari, to settle our tummies from the over-indulgences of the night before, and then we walked and checked his two gardens and chatted with his cats, six or eight of them, I recall. High over the terracotta rooftops of Rome, the gardens of Eugene's were like a little bit of paradise. Butterflies and birds found themselves in peace and harmony amongst the oleander, olive and fruit trees, roses, and a great herb garden. The cats were never a threat to the wildlife. The cats were his kids, all with different temperaments and characteristics like any other kids. The fumes and noise from cars never reached Eugene's rooftop.

One day on my walk over for lunch, I passed Largo Argentina, *Foro de gatti*, and to my horror all the street cats, hundreds of them that lived amongst the ruins of the Piazza, had been killed. The city of Rome explained that they with their claws scratched and ruined the columns and temples. Cats had lived there for hundreds and hundreds of years. (During World War II the cats disappeared but that was because the Romans were starving.) A very upset Eugene, with his ironic humor and anger at the same time, said that soon we would see laughing rats as big as dogs walking arm in arm down the Corso.

Eugene had a whimsical side. For example, when he was packing to leave for Mobile after quite a few decades in Europe, he put some chairs on hooks on the walls like a kind of surrealistic sculpture. He explained they were for his guardian angels to hang out upon.

He believed that some kind of revolution was on its way to Italy and Rome. He felt the tension in the air. So finally, after all those years in Europe, it was time to pack up, cats and everything else, and skip town for his old roots back in Mobile, Alabama.

His culinary expertise and cookbooks, like *American Cooking: Southern Style* by Time-Life Books, have taught and inspired me tremendously.

There ain't many people you can laugh and cry with. Eugene was definitely one of the very few.

This is my epitaph to my friend Eugene who inspired me and made me laugh.

Tammy explains:

To tell the truth, honey,
We need lotsa money.
We don't live like the lower trashes.
I like imported gin,
Must have soft human skin
For my sashes;
And we empty the till
Sending men to Brazil
To get, if you please,
The knees of killer bees
That I wear for my lashes.

Geoffrey Strachan

Geoffrey Strachan was born and went to school in Bishop's Stortford, England, where he studied French and German, acted in plays, and made puppets. During military service he learned Russian. He spent three years at Cambridge University reading Pushkin, Gogol, and Chekhov, as well as Moliere, Racine, and Kafka (among others) and writing lyrics for student revues. He spent a year in Paris immersing himself in Alfred Jarry, French *chansonnier* theatre, and world drama.

From 1961 to 1995 he was an editor with the London publishers, Methuen, where he developed the modern drama, fiction, and humor lists, introducing such authors as Alfred Jarry, Edward Bond, Joe Orton, Jakov Lind, Sue Townsend, Monty Python, Tom Lehrer, and B. Kliban.

He has translated many German children's stories. His translations from French include Cyrano de Bergerac's seventeenth-century science fiction epic *Other Worlds* and (most recently) Andrei Makine's novels of modern Russian life, *Confessions of a Fallen Standard-Bearer, Once Upon the River Lore, Dreams of My Russian Summers* and *The Crime of Olga Arbyelina.* He is currently attempting to re-learn Russian, in case Makine starts writing in it instead of French. He lives in Oxfordshire and goes to the theatre as often as possible.

Gooseberry Fools, Green Men, Elusive Troubadours:
Memories of Eugene Walter

Eyes are for seeing
Monkeys for treeing
Tea is for teaing
And Now is for Being

I first met Eugene Walter in Paris in May 1953. He opened my mind to many things. To the delights of monkeys, baroque music, and fireworks; to poetry and art as celebration; to caprice as the mother of invention. I had never met anyone quite like him. We did not see one another often in the years that followed but his books and spirit have never been far from me.

When we met he was living in the rue de Tournon, Paris, near the Jardin du Luxembourg, and we were both students in a French language and literature course at the Institut Britannique in the rue de la Sorbonne. I had just left school in Britain where I lived in rural-cum-suburban Hertfordshire and was on my second ever visit to France. Eugene told me, when we first chatted together, that he came from the "backwoods" of America. I'm sure he intended no disrespect to his beloved Mobile, Queen of the Gulf Coast, but I think he did not want me to suppose he was a city slicker from New York or any of those places up north. It was only by degrees, in subsequent conversations, that I realized he was a published writer associated with the new magazine, *Paris Review*. He gave me a copy of the first issue, launched that spring, which contained his haunting story set on the Gulf Coast in summer, *Troubadour*, his first to be published. The troubadour of the title is a small boy who treats an elderly pair to a fictitious life story before skipping away into the dusk like an elf. A note about Eugene mentions his having received the Lippincott Fiction award for his novel *The Untidy Pilgrim* and notes that it is shortly to be published.

I only caught up with this Catherine wheel of a novel—a little like Thomas Love Peacock crossed with an American Rabelais—and drank in the magical atmosphere of his Mobile when it was published in Britain in 1955. When was Eugene first in Paris? I do not know. But I was delighted, on reading the novel, to come across Laura Moreland's letter from that city where she says, "I just sit outside and think for hours at a time. That's what sidewalk cafés are for, you know...My favorite is two blocks from me, called Le Tournon from the name of the street. There are lots of people who sit at tables and play cards and others who write. They have a pretty red Irish Setter who chews tin cans..."

Certainly in the summer of 1953 Le Tournon—described in the back pages of the *Paris Review* as "a famous literary cafe"—seemed to be Eugene's *siège social*. We celebrated my eighteenth birthday there in June with a double coffee and Eugene gave me the second issue of the *Paris Review*, hot from the press, an exciting moment. He had now joined the panel of advisory editors. He delighted me further by giving me a copy of his *Monkey Poems*. Since early childhood I had always been enthralled by apes and monkeys in art, literature, and zoos. To receive from its author this sparky, literary, and artistic celebration of monkey-ness was an unbelievable delight. Like a surprise win on a lottery.

Eugene was so youthful and exuberant in manner that it never occurred to me that he was quite a lot older than I was. I think he had already visited England when we met. In our conversations he talked on occasion of the beautiful Suffolk villages of Long Melford and Lavenham which I knew from family outings. He also relished minor mysteries of British English. On first hearing an Englishwoman ask her husband: "Will you have your gooseberry fool now, dear?" he pictured a particular kind of jester (clad in green) being sent for.

Eugene was an amalgam of many beings: a Shakespearean fool was one of them. He wrote for the *Paris Review* about opera, music, dance, and art. He seemed to love all the arts and to practice many of them. He was playing the flute the second time I called on him, and during my weeks in Paris we saw the American National Ballet Theatre dancing *Graduation Ball*; the Théâtre National Populaire with Jean Vilar playing Shakespeare's *Richard II*, and also Moliére's *Médecin Malgré Lui* (the latter on Coronation Day). We watched a marionette play in the Jardin du Luxembourg. We visited the *bouquinistes* beside the Seine and bought eighteenth-century prints of animals. We heard a glorious concert of seventeenth-century music by Charpentier and Lully in the Abbaye de Royaumont, a ruined chapel in a green valley with shafts of sunlight flashing in (a magnificent combination of art and nature); and saw Lully and La Fontaine's tragi-comédie-ballet, *Psyché*, in Paris the same evening. He talked with fervour of a recent production of the baroque opera *Les Indes Galantes*.

Apart from introducing me to novel pleasures of the palate, such as Muscadet taken with sparkling Perrier water on the terrace of the Tournon and pizza (with cheese, tomato, and olives) eaten late at night at a Neapolitan restaurant in Saint-Germain, Eugene opened a door to me on the continuity of cultures between the old world and the new and on a mellow outlook shared between the people of European lands around the

Mediterranean and those of the southern states of America. It was a stimulating challenge to many of my north European assumptions.

His conversation and his work contain a huge range of reference—dazzling, mysterious, exciting—that I continue to explore. One of the poems published in the Rome-based international periodical *Botteghe Oscure* in 1955 is called *Green, Green, Grove*.

> *I saw the green man in the grove.*
> *The picnickers all dared me to prove*
> *I was not dazzled by my love*
> *Of dream, of summertime heat, of pine...*
>
> *I'll have his name: such is my dare*
> *To hear him speak it on the air,*
> *But meanwhile raise my bottle high*
> *To drink his face in the shady wine.*
> *He pierces me from the black dog's eye*
> *Of ghostly loins, he'd act through mine—*
> *He has no language but a sigh*
> *Yet he is fecund, he is loud:*
> *Green his ichor, fierce his blood.*
> *He'll haunt me in the black dog's eye,*
> *Until that moment when I prove*
> *As green as he is, in my own grove.*

As I read it now, this wonderfully mysterious and pagan poem is evocative for me of the carved foliate heads, faces with leaves for hair, leaves pouring out of their mouths, that feature in the churches and cathedrals of Europe (elsewhere, too) and were the subject of the late William Anderson's book *Green Man* and some of his poems. It also reminds me of the painter Cecil Collins, painter of holy fools, who painted himself as a "green man" in the '30s.

I went back to Paris briefly in the summer of 1954 and met Eugene again. We returned to the Abbaye de Royaumont, walking through the green July countryside on the banks of the Oise from L'Isle Adam. We drank champagne and ate camembert at the Tournon to celebrate the acceptance of an unpublished novel by Alfred Chester for translation into French. The Tournon's resident dog, Arnaud, was offered but refused the champagne and camembert. He must have been the one Laura Moreland described as liking to chew tin cans.

Eugene loved whatever happened in the theatre when the curtain rises. He recommended that I go and see a play called *En Attendant Godot* by a writer called Samuel Beckett, which had been playing since the previous year. That night with Beckett's anguished clowns was one of my great nights in the theatre. We also had a splendid night together in London—I believe it must have been in 1955—when we saw Noel Coward's camp, witty, and baroque musical play *After the Ball* based on Wilde's *Lady Windermere's Fan*, at the old Globe (now the Gielgud) Theatre, Shaftesbury Avenue.

I have no idea how much time Eugene spent in England in those days. 1955 was the year when Gaberbocchus Press of Chelsea published *The Shapes of the River*, a celebration of the Thames in London with haunting images by Gwen Barnard and exuberant words by Eugene.

> *Most people see only the Was of the Thames*
> *Like pomps, poops, periwigs, queens, quacks, quottements*
> *Romans, roysterers, rumbecks*
> *Frost Fairs, gilded galleons, Judge Jeffreys,*
> *all That Went Before ...*
> *Not so Gwen Barnard who sees the present everywhere like*
> *A lily on the stream*
> *Who reads only mote-notes, Light Reading*
> *But Highly Colored, and who says Take Take Take*
> *Oh Take the Was out of your eyes, and Let me*
> *Show you a Thames that never was, being so* is.

It was in the same year that Gaberbocchus also published Barbara Wright's witty English version of Christian-Dietrich Grabbe's delicious play, written in 1822, *Comedy, Satire, Irony and Deeper Meaning*. With "Drawings and Collages from contemporary papers by Dr. S. Willoughby." This volume and the "dozens of illustrations and vignettes, some with collage elements" was referred to in the announcement for the exhibition *Flashback*—drawings, paintings, and designs by Eugene Walter—held at the Museum of the City of Mobile in the summer of 1981. I cannot say if any of the originals were shown there.

But his eloquent translation (published by the Madaloni Press, Mobile, in 1983) of the young German romantic writer Fouqué's haunting, bittersweet tale *Undine* (first published in 1811), is one more shining demonstration of the truly international breadth of Eugene's European culture. As is the gloriously punning *Singerie, Songerie*, his delicious "masque on the subject of Lyric Mode" published by the Willoughby

Institute in Rome in 1958, a carnival caper around the theme of Hamlet—
here Amulet, in love with Verdine, daughter of Pollnone, sister of Tease.
Monkeys, birds and a phoenix promenade through the text which ends with
a poodle singing:

> *My corpuscles are waltzing*
> *The red ones with the white,*
> *I shall not be a-sleeping*
> *The whole of this night.*
> *O the waltz! O the Schmaltz! Bow-wow-wow-wow!*

Then more dancing and the triumph of Verdine and an Apotheosis featuring
the night sky with moon, stars, comets, and four monkeys as the four winds.
The whole is zestfully illustrated on huge handsome pages by Zev—clearly
a kindred spirit of Dr. Willoughby.

I do not know when in the '50s Eugene moved completely from Paris to
Rome. He was already publishing poems and stories in *Botteghe Oscure* in
1955 and 1956 and remained an associate editor of *Paris Review* at least as
late as 1956 (issue fifteen). By the autumn of 1959, when I spent nine
months in Paris as a post-graduate student he was already gone. During the
'60s and '70s we stayed in touch through correspondence—Christmas cards
and occasional letters and he continued to send me his books. In 1964 I
caught up with his novel, *Love You Good, See You Later,* which I enjoyed as
vintage Eugene Walter. By this time I was working as a young editor at
Methuen. It was my work there that gave me the opportunity some twenty
years later to renew contact with him rather more directly. Methuen was
then moving into the field of publishing new and already published novels
and stories in our own large-format paperback fiction series—Methuen
Modern Fiction. In March 1980 I noticed a review in the *New York Times
Book Review* of a new book of short stories by Eugene. This was only two
days after I had had returned to me (marked "address unknown") the card I
had sent him in Rome (no doubt at 18 Corso Vittorio Emanuele) the
previous Christmas. Where was he?

I traced him through his New York publisher and within weeks a letter
came through. He had left Rome and was back in Mobile:

"....*the sheer hecticness of Rome kept me silent. Much mail never
arrived, going or coming. The day I was tear-gassed in my own apartment,
having replaced the windows after friendly neighborhood bombs, not once
but twice, and tear-gassed for the second time, I started packing books. I
came over on a cargo, lucky to have a big cabin for two for myself and
felines; couldn't see subjecting the darlings to the horrors of air travel, bad*

enough for humans; dismal — sometimes deathly — for animals. I have nine cats. I no sooner had found a house and unpacked books than here came the worst hurricane we've had in over a hundred years and made a huge mess. I'm still drying out and digging out. But I wanted to settle down and write away from the confusions of Rome and that's what I'm aiming to do, given a little patience and a patched roof..."

Looking back on my years in publishing I realize that the early to mid-'80s was a period when, in a reasonably buoyant U. K. economy, Methuen, and I at Methuen (though it was part of a large and fairly tightly controlled publishing conglomerate) had greater freedom to experiment and publish unusual works I liked than either before or since. So the fact that Eugene's name was hardly known in Britain was no bar to the somewhat quixotic plan I then conceived.

In 1983 I was allowed to stop off in Mobile for a night on a trip that also included visits with authors in Connecticut, San Francisco, and Santa Monica, and I spent a memorable evening dining with Eugene and his cats. (I remember there was one that sat on the table and would nibble the flowers in the vase.) The food was prepared by Eugene himself and included salads grown in his garden. Out of that visit came the plan realized at last some two years later, to reissue his novel *The Untidy Pilgrim* and to publish a collection of his short stories. On that visit I also met a number of young writers—to whom, to my shame and chagrin—I was never able to offer any help at all in the UK.

In retrospect, Eugene's letter written after my visit is much too generous to me. But eloquent with regard to his own work on behalf of other writers:

"I wonder if you have any idea of the difficulties for a young writer here. The New York idiots return unread most unsolicited mss or simply toss them into the rubbish bin. Most agents charge fifty dollars just to read a ms! so that to meet and speak with a living breathing publisher is like sitting on Jupiter's knee for these young creatures. One more reason to have reviews and publishing houses right here in the South. I've published six of my own works by subscription and made money; all things no New York publisher would even look at..."

His long letter concluded characteristically:

"Well, I'm very excited about these things coming out in London and after my disappointments with the New York publishers (most of them are owned and sat upon heavily by such monopolistic entities as Exxon, whose directors wouldn't know a book from a boathook) this mere fact will

make it easier for me to complete half-finished works..." There followed a P.S. with love from all ten of his cats and a paw mark.

A few weeks later he wrote:

"Let's leave Pilgrim *as it is, I cannot find in the hurricane reshuffle in the attic and garage the bits and pieces I seek. Doesn't matter that much. But I'm madly revising and copying short stories and will send along. YES, I'd love to submit cover ideas and shall in two minutes.... I think we shall call the stories* Byzantine Riddles *in this new edition...."*

A few weeks later I received a postcard:

"Why don't we call the stories like this:
THE FLOWERY KINGDOM
*or **ARSE OVER TEACUPS?***
E.W."

Then, later:

"Dear Geoffrey, Rushing to Post Office: let's call the book The Byzantine Riddle and Other Stories.... *Batch of designs on my desk right now, working on ideas...."*

On January 3, 1984 he wrote:

"We've had the coldest Christmas since 1899 and all the pipes have burst, my kitchen flooded, I'm still without water, and everything is delayed... Designs are almost ready, I'll get them to post just as soon as I can finish one last one that has the monkey of 'Vodka' and really is my favorite drawing. Any book with a cat, dog, horse or monkey on the cover sells better than the same book without these creatures. I haven't stopped for Christmas yet. I cooked a small wild turkey, put it on the kitchen floor for them after I'd hacked out some breast and drumstick for me and amidst the floods and disasters they had a scene of wildest orgy..."

In May 1985 after a rather long gap I received another letter:

"No, I don't forget good friends and dear publishers nor do I forget dear friends and good publishers. I've been on a bumpy road since we were

last in communication. My roof, hastily and ill-repaired after the hurricane, fell apart in a big storm and books and pictures and cats had to be moved out..."

He was having health problems, too.

"I am impatient to get it all over with since I want to be in London for publication. I sent you roughs for jacket designs way back when; they came back marked 'undeliverable' and only later did I learn that the kind of sticky tape we have always used for parcels is now banned by the Post Office, since it gums up their latest machinery. BUT mystical powers have been at work or else your Master Philip Thompson [our jacket artist] is psychic: I had a monkey opening a Byzantine coffer in which you could make out a cat's ears and eyes in the opening! And I had a poodle on the novel. [Both featured in Philip's designs]....All the best and we'll get drunk in September..."

Sadly, circumstances did not allow him to visit London that autumn, but the books were finally published. Fernanda Eberstadt in the *Times Literary Supplement* described the reissue of *The Untidy Pilgrim* and the publication of *The Byzantine Riddle* as "a particularly unexpected pleasure" and hailed the novel as "old fashioned, not so much for the courtliness of its prose and its delicious rhythms but for its tribute to gentler virtues which one is unaccustomed to seeing honored in contemporary fiction: tact, courtesy, reticence, hospitality, right relations and the respecting of one's elders."

Colin Greenland in the *New Statesman* rejoiced in Eugene's "baroque and benevolent aestheticism" and the "pure pastoral dalliance beneath the cowcumber magnolia" and "love and leisure mediated by wit" of *The Untidy Pilgrim*. He rightly quoted Nonie Fifield's motto: "*Eclatez* with the fireworks and blossom with the rose: that's *my* message to the numbered and cubbyholed."

I don't suppose anyone has ever succeeded, or ever will, in numbering or cubbyholing Eugene and his wide range of genius—but having seen Eugene briefly late in 1986—as ever bursting with creativity—I was delighted to learn that in the autumn of 1987 he was to be *celebrated* in Mobile. "If I were even ten years younger," he wrote in advance, "it might all inflame my ego... I feel the best of it is that an ARTIST is being honored in our basically mercantile and military nation!" In favorable times I might conceivably have made it to Mobile in November of 1987 but the giddy spring of the mid-'80s was over. The conglomerate that owned Methuen had just been bought by a larger conglomerate which then sold off our list to yet another conglomerate (not *Exxon*) which grew bigger and then in 1997 sold Metheun to yet another conglomerate... But that is another story...

I stayed in touch with Eugene and early in 1988 he wrote:

"The celebration in my honour was fantastic, baroque, exhausting. The Archbishop sloshed Holy Water, the Senator orated, the Leviathan New Oriental Fox Trot Orchestra played, dancing till dawn, tables decorated with bouquets of collard leaves and miniature pomegranates (I'd jokingly said I'd leave if there was a gladiolus or scentless hothouse rose)...I want to thank you for writing to me in advance about Methuen's changes; no New York publisher is so considerate of an author and that's the truth...Every day I spend an hour sorting travel-and hurricane-shuffled archives, thinking of seriously working on memoirs. Did you know I'd once been stalled between floors in an elevator? — with Martha Graham? And that I ate peanut butter sandwiches on the upper slopes of Mount Parnassus?..."

In the last years cards passed between us and in 1995, frustratingly, Eugene made a lightning visit to Britain to give a television interview about Muriel Spark—but alas, his letter written in advance (using Methuen's address from eight years previously) was forwarded to me several weeks late—only after he had been and gone:

"...I've been all day shuffling papers after our two recent hurricanes, looking for what I hope is your correct address! Can't find it. Can't find your wonderful letter of a century ago which is worn thin from re-reading. Why don't you ring the BBC and find out where I'll be?..."

It turned out later that he'd been flown not to London but to Glasgow. I believe he had a night in London but no one at directory enquiries could give him the correct address or telephone number for Methuen (buried now in the heart of a conglomerate).

Over the years Eugene and I quite often lost touch, mislaid one another's addresses. Though his house in Mobile was undoubtedly more subject to hurricanes than any of mine in North London. But if he sometimes seemed elusive his was the elusiveness of a radiant spirit who was always there somewhere in the cosmos and would often suddenly pop up—casting his invigorating light—when least expected. A meeting with him, a card or a letter from him, or a reading of one of his poems or books, has always been like walking into sunlight after a long winter. The Muscadet is uncorked, the fireworks explode, and the laughter begins once more.

Gordon Tatum, Jr.

Gordon Tatum graduated from Murphy High School in Mobile, Alabama, where he was active in drama and music. At college at Birmingham-Southern he was also involved in drama and musical productions. He later attended the University of South Alabama and Bishop State Community College. When possible he took part in productions of Mobile Opera, Joe Jefferson Players, and Mobile Theatre Guild, and he served as soloist at various churches, particularly St. Paul's Episcopal in Spring Hill. He worked for *The Mobile Press Register* where he wrote, from time to time, about the talented Eugene Walter, then holding forth in Rome. After Eugene's return to Mobile, their paths crossed many times at the opera, symphony, and at community theatre playhouses. After thirty-four years at *The Mobile Press Register* as arts critic and Sunday Editor, Gordon Tatum now serves as public information officer for The Museum of Mobile.

Conversations Over a Picket Fence

Remembering Eugene Walter is not a difficult task. It is an easy thing to do. Most of my fond memories of Eugene involve pleasant days after his return to Mobile from the more colorful life with the world's famous jet setters in Europe.

Eugene returned to an apartment in the Oakleigh Garden District where he enjoyed life on Palmetto Hill. From time to time he roamed the neighborhood, stopping to admire flowers in bloom, speak to neighbors and, occasionally, chat with me over our picket fence at the home on George Street which my wife and I were restoring. These events were usually on a Saturday morning as our sons, then about two and five, played in the front yard under the watchful eye of Daddy.

Eugene and I had a few things in common, both having been born and reared in Mobile. While I was a product of World War II, he was actively involved in that endeavor. We both remembered fresh vegetables from home gardens and even fried chickens which a few hours before were family pets in the back yard.

There were discussions about street vendors, vegetable men hawking their wares, the musical ice man riding a horse-drawn wagon (but with rubber tires), and the ice cream man who back then did not have a recorded song to play over and over to the dismay of parents at mealtime.

Eugene had a number of works to his credit; however, my favorite was the Time-Life book on Southern cooking. I thought it read more like a novel than a collection of recipes. Mobile was certainly spotlighted. And cooking was just one of Eugene's many talents.

The arts and their growth in Mobile, certainly Mobile the city, were included in these momentous conversations. The city's movers and shakers were credited as well as its unsung heroes. All of this conversing was done over a picket fence on a fall or spring day with a gentle breeze blowing and the sound of young laughter in the background.

Favorite moments with Eugene? There were special times. That and the fact that I never accepted a kitten he often tried to persuade me to take. Later when we finally were adopted by a neighbor's tiny black cat I was tempted to name the feline Eugene. I instead opted for Kitty, but often think of the lovable, laughable elf named Eugene Walter who made my Saturday mornings more interesting.

Charles Smoke

In 1989, after working two years as an announcer, Charles Smoke became program director at WHIL-FM, the public radio station in Mobile, Alabama, for which Eugene recorded "Eugene at Large." The ten-minute segments aired weekly from September 1992 through Eugene's death in March 1998, featuring an eclectic mix of reminiscences, recipes, stories, poems, reviews, and more.

Mr. Smoke grew up in a variety of small towns in the Southeast and in Southern California, his Marine father moving the family to a new base about once a year. He earned degrees in English from Spring Hill College (BA, 1974) and Indiana University (master's, 1978); has taught elementary, middle, high school, college, and continuing education classes; and served as teacher and curriculum coordinator for the Upward Bound program at Spring Hill. He has lived in Mobile since 1978 and is involved in a number of arts organizations, including Mobile Opera and Mobile Symphony.

Charles Smoke is also a member of the Regular Readers Society, of which Eugene Walter was a charter member.

Endearing and infuriating. Eugene Walter could be both. And, for me, his embodiment of a number of contradictory qualities characterized his distinctive persona. For instance, he could demonstrate remarkable knowledge about some arcane subject (say, a minor Italian composer) and yet prove—or pretend to be—remarkably ignorant about some aspect of everyday life (say, re-tuning his radio). Or he could be completely reticent about some aspects of his life (his romances, if any) and exuberantly expressive about others. That last quality—his tendency to wear his emotions on his sleeve—had the potential to endear and infuriate.

One evening as we sat sipping port in his parlor, preparing ourselves for some outing (probably to the theater), he suddenly raised one finger—a request for silence. From the radio flowed music from Mozart's *The Magic Flute*. It was the first song of Papageno, the bird catcher, who prides himself on the ease with which he traps his prey but complains that he lacks the skill to catch a wife.

I regret that I don't recall which baritone sang it, but his identity may be irrelevant. I suspect Eugene was reacting more to Mozart's genius than the performer's. But whatever the stimulus, I had never witnessed such pure delight. Eugene threw back his head and laughed, clapped his hands, then clasped them, his eyes sparkling and fixed with rapt attention on a feathery vision in his mind's eye. For a moment, he conducted vaguely with one hand, and then he wept with unfeigned joy.

When the music ended, he removed his glasses and wiped the tears from his eyes. I felt a sudden self-consciousness—and privilege—at having seen Eugene so un-selfconsciously caught up in his pleasure, and I wondered if I ever felt as deeply and immediately or would ever be capable of revealing my feelings as openly.

Eugene's uninhibited displays, however, could prove less than endearing.

On one occasion, I accompanied him to the Bel Air Twin Cinema for a special matinee screening of *Carmen*, sponsored by Mobile Opera. He greeted friends and acquaintances, nodding and smiling, wearing his best public face. We settled into our seats, the lights dimmed, and the credits began over scenes of Seville: a religious procession and a bullfight.

"Shit! This is SHIT!" Eugene shouted suddenly, outraged at the shots of the bloody, beleaguered bull. Heads turned.

"DisGUSting! This is really shit."

Patrons of the opera frowned, stared in annoyance.

I attempted to shush Eugene, to assure him that the bullfight was staged, though I assumed that the director had probably resorted to actual footage of the sport.

He refused to be shushed. "This is really too much. TOO MUCH. UnbeLIEVable!"

Unable to glare him into silence, I sank back into my seat, straining for invisibility. His protests gradually subsided to a mutter until the credits mercifully ended and the opera began.

Of the various public humiliations I suffered thanks to Eugene, this was probably the most irritating. But even then I envied his freedom, his willingness to express what he felt and thought without restraint, the same openness I had seen in private, listening to the radio in his parlor. It's one of the things about him I remember most vividly and miss most acutely.

Monkey was I born, Monkey am, Monkey
evermore to be... Do you know who you are?

Jennifer Horne

Jennifer Horne's previous publications include a chapbook, *Miss Betty's School of Dance* (Bluestocking Press, 1997), and poems in *Amaryllis, Astarte,* the *Birmingham Poetry Review, Blue Pitcher* (poetry price 1992), *Carolina Quarterly, Dry Creek Review, Fan, Lonzie's Fried Chicken, Mockingbird, Noccalula, The Old Red Kimono, Poets On:,* and *Sycamore Review.* She has published a number of book reviews and essays in such places as the *Black Warrior Review, First Draft,* and *Poet Lore.* She received an M.A. in English and an M.F.A. in creative writing from the University of Alabama. For the month of January 1997, she was an artist in residence in the "Escape to Create" program of the Seaside Institute at Seaside, Florida. Jennifer works at the University of Alabama Press as an editor. She thinks often of Eugene's admonition to "combat dailyness" and misses being called "Blondina."

Herbs and spices found in Eugene Walter's kitchen shelves,
161 Grand Boulevard, Mobile, Alabama:

cumin seed,
sesame seed,
savory leaves,
saffron,
fennel seed,
thyme,
turmeric,
tarragon,
pickling spice,
poultry seasoning,
lobster boil,
gumbo filé,
fenugreek,
cinnamon sticks,
cinnamon sugar,
curry,
cardamon,
chervil,
cayenne pepper,
oregano,
chili powder,
caraway,
asafetida "yellow powder" from India,
vanilla beans,
anise,
juniper,
green peppercorns,
annatto,
vanilla,
pumpkin pie spice,
allspice,
truffes du perigord in a tiny yellow can

Pat Conroy

Pat Conroy is the author of a number of novels, among them, *The Prince of Tides, The Lords of Discipline, The Great Santini,* and *Beach Music.* Some of his works have been made into movies (*Tides* and *The Great Santini).* Among other things, he is currently working on a cookbook, an excerpt from which is his contribution to this collection of memories of Eugene Walter.

Mr. Conroy is married to an Alabama girl who keeps him "chained to Stern Duty and Deadlines," as Eugene would say.

On Eugene Walter of Mobile

When I moved to Rome, Italy, in 1981, I did not expect to meet the large number of American Southerners who had ventured there in their youth and never gone back to their homeland. They popped up everywhere and in strange contexts. The word "expatriate" took on a dark, smoky luster that it never had for me. To find the courage to give up everything that had made your childhood either immemorial or unbearable was a vanity of freedom I had never encountered. As an adult, I had found myself so haunted by my parents and my geography that I have spent a lifetime trying to write my way out of my addiction to memory. The American expatriate I had expected to meet in Italy, certainly; the Southerner, never. I thought all unhappy Southerners migrated to New York. Never did it occur to me that, for some of them, New York was just a stop-off point where they made their flight connections to distant points on the globe.

During the whole first year in Rome many of those disaffected Southerners I met said, "What a shame you missed Eugene Walter. A magnificent Southerner. More like a Renaissance man than a sadsack Alabamian. A novelist. A poet. An actor. He was in Fellini's *8 1/2*, you know. A songwriter. A translator. An Air Force cryptographer living in the Aleutians during the war. A famed gardener. And the best cook in Rome."

That I had missed the best cook in Rome caused me great anguish and keen regret. What was remarkable is that I rarely met a single American who had not known Eugene Walter and could not share a tale about this pixilated, garrulous, and perfectly whimsical enchanter. Rome had soured for him when the Red Brigades began to set off bombs in his neighborhoods and kidnap policemen he knew by name who were guarding the headquarters of both the Communist Party and the Christian Democrats, both of which were a block from his garden apartment. As for timing, my family and I passed Eugene almost in mid-air over the Atlantic. As we began our first day in Rome, he had ended his. Eugene returned to his roots in Mobile, Alabama, where he would live out the rest of his artful and over-achieving life. Because I listened so ardently to the plainsong of his nearly inconsolable friends, I always felt that I had missed one of the great opportunities of my life by not getting to sit at the feet of Eugene Walter.

"The food you missed," Alfredo di Rocca, the composer, would say, shaking his head sadly. "The meals were simply magnificent, spread out like works of art."

The great artist Zev, whose art works seemed painted with peacock tails and the dreams of preoccupied children, told me, "Eugene Walter was a walking civilization. He could do anything and knew everything. The conversation you missed! He didn't just *talk*. It was never just *talk*. It was grand opera."

I could not pass a restaurant without being told by some new friends that they had dined on *that* terrace with Eugene Walter or walked along the path of *that* park or sat in the shadows of *that* ruin talking to him about Camus or Sartre or Proust, all of whom Eugene had known and entertained and fed. I met some Italians who were in love with the whole state of Alabama just because Eugene Walter had sprung so fully formed and elegant from that deep South state. Many Italians were fully prepared to like me because they knew my native state of Georgia was contiguous to the one that had produced the incomparable Eugene Walter. His footsteps were numerous and broad and just by tracing them through his abandoned Rome, I realized the part expatriates play in defining the American spirit to their host countries. More than all the diplomats I met abroad, Eugene spread the joy and honor and wonder of being American and representing the essence of our finest selves as he told his incomparable stories and weaved his tantalizing web during his Roman years.

I never once saw Eugene Walter in Rome, but I felt his presence keenly. When my family returned to America after two years in Italy, I placed a call to him in Mobile and sent pleasant greetings and a hundred *ciaos* from a diverse and fervent group of friends from Trastevere to Parioli.

"You must come to meet me at once," Eugene said, after I had delivered the message from his Roman life. "There's friendship waiting here for you in Mobile. Time is swift and glorious friendship is one of the few condiments that make life both sweet and sour. What sign are you?"

"Scorpio," I answered.

"How dreadful. But it cannot be helped. I'll do the best I can to like you. Though I can't promise a thing. You are a large man with a weak voice, aren't you?"

"Yes," I said.

"Your family is not much, I would guess. Good solid peasant stock, but nothing to write home about."

"Exactly."

"Call your travel agent this moment," Eugene Walter said to me. "I know destiny when I hear her precious heartbeat."

I followed the call of destiny's precious heartbeat the following summer and found myself embracing Eugene Walter as though we had known each other for many years. He walked me through the dining room of a very fine restaurant where he was well-known. Every eye was on him. He was wild-haired and fixed you with dark, piercing eyes. His voice was honeyed and piping and his pronunciation was precise as befitted the actor and the linguist he was. He sounded like Nero with lines written by Truman Capote.

"Let us get something straight between us," Eugene said as we took our seats and the busboy filled our water glasses. "Your mother misnamed you. She was a frittery, vain woman who did not take the trouble to get your name right. You have never been a Pat and never will. It's a name for other people of no consequence. I will think of a name for you."

"Thank you," I said.

"No need to thank me. That'll come due when I find the exactly right name for you. Naming is one of the most important things. Ah! It's coming to me. I've got it. It's perfect. Do you want to hear what you should've been called all your life?"

"Yes," I said. "I guess."

"Lyon," Eugene said. "L-Y-O-N. You are Lyon and will always remain Lyon to me."

And so I did. Each time I called to check in on him in Mobile from that day on, Eugene Walter would say, "Greetings, Lyon. You evade me because you know you should be here in Mobile, living across the street from me, sitting at my knee and writing down every word I utter. It troubles you, Lyon. You could be my Boswell. Instead you are vegetating in a perfectly empty and licentious life in Atlanta, the whore of Georgia. Do you know the oldest thing I've ever seen in Atlanta is a traffic light or maybe a half-pound of rat-trap cheese? You belong to the ancient places, Lyon. You are an Etruscan and that is both your honorific and your tragedy."

In the restaurant that night, Eugene took the pepper shaker, unscrewed the cap, and poured the pepper into an ashtray on our table. When the waiter appeared, Eugene said, "Take this and flush it down the toilet of the men's room. It is dead dust and has no relationship to the sacred pods of real black pepper. This had the taste of talcum or black sand formed on volcanic beaches. Freshly ground pepper has volatile, tempestuous oils which only last about an hour after grinding. This oil is an aid to digestion. It also cleanses the blood, like garlic or cognac. Rid us of this sawdust, good man. What sign are you?"

"Sagittarius," the young man answered, removing the offending ashtray filled with the discredited pepper.

"Splendid," Eugene said. "Sagittarians are the blown kisses of the Zodiac, sweet-natured, but peppery like old-fashioned nasturtiums, not the sickly aromatic hybrids of today's tacky gardens."

I was in Mobile with my lawyer, Jim Landon, and we were staying with his sister, Sue Beard, in an area of the city near Spring Hill College. Eugene insisted that he would cook lunch for Jim and me the very next day, but he warned me that we should come prepared for chaos and surprise. Those were two watchwords of Eugene's life that he shared with me whenever I saw him in Mobile. He took the idea of whimsicality to almost absurd heights. Jim and I entered the shabby foyer of a nineteenth century house that Eugene was "renting for a song and the utter prestige of having me lease such a *déclassé* abode."

Cats moved throughout the house named with boisterous, T. S. Eliot flair. Boxes, piled to the ceiling, still bore the name of an Italian shipping company. Eugene brought an insouciance to the science of disorder. Jim and I cleaned off a sofa to make room for us as Eugene served us a glass of red wine.

Jim Landon possesses one of the most spectacular visual memories of anyone I have ever known. This lunch took place in Mobile eighteen years ago, yet when I called Jim at his law office at Jones, Day in Atlanta, he began speaking of it in precise detail.

"Eugene served us on beautiful Capo di Monte china, although I do not think the word 'china' is correct. It is simpler than that. Very elegant. Let's say plates. Yes, that will do fine. His wineglasses were thick, unwieldy, the provenance I would venture, Woolworth's. The tablecloth was lovely and I first guessed mohair, but upon further examination, I ventured it was cat hair. He served us barbecue chicken with a barbecue sauce I can taste to this day, taste but cannot duplicate. Pat, do you remember the orange slices floating in it, mustard and vinegar, and we just raved about it? Then a perfectly composed salad, dressed with balsamic vinegar and extra-virgin olive oil. We peeled our own oranges for dessert. You mangled yours, of course. I cut my peel very precisely in one continuous piece that sprang back into its original shape when I laid it upon my Capo di Monte plate. Afterwards, he served us a demitasse of strong Italian espresso. Then he gave us each a teaspoon of sugar moistened perfectly with angostura bitters."

"No wonder people think I'm a redneck, Jim," I said. "I never think about moistening sugar with angostura bitters."

"That is only the beginning of the thing, Conroy," Jim said. "I must take my leave now. I have real paying clients who actually require my legal services. 'Capo di Monte,' I believe you will discover, means 'at the foot of the mountain.'"

Eugene Walter sent me a paperback copy of his cookbook when it was published in November 1982. He had titled it with a baroque Eugene Walter-like flourish, *Delectable Dishes from Termite Hall—Rare and Unusual Recipes*. I read the book from cover to cover the day I received it, and it remains one of my favorite cookbooks in a library that has grown into a fairly extensive collection. There is not a recipe in the entire book that does not shine with a ray or two of Eugene's strange, piquant life. On every page, his complaints and prejudices about food and life spill out, staining the napery and the carpets with his vinegary opinions about everything. I have not come across a bad recipe in the book, and certainly not a dull one. It was Eugene who told me that as a cookbook writer he was always trying to disguise the fact that "my real job is to be a philosopher king or a prince of elves. If it has magic, Lyon, look for my footprints nearby. Promise me that, Lyon. Always."

But always is never long enough, and it is a word that runs out of time the way that life does. When I heard about his death in Mobile, I took down his first novel, *The Untidy Pilgrim*, from the shelf. I turned to the first sentence of the first page because I wanted the essence of the man to enter the room where I stood grateful to have known and loved him: "*Down in Mobile they're all crazy, because the Gulf Coast is the kingdom of monkeys, the land of clowns, ghosts, and musicians and Mobile is sweet lunacy's county seat.*"

Ciao, maestro. Whenever I feel magic in my life, I will look for your footprints. That is a promise, Eugene Walter, a promise from Lyon.

Jim Landon

Jim Landon is an attorney who lives in Atlanta, Georgia. He is a great friend of worthy causes, giving freely of his time and talent

It was the sort of baroque weekend that only a Mobilian could have taken for granted, and I certainly did not. Conroy [Pat Conroy] and I had arrived a few hours before he was to deliver the graduation address at the Julius T. Wright School, an assignment he treated less casually as each of my niece's beautiful classmates arrived in the kitchen to model their graduation pearls. He retreated in panic and emerged an hour later with a passionate exhortation that each of them beg the world to "teach me to dance!" which is still talked about in Spring Hill. (Yes, *Zorba* had been on the television in Atlanta the night before—luckily.)

And little did I suspect that our weekend would end two days later with lunch prepared by one of the great dancing masters. Eugene Walter was simply larger than most lives. His eccentricity would have been fey had it not been balanced with genius, as demonstrated by that memorable luncheon.

We entered his temporary lodgings (he had been home from Italy a mere two years) through a wide hall furnished with cardboard boxes of books and with cats. Lunch was served in a room whose floor held a large plaster deposit bearing an identical perimeter to that of the bare lathe spot in the ceiling. And the table, set with extraordinary Capo di Monte dishes, was anything but impeccable—but the cats appeared to like it. As if prophetically, the floor tilted slightly toward the kitchen, whence emerged, in time, the most superb barbecued chicken imaginable, the sauce containing large chunks of glazed oranges and lemons. A carefully chosen Gallo Hearty Burgundy was transformed by the menu. As their talk progressed, and stories of their separate experiences of Rome unfolded, the two writers finally realized that neither was hanging on the other's every word and relaxed.

Happily unnoticed, I peeled the orange which had been presented to me as dessert and, for the first and last time in my life, cut a continuous spiral peel from the stem to the blossom end, which snapped back to create an empty orange when the fruit was removed. It was a private delight, completely appropriate for the occasion. The orange was followed by a sugar cube doused with bitters—the world's most sophisticated sweet—and coffee, and a mad run for the airport.

There could not have been a better or richer introduction to the unique talent whose books, stories, plays, and columns—and, far too rarely, conversation—delighted me and my friends in the years that followed.

Donald Winsor

Don Winsor, a pentimento of remarkable poetry, was tutored by Roy Brown—the talented Headmaster of Plymouth Academy, Plymouth, Massachusetts; a professional orchestra conductor, upon retirement; and later in life, a consultant and creative writing instructor in Gainesville, Florida.

During the early Cambodian campaign, Mr. Winsor produced *Instant Thai*, a language publication provided by the military in Phanomsarakham, Thailand. Some of Mr. Winsor's works have been published in a variety of magazines, newspapers, and journals. His delightful poem *Senryr* (River Willows) appeared in the *Minachi Daily News*, Tokyo, Japan. Other poems written by Mr. Winsor are included in *Breakthrough*, Calgary, Alberta; *Hob-Nob*, Lancaster, Pennsylvania, *Bell's Letters*, Gulfport, Mississippi, *J. S. News*, Gainesville, Florida, and the subtle but charming *Frog Gone Review*, Mt. Clemens, Michigan.

Mr. Winsor has done political poetry, pre-published in Portlandville, New York, predicting the downfall of President Bush, and his new pseudo career at the bucolic broccoli farm. Mr. Winsor has self-published a variety of educational tracts, charts, and some scriptural poetry. His outstanding poem on apocalypse horsemen appeared recently in *The Remnant* as *Celestial Caballeros,* and was previously broadcast by radio Bonaire of the Netherland Antilles.

Mr. Winsor, who attended Lee College, has been a bodacious writer for over twenty-five years. He is from Gainesville, Florida, writes unusual poetry, and teaches eschatology.

A tribute to

Eugene Walter

The menu;

The muse;

and the memory:

UNDINE DESIGN

Pundit of peruse

Fine cuisine, ensues Eugene

Metaphoric mews.

David Walter

I was born in Mobile in 1946 to Francis and Martha Walter. Eugene's father was my father's older brother. When Eugene was a small boy he used to sit on my mother's front porch steps and listen to her play the piano. My father and mother met when my mother brought her outboard motor that she used for racing to him for repairs. Of course you can imagine that my mother, who raced outboard boats one minute and played the piano the next, was just the sort of person Eugene was attracted to. He told me that as a child he had a huge crush on her.

I grew up on Austill Lane in Spring Hill where we kept a milk cow in our back yard for a short time. I graduated from Murphy High School in 1964, joined the Marine Corp in 1965, and moved to Fairhope in 1968 after my discharge. I began my marine business then and have continued in that profession. For the last thirteen years I have been building artificial fishing reefs. Eugene always delighted in introducing me as "my cousin The Reefmaker."

Eugene was my cousin, but I did not meet him until I was twenty-four years old. We had corresponded while I was in the Marine Corps and found a mutual taste for the unusual.

Eugene returned from Italy to the United States in 1969 to do research on a cookbook. His expenses were paid by the company doing the cookbook. He already had the material he needed for the book but used the opportunity to tour the U.S. in style at someone else's expense. He contacted me and arranged to meet for dinner at a restaurant in Mobile. I was nervous at the thought of meeting my famous cousin. I was very much aware of my every move, and my conversation was stiff and superficial.

We were seated at a table, and I noticed a small sign next to the salt and pepper shakers that read, "Trudy is your waitress." No sooner than we sat down, Eugene looked around and, seeing no waitress headed our way, screamed at the top of his lungs, "TRUDY!" Every conversation and activity in the restaurant came to a halt and waitresses came from every direction, apologetically saying that Trudy was in the bathroom. After the initial embarrassment, I couldn't help but drop my defenses and enjoy the evening and the meal that Eugene refused to order from the menu.

Eugene left the next day and I didn't see him again for several years, but I will never forget that dinner.

Carolyn E. Haines

I first met Eugene at a party on Old Bay Front Road. He arrived with a box full of hot dogs from the Dew Drop Inn and a demand that everyone eat.

The first time I heard him perform was when he graciously agreed to read at one of the Second Saturday Series public readings at the old Lumberyard Café. I was barely thirty, unpublished, and awed by Eugene.

And then I had lunch with him. He was the most educated person I'd ever talked with for any length of time. And the most generous. He taught me many things, but one of the most important was that labels and categories are the tools of the small-minded who are trying to minimize others in an attempt to expand themselves.

Eugene gave me an incredible quote for the jacket of my first novel, *Summer of the Redeemers*. He read *Touched* and offered suggestions. He was wildly enthusiastic about my black cat detective, Familiar. I regret he didn't get to read *Them Bones*.

He introduced me to the habit of drinking port in the middle of the day—and the consequential necessity of "The Nap." And he gave me the phrase that excuses both behaviors—"we live in the sub-tropics, dahling." I use it every chance I get.

Ms. Haines is a member of the Deep South Writers' Salon and the Regular Readers Society.

Eugene: Magician, Enchanter, and Artist

It was a perfect October day, the kind of day that would have elicited an invitation from Eugene to "sit with me in the jungle and share a glass of port. It's—you know Mobile is the sub-tropics." Only this was the fall of 1998, and I was in Eugene's Grand Boulevard home with the executor of his will, Don Goodman.

I had dreaded the idea of "walking through" Eugene's house one final time. I had attended Eugene's funeral, but the Church Street Cemetery hadn't been one of "our" haunts. His home, though, had been the locale for most of our conversations.

When Don called to generously offer the chance for a formal goodbye, I almost declined. Don said a film crew was arriving the next day, and he also asked if I would help him make some decisions about preparing the house for the taping. Don wanted to recreate the place as Eugene had it— before he became so sick. And I think that, in his generosity, Don also knew how important it would be for me to say goodbye.

My tendency is to avoid confrontation with loss. The idea of going back to the place where I'd shared so many wonderful moments with Eugene was daunting. But I had so many great memories of that old house that I wanted a final visit. Closure, I suppose. At any rate, I bucked up and went.

Don had done a fabulous job of putting things in order, and I was indeed reminded of the days when I first knew Eugene. Those days when we would have dinner parties at his table, holding off several cats with one hand and protecting the butter dish with the other. As a cat lover, I was never put off by Eugene's tolerance for his beloved felines. The antics of the cats were sort of a bass rhythm to the melody of Eugene's wonderful stories and delicious food that he prepared back in the late '80s when we became friends.

This day the light was absolutely perfect. Golden warm light that would put Eugene in mind of days in Italy when he rambled the countryside, sampling food and wine and talking with goat-herders. It was the kind of light that Eugene could make magic with, transporting me to a time and place I'd never known and yet making me feel as if I were there.

Don had been working for most of a week, yet there was still a lot to do. We hesitated a moment on the porch, then opened the screen and stepped inside. My first inclination was to reach back and latch the screen door. How many times had Eugene urged all visitors to take care that his cats didn't get out? But the cats were gone. That reality was the first stab of loss. There was no longer a need to latch the door.

Eugene's walls, covered in the work of artists both young and old, famous and on the road to fame, were a testimony to his interest in all degrees of talent. Don had ordered some of the clutter, but the books and papers, the trinkets and tools of an artist were still there. Not for long, though. The house had to be emptied.

I asked Eugene one time to tell me one word that described his childhood. If we think about it hard enough, each of us can come up with such a word. Hauling a load of dirt in a wheelbarrow up a hill one afternoon at my farm, I stumbled and tipped the load. At that moment, I had a blinding revelation about the emotional patterns that were the fabric of my life. The word that described my childhood was responsibility. My destiny, or fate, or addiction, or curse—whatever you choose to call it—was to provide the best possible environment for the things I loved, in this instance, my horses.

Eugene's word was enchanted.

Though there were times I could gleefully have throttled him because his lifestyle choices were the exact opposite of responsible, I also envied him the magic and the freedom that were the biggest part of his spirit. And I needed so much the elements of enchantment that he interjected into my life. My biggest regret is that I didn't let him lure me away from my "duties" more often to play. I turned down too many invitations in order to finish a book or mend a fence.

Standing in his "parlor," knowing that he wouldn't sweep out of the kitchen with a glass of port in either hand, I looked around at the two chairs on either side of the occasional table and the place where his cat-clawed sofa had once been. I remembered the night we toasted marshmallows in the flames of candles, a moment of sheer whimsy.

With each of his friends, Eugene had a different relationship. With me he was never petty or petulant. Just as I learned to value the element of enchantment through Eugene, I also learned to differentiate between big and little talent and spirit. Eugene's generosity toward other writers, other artists, other performers came from the huge capacity of his own heart, and his own talent. He had no need to belittle others, or withhold the wisdom he'd learned. He gave that, plus praise and encouragement and hope to many, many people.

He also gave acceptance. There was only one trait that infuriated him— that of snooping. He despised anyone who plundered through his things. He was a private man who shared willingly to the extreme. But what he held private was sacred, and woe be unto the fool who tried to pry or plunder. We both agreed that anyone who came in the guise of friend but whose base intention was to pry should be pilloried and shunned forever.

Don and I talked about these things as I read the titles of books on Eugene's shelves, recalling tidbits of plot or character that Eugene had shared with me. He loved mysteries and British authors, but he was a loyal and avid reader of Southern writers.

Once I'd made my tour of the "parlor," I went into the "Cat-Free room" where I came face to face with the life-sized Dolly Parton cutout. Eugene loved Dolly! He kept her cutout in this room where he kept his most valuable treasures, not excluding the mannequin hand that reached out from behind the sofa. I looked at what must surely be the shrine for Tallulah Bankhead's pubic hairs—but I didn't touch it. Those things are best left for scholars and historians.

Don called my attention to the French translation of one of my books on the coffee table. Eugene's generosity to me and a thousand other writers and artists was captured in that grand gesture. He was never shy about calling attention to his friends' works. He gloried in mischief, such as when he created a pseudonym for me. He did reviews of my books on WHIL, and was fond of saying things such as "she's also written the *Pirate Maiden* under the pseudonym of Hippolyta Haines." Hippolyta was his secret name for me—a name derived from my love of riding horses and the outdoors.

In a moment of whimsy, Don turned on the dancing hula girl that delighted Eugene with her hip-waving antics. Eugene adored her. Somehow, through wars and politics, parties and hard times, Eugene managed to retain the wonder of a child. One of his greatest talents was that he could infuse his friends with that magic. I had the most vivid memory of the mischief and delight on Eugene's face when he showed me the hula girl for the first time.

When we sat in the "Cat-Free" room, Eugene often entertained me with stories of his time in Europe. He'd spin out the names of celebrities—a galaxy of stars who clustered in Europe during his thirty years there. Like everything else with Eugene, he made those people as real and accessible as he made himself.

His recounting of his stories had nothing to do with embellishing his own life. Eugene had no need to cling to the past. He lived in the moment in perfect contentment. Or so it seemed to me. Yet he could make the past come alive, and he included me in that world.

The next room was his study/office. I had spent almost no time there, only occasionally looking up something in his complete *Oxford English Dictionary*. There was never a time that I needed a word that I couldn't pick up the phone (except, of course, during his nap time—which was forbidden and elicited extreme displeasure) and ask for his help. A French term?—call Eugene! Help with a recipe—dial the master chef! A gardening crisis—there was no facet of herbs, shrubs, trees, or flowers that Eugene couldn't help with. And if he didn't know, he knew how to get the answer.

There were even times when, in plotting a mystery, I needed a deadly plant. Eugene was the source. He had an amazing knowledge of vegetation. Not to mention that he could walk into his backyard and return with a garden salad fit for a king.

One of my favorites was a plant he called "the angel's armpit" because of its smell. He would tell me to fetch some, and I would gladly oblige.

In my yard in Semmes I have some of his plants. A maple, a tallow, an oak, a beautiful wild rose. Not all of the plants he gave me survived. But Eugene was never one to point the finger of plantocide at a gardener who tried.

In the dining room Don had uncovered some of the fanciful dishes that Eugene loved—hand-painted Italian pieces of ceramic artichokes, asparagus, and other vegetables. We talked briefly about a display for the film crew. Then I suggested that we go outside on the porch.

It was not that the house was empty of Eugene. Far from it, the house was full of him. So many memories. So many moments that we shared as we discussed writing or a movie or a book we'd both seen or read.

Don and I sat on the front steps, shaded by the tallow trees that had been a bone of contention between Eugene and the power company whenever they came to cut them back. Eugene had fought for those trees. I doubt it will be long before they are removed without Eugene there to protect them.

It's just one more aspect of him that I'll miss. You could count on Eugene to say what he thought—and what he felt. Usually tempered with kindness, but occasionally with the spice of razor-sharp intelligence.

Kindness and wit are a rare combination. He would approve of my deduction that it's easy to be stupid and kind. And then he would point to certain Alabama politicians who'd achieved not even that dubious combination since they lacked the capacity for kindness.

I was not at the hospital when he was taken there the weekend he died, but I've been told that when the doctor asked him if there was anything he was allergic to, he said, yes, only one thing. Fob James.

I miss him greatly.

Crepe paper and tin foil: Celestine got
the rôle of Queen because "I was the
biggest girl in the third grade — too
big to be a regular fairy..."

Nancy Hartley

Nancy Hartley has been a Special Education/Career Tech teacher at Augusta Evans School in Mobile, Alabama, for the past twenty-five years. She has an education degree from the University of South Alabama.

She first met Eugene when, with mutual friends Joe and Donna Camp, he attended a dinner party at Nancy's home. His unique, delightful personality made a lasting impression.

Eugene, being a consummate gardener, was interested in her job working with "special needs" students in a greenhouse setting. One of the manifestations of his interest in the "poor dears" was to bring items by the school which he thought could be helpful. Nancy admits she still does not understand how the bag of used kitty litter was supposed to be used in their program.

Most people would be surprised to know that Eugene was interested in helping the "special need" students at Augusta Evans School. The greenhouse program is certainly richer because of Eugene. Our herb beds sport many herbs and flowers that he shared and enjoyed. We have several rare plants that he gave us. (Oh, if I could have said "rrrare" with as many R's as Eugene put in.)

He often had his "grocery store drivers" stop by our classroom with a trunk full of goodies for "those dear children." The students would let me know that Eugene had arrived in the parking lot. He would yell out "yahoo" several times and we would come running. I really think deep down the children frightened him, but he wanted to do for "the dears."

He so loved to send us empty cat food cans, the expensive brand with a strip of aluminum foil around the top. Eugene thought it would help the kids' motor skills to remove the foil and later we could use the cans to start seeds.

My greatest regret is that we never realized the herb booklet he wanted to produce. It would have featured his recipes and line drawings regarding the herbs that we raised for sale in our greenhouses. We talked about it often and planned to do it soon. Alas.

We have in our flower beds lots of wonderful plants that Eugene gave us—and lots of odds and ends around the class and greenhouse areas. My favorite is a pool cue. Early, early one winter morning before Eugene died, as we met in his back yard and walked into the garage, he picked up the stick and with a wink said, "Tie your tomatoes up with this. Truman Capote and I played pool with it."

I still have the cue, of course. It sits in my classroom and reminds me of the wonderful times we, my class and I, shared with "Uncle Eugene" when he paid us a visit.

Yahoo!

Cammie East

Mary Cameron Young Plummer East, generally known as Cammie, is the daughter of Cameron and Mary Francis Plummer, longtime proprietors of the Haunted Book Shop. She grew up in the book shop, mainly, where there were many kind and nurturing adults who took good care of her. Eugene was among them.

Eugene was one of "the Hants" of the shop in the late '40s, and worked in the shop until Cammie's father discovered what Eugene's idea of conducting a sale was. When asked the price by a customer, Eugene replied, "Well, I don't know. What do you think you ought to pay for it?"

Cammie graduated from Julius T. Wright School for Girls in 1963, and attended Wellesley College from 1963 until she left to marry P. D. East in 1965. She has a B.A. in history from the University of South Alabama. She has worked for the *Mobile Register* since November 1974. She is "an accomplished dilettante, able to summon many bits and pieces of insignificant trivia on many subjects, but nothing of great significance to anyone."

Widowed since 1971, she still resides in the home she shared with P. D. in Fairhope. Eugene was one of the enthusiasts and supporters of P. D.'s *Petal Paper.*

My first real recollection of Eugene Walter comes from the day about 1970 when my mama called to announce that he was in town from Rome and was doing research for the Time-Life cookbook. By the way, she said, could she bring him over to our house for lunch! (You'd best believe that's intimidating for a cook of my caliber.) Foolishly, instead of whomping up a batch of chicken salad and deviled eggs, I did what passed for a company dinner, complete with little store-bought frozen shrimp in a cream-dill sauce. Eugene was warmly appreciative anyway. (I dare say he privately thought my cooking would do in my husband, P. D.)

And then there was the time Eugene had a yard sale at the Cox-Deasy House on the grounds of Oakleigh, where he first lived upon his return to Mobile. I think he thought I'd inherited Mother's keenness about sales and pricing. I hadn't. But I went, although not so early as the first eager yard-salers who just about broke down his door at six a.m. Most memorable of that day: the part-time Baptist preacher, decked out in a gold polyester jump suit, who bought everything in sight, then haggled over the fifteen-dollar price of a Venetian glass chandelier that would have probably brought at least fifteen hundred dollars at any local antiques store. (But I didn't know that then, either.)

I did see a Venetian mirror in a bentwood frame, marked fifty dollars, that I bought from Eugene a few days later. I don't know whether it was a bargain or a treasure, but it was one of those objects that haunted me after I saw it. I loved it then, and do, even more, now. As I still cherish the toy box he made for me in 1947, from a wooden crate that had been used to ship books. He painted it, labeled it "Cammie, *sa boite a joux-joux,*" and illustrated on it a Plummer family enhanced by a sibling for me and a fluffy puppy, neither of which ever materialized. I used the toy box as a coffee table for years, and now it's at the foot of my bed.

Another time, I went to have lunch—I picked up some of Pollman's finest ham-and-cheese po-boys on the way, as I recall—with Eugene at the Cox-Deasy. It was during the time when he and the historic ladies had fallen from each other's favor. When I came back to the office after lunch, I'd had a call from one of the ladies, telling me that I'd "been seen coming and going from Eugene's house," and hoping that I wasn't planning to do a story. (Only after I'd left Wellesley to marry P. D.—when folks in two counties counted months up through and past nine with an equal absence of titillating outcome—had I ever previously known myself to be the subject of such speculation and scrutiny.)

It was mildly delicious, I'll admit, to be at the center of even so small a "scandal" with Eugene, however tiny the teapot that spun the tempest. I informed the dear soul that I'd known Eugene since before I was born and didn't consider having lunch with an old friend to be an appropriate subject for any inquiry. And then Eugene and I had a good giggle about it.

I am glad that one of the newspaper's editors sent me off this past February 1998 to pick up Eugene's chapter of *The Name of the Azalea*, [the serialized Mardi Gras mystery published in the *Mobile Register* with each chapter written by a local author] which some here have suggested was probably his last published work. I privately chafed a bit at being an errand person, but was happy to have an excuse to go and visit, even briefly. That was just before Mardi Gras, and I took him some seasonal gifts I'd received—an incredible Carmen Miranda-out-of-Bourbon-Street string of plastic beads adorned with bananas and other fruits, as well as a string of gaudy red hearts, both of which he promptly donned. What I saw at Eugene's house bothered me, but reassured me at the same time. I am sure that he knew then that the end was near, as did I. He was unhappy about his difficulties with his vision, and was weary of dealing with doctors and hospitals, but was calm and level. He was not too weary to instruct me on the fine points of the difference between "carnival" and "Mardi Gras," and asked me to get someone to clean up the errors he'd seen in others' segments of the story.

He talked of affairs he'd put in order, told me I should be writing, and gave me a print inscribed *"To the ever-dancing Cammie, from her crotchety Uncle Eugene."*

The same editor and Mike Wilson, one of the more able reporters here, were eager to meet Eugene. I offered to introduce them, but suggested that we not wait long. I bought a bottle of the best port I could find, and, finally giving up on the busy editor and reporter who couldn't make it, tried to take the port by in the week before Eugene died. I never telephoned at the right time to get an answer.

So Tuesday morning, after hearing Monday of Eugene's death, I took the bottle out of the trunk of my car and sat it on what passes for a liquor cabinet at my home, where it will be the font for a toast at an appropriate moment.

you can't have everything:
personally I'll settle for sex,
vodka, and Guerlain.

Jo Ann Breland

Jo Ann Breland is a native Mobilian and a graduate of the University of Alabama. She uses her communications degree mostly in positions at various radio stations. She has worked at WHIL Radio in Mobile, Alabama, since December 1986 as an announcer and Public Service Director. Her dabbles-on-the-side include writing, sewing, photography, and acting. She made her stage debut as a teen-ager at the Pixie Playhouse in Langan Park in the lead role of the play *The Unwicked Witch*.

The best moments of my life come from my pets...six cats (one adopted from Eugene in 1995) and two dogs. They do something every day to make me laugh, and I can't imagine my life without them. That love of animals and of the arts were the common threads that ran through my friendship with Eugene Walter. And, as Eugene would have said, "Of course, my dear, you ARE a Sagittarius!"

I met Eugene when he was living at the house on Palmetto Street. Becky Paul Florence took me to visit him when he needed help creating an outlandish costume for his portrayal of Santa Claus at the annual Christmas celebration at Oakleigh (yes, Virginia, there WAS a Santa Claus named Eugene). I had never met anyone at all like him. I thought him charming, messy, and fun...and had never had food quite like what he served to Becky and me that evening.

My favorite works of Eugene's are his squiggles. Several of them are framed and hang on my living room wall circling a picture I took of Eugene cradling his cat Boudina.

Eugene used to call me "cat mother" or "Auntie Jo Ann" because I used to take care of his kitty family when he would go out of town on speaking engagements. Since I tended to the cats so often, Eugene swore that when they heard me on WHIL they would run into the living room and look at the radio because they recognized my voice (which I chose to believe).

Along with my kitty care-taking for Eugene, I used to also do some surreptitious house cleaning...just do it and not bring attention to the fact that I did. One time, I got ambitious and took home to wash a somewhat odoriferous blue throw rug that was in the living room. I washed it and it fell to pieces in the washing machine. Feeling bad that I had obliterated some of Eugene's property, I went to K-Mart and bought him a couple of fake, but nice-looking, Oriental rugs to replace the one I'd disintegrated.

When I next saw Eugene he didn't say anything about my house cleaning, or the new rugs, so I gulped and said, "Eugene, I took home that blue rug of yours to wash it and it fell apart in the washing machine, so I got you these two rugs to replace it."

He said, "Well, what did you do with my rug?"

"Threw what was left of it in the garbage," I said.

"I need it," Eugene countered.

"It was in little, teeny pieces, Eugene! What would you need it for?" I asked.

"Theatrical purposes," Eugene said firmly.

Joseph Sackett

Joseph Sackett is a retired Marine Corps officer, a former aerospace engineer, and a writer of fiction and non-fiction.

During his Marine Corps career, he flew A-6 Intruders from various land bases and aircraft carriers. Numerous squadron deployments took him to the Far East and the Mediterranean areas of Southern Europe and Northern Africa. Many of his "sea-stories" formed the basis of his first novel.

As a freelance writer, Mr. Sackett has written articles on politics, military issues, the defense industry, and items of Southern general interest. His weekly About.com features can be read at http://mobile.about.com. *Gray Ghosts* was published in 1995. His latest novel, *Present in Spirit*, was published in 1997. *Historic Homes of the Oakleigh Garden District*, a non-fiction book, was published in 1999. A third novel is in progress.

Charmed by Southern ways and traditions, Mr. Sackett and his wife now live in a post-Civil War Creole cottage in Mobile, Alabama's Oakleigh Historic Garden District.

Mr. Sackett met Eugene at a plant sale. At that meeting, a discussion of the wickedness of the New York publishing world ensued. When both parties concluded they were on common footing, a friendship was born. Soon thereafter, Eugene assigned Mr. Sackett weekly chauffeur duties.

The Santa Fe Oak

"My goodness, would you look at *that*." Eugene pointed to the side of the road.

Glancing to my right, I spotted the subject of Eugene's attention. A middle-aged woman of fifty or so was about to cross Old Shell Road. Her long, flaming red hair was a bit lascivious for her age. Her skirt decidedly too tight and short.

Eugene wiggled a gnarled seventy-five-year-old finger in the woman's direction. "If I were a few years younger, I should like to engage in a few moments of sociological research with *her*. She *must* be French."

I repressed a grin as the woman faded in my rearview mirror. "We have too much on today's agenda, Eugene."

"I know, I know." He turned and smiled wickedly. "She was something, though. She brought back memories of Europe. Ah, yes..." Eugene looked beyond the live oaks lining Old Shell Road. "That's one thing that's so wonderful about Mobile. You turn a corner and a flash of Europe strikes you when you least expect it."

"My sentiments exactly, Eugene." We drove on.

For the next two hours, I transported Eugene to various commercial establishments—the dry cleaner, the post office, the print shop, a trip to the Eclectic Art Gallery for book and squiggle replenishment. After a leisurely domestic re-supply at Delchamps (before the Jitney Jungle scandal), Eugene announced his readiness for lunch. "What'll it be? Chinese or Dew Drop?"

"Your choice, Eugene. I could do either."

"Let's be worldly, then. Hong Kong Island! I'm paying, of course. It's the least I can do to repay you for your kindness. You're the last of the Christian martyrs, you know. A model of patience."

I grinned but said nothing as I steered the car west.

"Heineken, my dear. With a glass."

The waitress smiled, then turned to me. "And you, sir?"

"Iced tea, please."

The young woman smiled once more, then hustled away to fetch our drinks.

For the next hour, Eugene and I swapped stories, periodically agonizing over the wickedness of the New York publishing world. Throughout our sitting, we consumed various bits of oriental buffet items, ending of course with Eugene's favorite part of the meal—soft ice cream and almond cookies. At the meal's conclusion, our waitress presented the check. I covertly slipped it to my lap.

"I saw that."

I waved my hand. "I've got it, Eugene."

"But you got it last time." He shrugged. "I won't argue. It's not polite to argue over food. French manners, you know." Eugene paused for thought. "In lieu of monetary restitution, I have something in my garden for you. I want you to take it home with you. It's getting too difficult for me to tend my plants these days. I can't bend like I used to. I have a rather unique lost child who needs a home—and I've been saving it just for you."

My eyes widened. Eugene knew I was a sucker for plants. "I can't wait."

"All right then. You pay the check, then we'll go home and have a finger of Port. After that, I'll fetch you something special from the garden."

After two Ports in the No-Cat-Room, Eugene escorted me through the kitchen to the backyard. On the way, he grabbed a cardboard box, stuffing the bottom with damp newspaper signatures. "It's over here, Joseph." He waved me to his position. "You'll need to grab a shovel to dig it out. I'll be keeping the pot."

Soon I was standing before a rather odd-looking potted tree. More than a mere sapling, the thing stood four-feet tall with oversized, rather unhealthy looking spotted leaves.

Eugene beamed. "It's a Santa Fe oak. It's very rare in these parts. Will you take it?"

I concealed my uncertainty. If the oak was imported from Santa Fe (as the name suggested), what chance would it have of surviving on Alabama's Gulf Coast? Situated beside the Sangre de Cristo mountains, Santa Fe's arid climate was totally unlike Mobile's. I punted. "I didn't know they had oak trees in New Mexico."

"Of course they do!" Eugene furrowed his brow, studied my reaction. "Now, will you take it?"

I forced the look of a proud father. "Of course I will. I'd be honored."

Eugene smiled and shook the cardboard box in an approving manner. "Good!" He stroked a spotted leaf and spoke to the tree. "You're about to have a new home, young orphan. Joseph will take good care of you. I have utmost confidence in him."

A guilty vision of dry lifeless branches snapping before Gulf Coast winds and hurricane downpours flashed through my mind. I forced the scene away. "She'll be in good hands, Eugene. You can count on me."

An hour later, the sickly spotted Santa Fe oak stood transplanted in my back yard.

The months passed. In November, Eugene's oak shed all its leaves. By December, all traces of suppleness and vitality had left the tree's humble branches. I worried that the oak had not survived the transplant or had rejected Mobile's climate. I thought about confiding with Eugene and asking for advice, but decided against it. Eugene's own health was beginning to fail, and his aged but honored cat, BW, had just passed away. Eugene had given me the Santa Fe in good faith, that I might properly care for it and relieve him of that small burden.

By late February, Mobile saw the first signs of an early spring. Azaleas bloomed early glories. Pin oaks sprouted greenery, challenging the splendor of Mobile's celebrated live oaks. By early March, crepe myrtles sprouted delicate sprigs and botany inspectors noted early evidence of furry pods forming amidst green waxy magnolia leaves. By mid-March, my Japanese maple burst forth a coat of fiery red leaves. The last to leaf out, the red maple had always defined the time-sequenced threshold of what was going to bloom and what was not. Clearly, the Santa Fe oak was not. Not a sign of life. Nothing but dry brittle branches forming the exoskeleton of a tragic soul lost to winter in a foreign land.

In mid-March, I called on Eugene for our monthly tryst to the Regular Readers' Society. More than the previous year, the winter of 1998 had aged Eugene. Slow afoot, he was nonetheless in good spirits that day. We discussed Bob Bahr's book on creative fiction. Eugene ate potato skins and sipped a Heineken. After the meeting, I took Eugene home and, as usual, we adjourned to the No-Cat-Room for a Port and a few final moments of lively discussion. It was the last discussion we would have.

Eugene took ill and passed away two weeks later. My confidential friend and supporter was no more. On April second, a lively Excelsior funeral allayed the grief I had experienced while seeing him on his deathbed. Fittingly, Eugene was laid to rest in Church Street Cemetery beside Judy Rayford and Joe Cain.

The day after the funeral, I sat on my back porch contemplating a weekly routine without Eugene Walter. The thought was depressing. While staring at my rear garden, I was distracted by a squirrel scurrying down a tree to investigate an unidentified morsel on the ground. I chuckled as I recalled Eugene's story of feeding dry figs to the squirrels—just to note their reactions. That's when I detected a faint bit of greenery where none had been before. I rose from my wicker to investigate.

As I approached the source of my curiosity, the bit of greenery turned to multiple tiny green buds on an otherwise barren silhouette. Closer evidence confirmed my unlikely conclusion. Eugene's Santa Fe oak was alive! Despite contrary indications, the tree had survived winter and had come back to life! I looked toward Church Street Cemetery. In some magical way, Eugene's passing provided the energy to boost a lifeless essence into a modest springtime celebration—a sly squiggle of nature that only Eugene could produce.

There is a homeless fellow who strolls Government Street, talking to the trees. Many of you know who I mean. Most people say he's crazy. They're probably right. But I too must confess to talking to a Santa Fe oak now and then. The oak still doesn't look like much. It's only five feet tall and its leaves are disproportionately oversized for its modest branches. But a friend gave it to me to care for— and I'm doing my best. Thanks, Eugene. Someday, I'll see you again.

A cat's eye view from Eugene's back porch
(Photo courtesy Walter Reinhaus)

Roy S. Simmonds

Mr. Simmonds is a British writer who has written on John Steinbeck and is considered a major authority on that literary figure. He is also the author of two books on the Mobile novelist William March.

Mr. Simmonds developed a fondness for Mobile and the deep South through the writings of Mr. March, which was furthered by his discovery of Eugene Walter's work.

He came to Mobile in 1988 to join in the celebration hosted by Auburn University and the City of Mobile in which Eugene Walter was honored as "the Renaissance Man."

Two Lunches, Two Brief Meetings and a Handful of Correspondence:

Memories of Eugene Walter

I first met Eugene Walter in Mobile in the early spring of 1986 while I was visiting that welcoming city for the "Salute to William March" program. I had arrived hoping that during my brief stay I would have the opportunity of meeting Eugene, for I had long admired his work and was both anxious and curious to meet the writer who had so vividly and often (I suspected) idiosyncratically brought alive for me the sights and smells of the city of his birth in his novels *The Untidy Pilgrim* and *Love You Now, See You Later*, and in the short stories collected in England in the volume *The Byzantine Riddle*. The desired meeting was brought about through the true Mobilian hospitality and generosity of Mrs. William S. Burks, Jr. when she invited both Eugene and me to lunch at a restaurant of (so I understood) Eugene's choice, the name of which I never really ever recorded in my mind, but which, if I remember correctly, was situated somewhere close by the defunct Gulf Mobile and Ohio Railroad terminus. At least, the photograph I took immediately before the two I took of Eugene at table, his glass upraised in greeting, is a view of the grandiose but deserted facade of that station building.

I do not possess by any stretch of imagination the gift of total recall, so there is sadly no way in which I can here reproduce the conversational jewels that Eugene regaled us with during the course of the meal. Suffice to say that the three of us had a most enjoyable time: good food, fine wine, and witty and wise discourse, as always, from Eugene's lips. The man had a fund of stories that held Nell Burks and me enthralled and frequently shaking with laughter, although, in a more serious vein, he had some rather uncompromisingly forthright opinions to express on certain local issues. I was particularly anxious to hear from him about his involvement in the early days of the *Paris Review*, and of his time in Italy and his work with Fellini and the Princess Caetani, founder of the poly-lingual magazine *Botteghe Oscure*. I inquired if he had any plans to write his literary memoirs, giving the lowdown on some of the writers and artists he had been telling us about. It would be a fabulous book, I urged. He did not, however, feel the need for any urgency in the matter (although he admitted he had a possible title, *My First One Hundred Years*) and dismissed the whole idea as being something he might get around to doing someday. When I mentioned that I was a subscriber to the *Paris Review*, but that my collection was missing some of the early numbers, there was no hesitation in his reaction. He offered, if I let him know which numbers I didn't have, to check if he had spare copies at home, which he would be only too glad to let me have.

Shortly after I arrived back home, I wrote to Eugene and advised him of the numbers (there were eight of them) I still needed to make up my complete set. He was as good as his word, for a few weeks later I received a letter from him postmarked June sixth:

*I very much enjoyed meeting you and sharing lunch with Mme. Burks (whose secret name is Yoga Mae Pom-Pom). From your book [*The Two Worlds of William March*] I learned that I was born only a few steps from the birthplace of Bill Campbell [William March] (Conti and Bayou for me). Do you think there's something in the water? I must apologize in taking so long to answer your nice letter of March 18. I had been suffering all manner of malaises and finally thought to check with my dentist who turned pale when he saw some root canals that were done in Italy. So with extractions and antibiotics and painkillers and all that ro-ra I've been more or less out of the picture. Then, too, I had to seek in some hurriedly hurricane-packed boxes to find those* Paris Reviews. *Well, I'm so pleased to tell you I found Nos. 1, 2, 6, 7, 8, 11, and 13. That leaves No. 4 you still lack. Why don't you write the New York Office of* PR? *I know that most of the earlier nos. have been reprinted and are available either from our office or a certain bookshop. I'll take these to the post tomorrow. In return perhaps you could locate a reading copy (I don't care how battered) of* The Book Without a Name *by Lady Morgan (1840s or '50s). I had it for years and it vanished in some move from someplace to someplace. It used to turn up everywhere in London ... .*

Nell Burks so enjoyed meeting you. She's on the Riviera now. I'm dealing with workmen dealing with what last Fall's hurricanes Elena and Juan dealt us. Later, in peace and quiet I shall enjoy your book at leisure and do a proper review. I read the mss. [sic] long time ago and was very impressed. All good wishes and let me hear from you.

Mille fleurs,

Eugene

The package of *Paris Reviews* arrived on July fourth and I wrote a long letter, in which I thanked him for the magazines and reported that up to then I had had little luck in tracing a copy of *The Book Without a Name*. The search, I assured him, would continue. I wrote him again on August twenty-sixth, apologizing for my silence, occasioned by the fact that I had still not been successful at all in my searches through the London secondhand bookshops, but that there were still a few others that I could try. In mentioning that my latest work, *William March: An Annotated Checklist*, had just been accepted by the University of Alabama Press, my fingers stumbled over the word "Annotated," which came out as "Annotted." The error obviously appealed to Eugene's sense of humor, as evinced at the beginning of his next letter, which he sent just after Christmas.

> *I don't think I told you how glad I was to hear that the* William March A Knotted Checklist *is to be published. Much needed, I'd say. Auburn University is going to honor me in the same way it did Bill Campbell, with testimonial dinner etc, et al..*
> *.. Meanwhile I am working on the mss. of a collection of comic (I hope) and satirical (I know) poems called* The Pack Rat & Other Antics *to bring out as soon as possible. I don't care in what condition* The Book Without a Name *[is], even a Xerox will do. I just want to have the text. In the 40s it cropped up in London and Edinburg catalogues.*
> *Every good wish for a prosperous and entertaining New Year and*
> *Mille fleurs*
> *Eugene W*

I replied on January seventh, congratulating him on the forthcoming testimonial dinner and telling him that Nell Burks had sent me an invitation to the buffet supper she gave to the Auburn organizers, Leah Atkins and Bert Hitchcock, on November 18, which unfortunately I was unable to accept.

> *... The things I am missing here in the backwaters of Essex! I hope that Auburn will let me know when your great day will be, so that I can be with you all in spirit if not in the flesh ...*
> *... Your new book sounds delightful. Please let me know when it is published in the States—or will it be published over here as well? I am still pulling out all the stops in trying to find a copy of* The Book Without a Name. *I have several bookdealers searching for it and with all the activity I have created something <u>must</u> turn up soon. If not, I'll see if I cannot somehow get a Xerox made for you, although this too may present some difficulties.*

Again, there was silence. I wrote another letter on June twenty-second, confirming that I was returning to Mobile in November, with my wife this time, and that I was looking forward to meeting him and Nell Burks once again. I was hoping to play some part in the celebrations in his honor on November twenty-first and twenty-second.

Today at one of the large London book fairs, I again tried to find that elusive copy of The Book Without a Name. *I have come to the opinion that booksellers aren't what they used to be. Most of those I asked about the book thought I was pulling their legs, two had heard vaguely about the book, and one, a man from Ireland, said he had several of Lady Morgan's books back home, but not a copy of* The Book Without a Name. *However, he did show more intelligent interest than anyone else, and I have given my name and address in the hope that he might be able to turn something up.* The Wild Irish Rose *[one of Lady Morgan's romances] has recently been published over here in paperback. Is this of any interest to you?*

... Has The Rat Pack & Other Antics *been published yet? Are you still working on* My First One Hundred Years? *Is the novel version of* The Blockade Runners *finished? ...*

Eugene mailed a reply on July thirteenth:

I was happy to have your nice letter. I called Nell Burks and shared it with her ... I sent the collages which illustrate Monkey Poems *to the press in Texas by United Parcel Service which was created to avoid delays, damages, and losses of the U. S. Postal system but the packet arrived smashed, even though it was marked 'fragile' and insured for a small fortune. Luckily I had put everything between layers of heavy pasteboard...*

Odd about The Book Without a Name: *during World War II and just after it cropped up in a number of catalogues. I'm sure it will again. Yes, thank you, I'd love* The Wild Irish Girl. The Pack Rat *comes out Sept. 1, and* Monkey Poems *shortly thereafter. I'll give you a review copy of* Rat, *of course, but I don't know how they will do about* Monkey. *If you're interested you could write and ask them simply to reserve a copy until you come over.*

To give you a hint or a preview I'm sending under separate cover a shuffled mess of proofs of Rat *for (I hope) your amusement. Do you have* The Pokeweed Alphabet? *Nell has extra copies and will send one if you don't have it. I'm trying to work on a book of memoirs but have been delayed by dental problems, the ro-ra over the celebration, etc.* Negative Capability *is publishing a supplementary volume with bits of autobiography, new poems, a story, drawings, etc. This is a new typewriter; I haven't*

tamed it yet. It is only 9:30 AM but the reading is 83F. I find it too hot and humid to work in the garden and it has turned all jungle ...
                    All best
                        Eugene

I sent *The Wild Irish Girl* over on July twenty-fourth, enclosing a note to tell him that I was over the moon at having picked up "the other day right out of the blue" a copy of the 1953 Gaberbocchus Press edition of *Monkey Poems*, and followed this with another long letter on August 6, thanking him for *The Pack Rat* proofs. I told him that Leah Atkins had sent me copies of *The Likes of Which* and *Jennie, the Watercress Girl*, and that I had obtained a copy of *The Pokeweed Alphabet* from the Haunted Book Shop the previous year, reminding him that Mrs. Plummer kindly got him to sign it for me [he had written on the flyleaf: "for R. Simmonds from E. Walter (he will understand the message!)"], and that I had also picked up copies of *Undine* and *Delectable Dishes from Termite Hall* at the same time, both of which he had also signed. In the latter, he had written: *"For the amazing Simmonds, the famous long-distance biographer, from the amazed Eugene W."*

In Mobile, things were already obviously moving at a fast pace and I received no reply to this last letter, although a signed copy of *The Pack Rat* arrived early in October, bearing the message: *"For Roy Simmonds, with every good wish from Eugene Walter. See you soon!"* I wrote again on October 10, thanking him for the book, looking forward to his new book, *Adam's Housecat*, and hoping to have news of it and of his book of memoirs when we met the following month. He sent a postcard on October twentieth:

We are all so busy. Monkey Poems *delayed in BINDERY—all hard work. Nell sends greetings. Look forward to meeting Mme. Joyce & seeing you again.*
                In haste,
                    All best
                        Eugene

The visit of my wife and me to Mobile was for us a memorable event. We met up with Eugene on the afternoon of November 15 at his autograph party in Billie Goodloe's Books & Co., but, of course, there was little opportunity on that occasion to make much more than fairly superficial contact. Eugene was in great form, clearly lapping up all the attention he was being given. The confines of that friendly little bookshop exploded with bonhomie. As, so it seemed, did the whole of Mobile during the next few days.

Two days later, Nell Burks once more acted as gracious hostess at a lunch she arranged for Eugene, Joyce and me, and Rod Jackson at the Riverview Plaza. The five of us ate and talked and laughed for two hours, and Eugene presented me with a generous portfolio of some of his "Squiggles" prints, an exhibition of which had been opened at the Townhouse Gallery of the University of South Alabama the previous week.

Those of us who were there will never forget the Gala Dinner in the Plantation Ballroom of the Riverview Plaza Hotel, on the evening of November twentieth. Eugene's grand entrance up the hotel's long, gleaming escalator and his triumphal progress between the two lines of laughing and applauding guests on the crowded verandah outside the ballroom was truly a sight to behold. If my memory serves me right it was all conducted at a fairly spanking pace, and in no time at all Eugene had disappeared with his entourage behind the closed doors of the ballroom. We lesser mortals waited outside, while the official photographs were being taken within, and when at last we were invited in we were confronted by the breathtaking sight of that vast array of round tables, stretching away in every direction, each table with its pink tablecloth and each, at Eugene's special request, with its centerpiece of collard greens. Yes, indeed, it was a night to remember!

Thinking back on those heady days in early November of 1987, I get the impression that all the public flamboyance and the occasional outrageousness on Eugene's part was simply a cover for what was, at root, an underlying shyness and a very real compassion. Certainly, other than on the night of the gala diner, he contrived to maintain a strictly background posture. On the afternoon of the day following the gala dinner, there was held at the Bernheim Hall a literary forum ("Discussions of Walter's Works") followed by performances and readings of his works (*Monkeyshines*). Eugene was, however, conspicuous by his absence. I recall that during a break in the proceedings I slipped out into the foyer to retrieve a book I had left behind on a sofa before the program had started. Eugene, a lonely figure, was standing on his own, gazing out through a window. I urged him to come in and listen, but he declined, saying that it would be all too embarrassing. "I'll come in later," he promised, but, even then, I had the feeling that wild horses could not have dragged him into the auditorium.

After the conclusion of the Celebration, my wife and I traveled to Tuscaloosa, Athens, Murfreesboro (for Thanksgiving dinner with friends),

Birmingham, and finally Atlanta, where we caught our plane back to England, arriving home on December fourth. I eventually wrote to Eugene on December fifteenth, regretting that there had been no opportunity for the two of us to get together for a quiet talk. It was well over a year, early April 1989, before I next heard from him:

I apologize for long silences; I get so involved in dailyness that correspondence suffers. I've heard you've been ill and I am indeed sad to hear so. I hope all's on the mend by now. I'm mailing the Neg. Cap. [Negative Capability] which took forever to come out (a year and 4 months late) but it sold out before publication and is being reprinted e'en now. I'm sending as well the Haunted Book Shop's reprint of my very first book, from 1946, Jennie, the Watercress Girl. I've been very involved with a new weekly paper, doing a column and reviewing books, etc., and with a project of a friend, Fred Baldwin, a gifted composer, actor, esprit, who has taken an old Creole firehouse downtown to turn into a theatre ... . The Creole firefighter groups were elegant clubs really with highly polished fire engines downstairs and ballrooms upstairs for Carnival. This building is about 1840ish and looks like such in London really, four squat Doric columns downstairs, red brick body, classical pediment, etc. We envision concerts of new music by Southeastern composers, new plays by young Southeastern playwrights, a repeat of that Monkeyshines programme everybody enjoyed so much, all that. And readings, and exhibitions, and revues.

Let me have a squeak from you; I hope that your medical problems have become only a memory. Sweeping bows and compliments to Madame and deepest good wishes and mille fleurs from

Eugene

I replied on the fifteenth of April, assuring him that I had recovered well from surgery and thanking him for all the goodies he had sent. I regretted yet again that there had been no time in November 1987 to visit his Aladdin's cave at 161 Grand Boulevard and asked when it was going to be possible to read his teeming memoirs. His reply was written a fortnight or so later, on May Day:

I was so happy to hear from you and hear of your good progress. I suffered two bouts of an elusive and virulent form of tropical WHAT? which the epidemitoligists think Cuban soldiers brought from Africa and the worst part was the weeks and weeks of strange lassitude which followed so I sympathize with your post-operative lassitude. I find that small luxuries are always a help. I've worked with the dusting and straightening up but NOT MODERNIZATION of the Haunted [Book Shop]. I think you'd approve. I'll pass on your greetings. I've just been up to Montgomery to read at a festival celebrating the improvements at the state archives. Met some delightful critters who run bookshops up there. What is so amazing is how shops and critics and scholars are "discovering" me for the first time. National Public Broadcasting is coming later this month to do a TV color special on my household and myself (I suppose) so I am busier than sixteen beavers and eight squirrels attempting to transform my natural author's squalor into a more seemly picturesque disorder. And I have to curl out the eight bush-tails and polish a little brass. I always find that if the brass is polished nobody but nobody notices the dust curls copulating under the sofa... . Nell has been working on a series of little guidebooks to Mobile. I've been trying to face up to a final revision of my novel Adam's Housecat. *And sifting through a lifetime of material, all unpublished. And so it goes. This is in haste, to send best greetings to you both; I was so glad to have your news.*

more later, keep me posted.
mille fleurs
Eugene

I replied on May twenty-first, expressing my relief that the Haunted Book Shop wasn't being ruined, and hoping that the TV program went well. I trusted that the revision to *Adam's Housecat* would not be too long delayed— "nor, and I am saying it again, your memoirs of New York, Paris, and Rome in those exciting days of the '50s and '60s."

There was another long, long delay before I heard from him, this time a postcard dated September ninth, 1991, bearing the message: *"Dear Frens, Hey, how you? Send me a squeak & I'll return with a salvo. All best. E.W."* He sent at the same time an order form for his recording *Rare Bird*.

I replied a month later. I apologized for having been disgracefully out of touch, but excused myself by telling him I had been busy, putting the final touches to a two-hundred-fifty-thousand word book on Steinbeck, asked if *Adam's Housecat* had yet been published, and enclosing an order for *Rare Bird*.

The *Rare Bird* cassette arrived in due course, but no further letter. Another postcard turned up early the following March: *"Please say if I have the correct address. Want to send you my new book. How are you both? Best S'uthun-fried good wishes! best, Eugene."* To which (in part) I replied on March tenth, confirming that he did, as was evident, have my correct address. I assured him that I was in good health, and that at the moment I had three books seeking publishers.

I am much looking forward to reading your new book. Is this, I wonder, Adam's Housecat, or something else that I do not know about? As I have told you before, I hope that you will, if you have not already done so, get around to writing your memoirs. That would make a terrific book. I much enjoyed the Rare Bird *cassette. It was good to hear your voice again and the readings were perfect, as of course they could only be.*
Say Hello to Nell for us, and to all our other friends in Mobile. If sometime you could send a newsy letter, my cup would runneth over!

Eight months passed, and then I received a card from him—a combined flyer and order form for a new edition of *The Pokeweed Alphabet* that had been published by Crane Hill Publishers in Birmingham and described as: "An illustrated nonsense alphabet to charm even the nastiest old crank! It's Eugene Walter's phabulous paperback primer of linguistic glee! (Rumored to also reveal the meaning of life!)" With his pen Eugene had crossed out the word "also" and had written a message in the space reserved for the name and address of the person ordering the book:

This book and Hints & Pinches *will reach you shortly. All best—E.W.*

Three months later, no books having arrived during the interval, I wrote, expressing my concern that I had not heard from him for some time, and wondering if perhaps the anticipated books had gone astray in the mails. I hoped that all was well with him and asked about the memoirs. A copy of *The Pokeweed Alphabet* arrived a month later. It was inscribed; *"For the dear Simmonds, with cat and monkey good wishes from Eugene Walter."* I wrote the day after it arrived, sending my thanks and telling him how my wife and I had enjoyed turning the pages and chuckling, constantly amazed, as always, by his wicked inventiveness. *"Keep well, Eugene,"* I wrote, *"and keep working and continuing to delight us. We need such joyous works as yours in this mad world! .... MANY THANKS!"*
This time he replied, on March twelfth, 1993, obviously as soon as he received my letter:

I was so happy to have your nice letter and glad the book arrived. Oh, yes, there will indeed be more. The day I turned 70 I decided to open all the boxes, make clean copies of all the mss. and Devil take all publishers and agents even if I don't.

Your queries: some of the illustrations are my drawings, of course, and many are really collages made from illustrations in late Victorian reviews, like Leslie's *and* Harper's.

But the real news is that you're working on a novel. I think that's great. ALL literary historians and critics, and commentators and anthologists want to write "creative" texts; all "creative-writers" die to write commentaries and criticisms, etc. It's part of the bi-<u>hex</u>uality of writing types. Change tracks with relish.

I haven't heard from Leah [Atkins] or Bert [Hitchcock] but I know they're busy. She's been wildly admired for her War of Secession lectures. I've begged her to make a tape.

> *All best, more later ...*
> *Eugene*

But there was to be no more. I wrote again on the thirteenth of August that year, and then I became ultra-involved in revising one book and proofreading another, and then trying to write yet another. I imagined that he was similarly engaged.

Then earlier this summer, [in the summer of 1998] while I was glancing through the contents of the just-delivered June twenty-second and June twenty-ninth double issue of the *New Yorker*, I caught sight of his name, and turned immediately to page sixty and plunged with all the delight of old into his lovingly recalled memories of his Mobilian childhood, *Secrets of a Southern Porch*. As soon as I had finished reading, thinking that I must write and congratulate him on the piece, I looked up the Contributors column and it was there that delight became sadness when I learned that Eugene had died in March. The one consolation was the news that at the time of his death he had completed an oral history of his life.

I pondered on the fact that I had never got to know him as well as I would have liked: two lunchtime meetings, a few words exchanged at an autograph party and in the foyer of the Bernheim Hall, and a mere handful of exchanged letters are little enough on which to base a knowledge of that unique, compassionate, maverick, sometimes cock-eyed personality that was Eugene Walter. But then, I still have the books, and for these I am overwhelmingly grateful. I have only to read a few lines such as these plucked almost at random from *The Untidy Pilgrim*—

"Just north of the downtown business district of Mobile are some shady streets bypassed in the town's westward growth. Many of them are still

shaded by the fine stands of live oak, and are comprised of handsome town houses built between the 1840's and the 1880's. The best-looking are the oldest, built of rosyred brick, and ornamented with fanciful iron lace galleries, and balconies; with fences of this same crazy curlycue work enclosing the gardens.

Or—Mobile was at its loveliest. Long after sunset the sky still held an apple-green glow tenaciously, giving up only for that luminous and velvety blue that colors the very air, and makes windows and street lights seem more yellow than usual. The streets of Spring Hill were all slumbering darkly, save for an impromptu breeze now and again that seemed to turn round several times in a single treetop like a restless bird settling itself to roost."

—and I am transported back by his genius to the Gulf Coast and can imagine myself once again walking along Church Street or Government Street. It is magical writing and in its very heart, like a throbbing light, is the love that he always felt for the city of his birth even when he was far, far away in Alaska, England, Paris, or Rome. The pure joy that is in his work, be it prose, poetry, or art gives joy to the reader and the beholder. It is infectious. It is a joy of living.

Fantasizing, I like to picture him now, surrounded by every one of the beloved cats that he ever owned, gazing down at us all from his monkey heaven, with that somewhat bemused and slightly mischievous expression he so often had—and perched, not on a white cloud, but on a large sack of celestial collard greens.

James White

I met Eugene Walter shortly after I moved to Mobile from Los Angeles. He was most complimentary of my first novel *Birdsong*, which had come out years before. He never mentioned any of my later novels to me, but a mutual friend said he told him that I should buy a bottle of Scotch, drink the whole thing, and write another book like *Birdsong*. I liked and admired Eugene and always made sure that USA's writing program asked him to speak each year at various writing activities we hosted. I did so because he was a wonderful speaker and he needed the money. Eugene had a chip on his shoulder about professors and universities in general; his spontaneity and honesty made him someone who brought education with him wherever he went.

Mr. White is the director of the Creative Writing Department at the University of South Alabama. In addition to the novel Birdsong, *he is the author of* The Persian Oven, California Exit, *and* The Ninth Car.

On Eugene Walter

Eugene Walter's charm and wit were obvious to anyone willing to see them. I resisted a moment early in our acquaintance because during our first lunch at the Dew Drop Inn, he introduced me to everyone coming to our table as James "Smith." But over the years I got to know him better and gladly appreciate his individuality (for want of a better word).

Eugene had the kind of education that would be impossible today because of our bureaucratic schools and materialistic way of life. He had learned the love of literature and history from spinster teachers who made the subjects they taught the love of their lives. He looked past making money and seeking fame and focused on what interested him. His eye was leisurely and piercing—he knew history and enjoyed calling a spade a spade. I would imagine that to someone educated to hunt money, Eugene could seem superficial and perhaps at times silly. But he was one of the bravest people I've known.

The simple logistics of his life would have frightened most people. When he returned to Mobile from Italy, he didn't get off the boat and attempt to find a paying job. Instead, he continued his life that was, from one aspect, carefree, and found the support of others. I don't think I know anyone else who could have managed this as Eugene did. It took guts. It meant that he was uncompromising concerning how he would lead his life. He chose to continue cultivating his mind and the people around him, and, in an important way, teaching sophistication to anyone who crossed his path. He was like the spice of his own cooking. He made ordinary life a celebration.

Everyone has Eugene stories, which is what he was all about. He realized that one's history or past is a means of touching someone else.

Moments with Eugene that I especially remember are his playing non-existent musical instruments in his first reading at the University of South Alabama after I became Director of Creative Writing, his efficiently removing a steaming cat turd off the top of a newly reupholstered chair at his home, and a moment when he told me that he never had a lover. (Perhaps he's in love with life, I thought.)

I'd like to thank him now for the generous praise he gave my son Jules at the very outset of his young painting career. Jules was one of many whom Eugene aided and encouraged—he gave creative people his support, which was also his love.

The evening of Jules's packed one-man show at Bay Rivers Art Guild, Eugene arrived with a flourish, wearing tinted glasses, ready to party.

Eugene's being there was a kind of success for the event. At one point, Eugene crossed over to me and asked to speak with Jules privately. "That painting," he told him, pointing to an oversized self portrait with gold leaf, "should be in a show in *Paris*." This was a lovely thing to say, and something probably no teacher would ever say to a young artist. Having taught writing for years, I probably wouldn't risk spoiling the young writer (which perhaps is why he occasionally criticized professors and academics). Eugene's praise, as Eugene, was extraordinary. A few minutes later, I heard him say to someone else, "*That* painting could be in any museum in Europe." He was more than willing to encourage and support new talent, and create a moment of elan.

Something elusive about Eugene kept us from being close friends, but I cared for him and wish everyone in Mobile who can't now, could have experienced his remarkable self.

Dr. Willoughby's message to all.

Dr. Frances Gardner

Dr. Gardner is retired from the University of Mobile (formerly Mobile College). During her tenure she was instrumental in having Eugene's works displayed on the university campus.

Eugene Walter at the University of Mobile

The University of Mobile was fortunate to feature the work of Eugene Walter on two occasions. The first was a show on our campus of Eugene's paintings and drawings produced over a period of more than fifty years. This exhibit was part of the unforgettable *Celebration of Eugene Walter; Renaissance Man.* Professor Mack Clark, chairman of the Department of Art, says that it was the largest collection ever displayed in the Fine Arts Building.

The works ranged from black and white drawings to others in the vivid colors so characteristic of Eugene's work. They covered a wide range of subjects from his beloved fanciful cats and monkeys to a lovely painting of a beautiful young woman standing by a building characteristic of old Mobile plying her trade—one not generally acceptable in better social circles.

The second event featured Eugene in person. Some years ago, the College of Arts and Sciences established the annual Patricia Boyd Wilson Lecture Series in the Arts and Humanities honoring our dear friend, the late Mrs. Wilson. We agreed that it was highly appropriate to have Mrs. Wilson's friend Eugene as the speaker one year. It was an unforgettable night. He read from *The Untidy Pilgrim* and other works of fiction. But the program consisted mostly of readings from his poetry, including *The Quarterback's Lament* and *The Cockroach Cotillion.* I, like the other admirers of Eugene's work, always think of that wonderful, fanciful little poem each time I see a poor little creature lying on his back on my porches. My thoughts turn not to the efficiency of my exterminator, but to a wonderful party I hosted unknowingly the night before. As I recall, Eugene ended the performance with his unique rendition of country music straight from Nashville.

These past few days I have pondered the gifts Eugene gave our students and guests that night. They are numerous. Perhaps the most obvious was his dispelling the common notion of many young people that poets and artists of all kind tend to be stuffy old people. Eugene was fun. But perhaps far more significant than that was his taking them with him to a wonderful world of fantasy—child-like fantasy. Some of them had forgotten it after they left Alice in Wonderland and said farewell to the Wizard of Oz. Their current world of fantasy was centered largely on the noisy world of *Star Wars* and alien invasions. A reminder of the reality of the world of fantasy, be it encountered with aliens from other planets or sirens singing on the rocks, was Eugene's gift to our students and guests—and to me.

Sondra Maniatis

At the age of four, Ms. Maniatis, a native of Greece, came to Mobile where she was raised and educated. She received her bachelor's in history and French from the University of South Alabama where she was awarded a Fulbright Grant her senior year. She left for France to teach English in a French *lycée* and attended the *Université d'Aix-Marseille* where she studied French language and literature. Ms. Maniatis taught English as a second language on the French Riviera and worked annually at the Cannes Film Festival as an interpreter. She spent a subsequent year studying German at the Goethe Institute of Nüremberg. Ms. Maniatis received her master's in French from Emory University. While there, she received the prestigious Anna Amari Perry Award for excellence in French teaching and scholarship. She was also active in theater while a graduate student. She is currently chair of the Foreign Language Department at UMS-Wright where she has taught French for fifteen years. In 1995, she was one of fifteen teachers nation-wide to receive a grant from the NEH to study theater in Avignon, France. Ms. Maniatis is also a human rights activist for Amnesty International and has been working to free prisoners of conscience from Peru. She is married to Mobilian Clark Powell and has two children.

Three years ago UMS-Wright published its first issue of *Feu-Follet*, a French literary magazine featuring original student poems, essays, short stories, and artwork. Our inaugural issue was made unique by a contribution from the Pulitzer Prize winning author, William Styron, who allowed for the first-ever publication of an original work in French. I knew that student writing, artwork, and layout would only get better with time and experience. But how could we find another famous bilingual author to contribute a never before published work?

Just like coaches, French teachers also have to keep impressing the headmaster, board, and parents. So I anguished after that first year, until one evening at the Alliance Française I met Mobile's Eugene Walter. He was delivering one of the funniest lectures I had ever heard on a thoroughly dull and academic subject: poetry in translation. He read his own translation of select French classics and even some original works written directly in French. I was impressed by Mr. Walter's ease and grace in a highly nuanced idiom. But I was especially charmed by his wit as he covered everything from Mobile's neo-colonial structure to Isak Dinesen's drinking habits. That is when I decided to approach him about contributing to *Feu-Follet*. Jim Whitman introduced me as Sondra Aubert and I received a healthy dose of the Walter charm as he gazed at my profile and sighed, "Exquisite Hellenic. But Aubert, that's a French name, *n'est-ce pas*?"

"Only by marriage," I replied. "My birthplace is Amphyssa."

"I must put you on my mailing list," and he handed me a glass of red wine.

I had heard that Mr. Walter was terribly sympathetic to anyone with a literary bent and I suspected that he wouldn't refuse a sincere request for help, especially after this first French contact. But I decided that a request for a student publication should come from the students themselves. Yet when I explained a little about Mr. Walter's background to the two students who were to contact him, they were sure he would refuse. "A founding contributor of the *Paris Review*, a recipient of the Lippincott Prize for Fiction, an intimate of Federico Fellini! He will never have time for us!" they protested. Wrong!

Robert Mitchell, my editor, came to class the next day somewhat awestruck. A been-everywhere, done-everything, sixteen-year-old prep school stereotype, he thanked me repeatedly for suggesting he call Eugene Walter. "You can't imagine what it was like talking to him, Madame," Robert exclaimed. "The man knows everyone. He's worked with all the big guys. And he wants to help us with *Feu-Follet*. But not over the phone." That evening, Robert and Thad Inge, another upper level French student, were graciously invited to Eugene Walter's home on Grand Boulevard. They returned to class the next day bragging about how they had shared an *apéritif* with Eugene, straight scotch poured into an eight ounce glass, as they sat in his parlor. He had shown them original drawings, manuscripts, photographs, and turned their heads with tales of New York, Paris, and Rome.

The class was mesmerized as the day's lesson gave way to something much more immediate, exciting, and real. Thad and Robert, as well as other aspiring writers in the class, felt that they had brushed up against a brightly shining star. Enhanced and still glowing from its contact, they imagined themselves bigger than life. They too would travel to Europe, suffer for their art, emerge purified and ready to write. Although they did not make it to Paris that year, these students did write and beautifully so. The idea of working with someone like Eugene Walter and having him read their work made them all reach for something higher. Mobile author Jim White said of Eugene that he was the last of a generation educated in a world where the word was everything. Something of that vision was undoubtedly transmitted to my students who have remained transformed by the encounter with a truly magical presence.

SOPRANO: Rare bird, but not an endangered species.
Known to petrify conductors, infallible in quelling
choruses and orchestras. Feeds on caviar, champagne,
cornbread and flattery.

Bert Hitchcock

Bert Hitchcock is a member of the English faculty at Auburn University, where he is presently Hargis Professor of American Literature and has served as chairman of freshman English and department head. A native of Demopolis, Alabama, he holds degrees from Auburn, the University of Oregon, and Duke University. He has written articles on American writers for such reference works as *American National Biography, Reference Guide to American Literature, Contemporary Fiction Writers of the South, Dictionary of Literary Biography, The Companion of Southern Literature,* and *World Book Encyclopedia.*

**Dr. Bert Hitchcock delivered this speech on the occasion
of the Grave Marker Dedication for Eugene Walter**

1 May 1999

I first met Eugene Walter on the Saturday evening of August 1, 1986. My memory, I know, is not to be trusted and my scholarly notes are sometimes less than satisfactory. But for this matter the latter are clear and definite. The two of us came to our dinner appointment with more than a little apprehension. I was the objective, independently-minded (high-minded, I'd like to think) scholar who did not really wish to have much personal contact with the subject of his forthcoming critical essay, and who was doing so only because of a forceful push from a chief editor. Eugene, for his part, was to be talking to the person contracted to write an introduction to a novel of his that he did not want reprinted—a publication (he was clear) that he considered piracy.

So it came about that I went to number 161 Grand Boulevard.

Where, of course, I was graciously and generously received.

Eugene said later that what he was expecting was a dapper Anglicized little pencil-mustached college professor, not the (and I quote) "Scottish leprechaun" who showed up. I don't quite know what I was expecting—nor perhaps, still today, what I got. The salutations and signatures of our subsequent correspondence would transform over time from "Mr. Hitchcock" and "Mr. Walter" to "Bertolino" and "Nuncle NuGene," to "B." and "E." and "Cranky Colonel Pop-a Gut." Superficially evident here, the change was for me actually much more profound.

The title for my remarks today, "Eugene in My Life," might better read "Life in My Life." I don't want to exaggerate or be overly dramatic, but the term that comes to mind is the acronym C.E. that has recently come into scholarly use to designate what we historically used to call A.D.—or as in the abbreviation B.C.E. instead of B.C. Its meaning is "common era," or "before common era," and this usage seems compellingly suggestive for the time line of my personal interior history. Here, there is a kind of continental divide: before meeting Eugene on one side, and after meeting Eugene on the other. To designate my two eras, a reversal has to take place, however, because for me individually what was before Eugene was common, and what followed was uncommon. What I'm talking about, or trying to now, is my own very personal perspective or outlook—my perceptions of life and living and how to experience it. Moving into the Uncommon Era, I began for the first time to have some real and not just notional understanding of the right brain-left brain business. Certain bounds, or bonds—professional and cultural—that had appeared to me THE realities and THE horizons, no longer seemed, or were, that. I, the academic literary historian and scholar, began to see, and feel, the *art* in literary art, to intuit the *human* in humanities, in ways I'd never conceived before. Some things—love and fear included—William Faulkner once wrote, "are just sounds that people who never... loved nor feared have for what they never had and cannot have until they forget the words."

Am I being clear here? It's hard to be clear, here. I think now of Walt Whitman. Evidently, I didn't resign my professorship and Go on the Road, did not swap wool tweed for metal-buttoned denim. Like the "Good Gray Poet" though, I discovered a new mode of traveling and glimpsed wonder-filled brave new worlds. Just as Whitman talked once of science and facts, I must speak of senses and spirit and non-factual truths. Addressing artists rather than scientists as Whitman did, I would also declare that although "Your facts [or non-facts, but truths]... are not my dwelling, / I... enter by them to an area of my dwelling." And this area of dwelling, this new manner of seeing, of living, became for me, thanks to Eugene, an uncommon one.

As things turned out, way back then in late 1986, my academic subject took issue with only one paragraph in my manuscript introduction to *The Untidy Pilgrim*. I had used the word "whimsical," and Eugene contended that among the things he was rejoicingly free of, this was one. *"High spirits and sweet lunacy, yes, whimsy, not,"* he wrote.

Of course, he was right, of course, of course.

I, still, am not capable of poetry. But I think of lines by two poets.

First, Jean Garrigue:

But now the account's at an end, what moral comes?
Green was the wind and world and green my heart.
I speak of simple, incommodious things like joy.
At least, in a world of cold acceptance
I dream a sanguine innocence may come
As does the rain or from the mountains, doves,
And every generous action move again
The springs of some gay spontaneity.

And, again, old Walt Whitman:

Good-bye my Fancy!
Farewell dear mate...
I'm going away, I know not where,

Or to what fortune, or whether I may ever see you again,
So Good-bye my Fancy.

...

May be it is yourself now really ushering me to the true songs (who knows?)

...

Good-bye—and hail! my Fancy.

Don Noble

Don Noble has been a professor at the University of Alabama since 1969. He had the good fortune to meet Eugene Walter when he interviewed him for *Book Mark,* an Alabama Public Television show that Mr. Noble hosts. After that "Eugene and I met from time to time but never often enough."

He smiled understandingly—much more than understandingly. It was one of those rare smiles with a quality of eternal reassurance in it, that you may come across four or five times in life. It faced—or seemed to face—the whole external world for an instant, and then concentrated on you with an irresistible prejudice in your favor. It understood you just so far as you wanted to be understood, believed in you as you would like to believe in yourself and assured you that it had precisely the impression of you that, at your best, you hoped to convey.

The above is of course from *The Great Gatsby* by F. Scott Fitzgerald. In the quote the narrator, Nick Carroway, is attempting, as he does through the novel, to explain what was so special about Jay Gatsby, why he was so "great." The answer in part to why Gatsby was so special is that he made the people around him feel special.

So it is with any attempt to remember Eugene Walter and what made him so special; he made *you* feel special, honored, talented, important, especially important to *him*.

Of course, with Eugene, nothing was ever that simple, but more of that in a moment.

In the spring of 1990 Brent Davis and I made a little series of interview shows. They were awkward enough, God knows, but we were hopeful that with a little practice and more preparation I could conduct a better interview, and we plunged naively on, receiving funding for a series of shows with Alabama writers to be called *Alabama Bound*. There had been a book published by this title, we learned, but it was about Alabama prisons and prisoners and we thought the overlap and confusion with writers would probably be minimal. Brent and I set about producing the series, with no idea of including Eugene. To my shame, I had not heard of Eugene, who had been back in Mobile for over a decade by this time and had already been honored as Mobile's "Renaissance Man." I might not have heard of Eugene for some time longer to come had it not been for Katherine Clark, author of *Motherwit* and my colleague in the Department of English at the University of Alabama that year. Katherine told us in no uncertain terms that we must include Eugene and gave me copies of *The Untidy Pilgrim* and *The Byzantine Riddle* to read. As Eugene often put it, "Weeeell, that was that!" I was hooked. The work is whimsical, delightful, entertaining, mildly naughty, idiosyncratic, in fact, in style and tone, *unique*, and one does not stumble across that every day. I *was* hooked, and that *was* that.

Before the actual interview, it seemed wise to meet Eugene face to face and get some sense of the person. His old and good friend and colleague from the *Azalea City News,* Becky Florence, arranged that, and we met one evening in Maia's Chinese restaurant out near the interstate. It was the first of a string of meals shared, evenings which had a certain similarity. Wherever we were, Eugene *loved* this restaurant. He *adored* certain dishes there. When we actually ate the dishes, though, they were not quite up to snuff, a little disappointing. There was never as much talk about food with Eugene as I had expected, and hoped for, since he was the author of the Time-Life's *American Cooking: Southern Style* and lots of other writings on recipes, herbs, spices, and so on, but there was enough so that one knew the cuisine was often a disappointment and Eugene could have done it better.

At his place on Grand Boulevard, however, when Eugene cooked, the meals were somewhat odd. Whether Eugene could not afford expensive ingredients or whether he was just bored with "conventional" food, I do not know. What I do know is that I was fed interesting, surprising salads with tart, even bitter little herbs from the back yard in them. I was fed some kind of barrel-shaped pretzels with peanut butter, I think, in them. (Eugene thought these were a real "find.") For dessert one evening we roasted marshmallows at the table, over candles.

The setting for those meals was also unusual. As all visitors knew, Eugene had lots and lots of cats. One of these cats was, so to speak, arboreal. Eugene had arranged, pardon the expression, catwalks, in the kitchen. These were pine boards that ran from the tops of cabinets to the refrigerator, to above the stove and so on. One cat apparently lived up there, near the ceiling, and had his food and water dishes up there, and his litter box too. Standing in the doorway to the kitchen one evening I watched Eugene sauteing while cat hair and other items drifted gently down onto the stove and sometimes into the pan.

Another of Eugene's cats, as all visitors noticed, had some kind of skin condition—mange? Leprosy? Who knew? As we sat in the living room having some bourbon before dinner I glanced into the little dining room and there, curled up asleep on the dinner plate that was to be mine, wouldn't you know it, was the cat with what I will daintily call the running sores. When we went in to eat Eugene *very* gently put the cat onto the floor. There was no hint of discomfort or any reprimand to the cat. When his (Eugene's) back was turned, I wiped my plate with my napkin and we all moved forward. It was not a place where one felt it appropriate to be fastidious: we were having an *adventure.*

Eating out was also an adventure, as noted. One evening Jennifer Horne and I took Eugene to eat at Hemingway's, near his home. He had chosen the place. It was his current favorite. At the start of the meal Eugene ordered a salad with capers as one of the ingredients. The salad came. Eugene studied it and summoned the waiter: "This salad should have more capers." The waiter took Eugene's salad back to the kitchen, put on more capers, and returned. "No, no, no," said Eugene. "Bring me the capers and I'll put them on." The waiter consulted with management and in a moment brought out a little bowl into which had been dumped what must have been at least a full jar of the little three-and-a-half ounce, two dollar and fifty-nine cents jars of capers. "Good," said Eugene and added a teaspoon of capers to his salad. We ate on. The meal was fine. We came to the end. Eugene's appetite was not so good at this point and he asked for some take-home cartons for his remaining fish, vegetables, rolls, everything. Including the capers. The capers went into their own small styrofoam container and when we got home Eugene put all the little boxes into a refrigerator which, I noticed was absolutely packed with little styrofoam boxes. I had the impression that Eugene never got around much to finishing off these doggy bags; he just wanted them to be there.

When one took Eugene to dinner one felt special. Driving from Tuscaloosa as we did, we had no idea what Eugene's day-to-day life was like. I can tell you though that the impression one got was that it was a desert for him between visits, that no one else ever took him to dinner or anywhere else. Only after his death did it become somewhat clear to me what a large, complex network of friends and supporters Eugene had in Mobile, to drive him to the post office, the grocery store, doctors' appointments, to take him to lunch, and so on. Many of them must have felt the same way I did at being a part of Eugene's life: special.

Eugene was probably the most generous writer in his comments on other writers, of any writer I have ever spoken with. A number of years ago I spent a little time with Richard Yates, author of *Revolutionary Road* and a number of other fine books. Yates admired no one. Mailer was no good. Updike was no good. Everyone *else* was overrated. *He*, Yates, was undervalued and unfairly ignored. Eugene, who had quite a body of work to his credit, actually *was* undervalued and largely ignored in the world of letters. He *did* have a right to be a little bitter if he chose, but he wasn't. Eugene praised writers always, veterans and neophytes alike. Had I read Muriel Spark? I had. Good! Did I know Charles McNair's new novel, *Land O'Goshen*? It was brilliant. Was I reading Carolyn Haines' cat-familiar mysteries? I must, they were so clever. Eugene was a booster for the literary arts with his every breath—in conversation, on the radio, and of course in print. This is not as common as one might think.

On the day of the actual interview we arrived at Eugene's at nine a.m. and the crew set up in the back garden. Eugene offered everyone applejack on this hot, close, humid morning in June. The crew refused. "Media people who don't drink!" said Eugene. "My, my." I sat and chatted with Eugene for the hour it took to set up and we sipped applejack. During the interview, in the hot sun, we kept our glasses under our chairs and sipped during breaks. The interview went beautifully. Here's a writer who is not afraid of the camera, I naively said to myself. It was only during and after the interview that I learned how intensely he had been connected to Italian film-making and how much on-camera acting he had done. Eugene had been on camera hundreds of times, in how many films? Twenty? Forty? A hundred? I never have been clear.

During the interview he was animated, articulate, fully alive, the perfect interviewee. The stories seemed spontaneous and fresh, sometimes as if my questions had reminded him of matters or anecdotes he hadn't called to mind in years. Later, Fred Baldwin and Ted Dial and others would tell me that these stories were Eugene's stock in trade; he had been regaling Mobile parties with these anecdotes for a decade. But they were newly minted as far as I was concerned. The temptation was to feel fooled: I felt special; Eugene was *acting*. There was really no contradiction.

Eugene often said, "I combat dailyness." He gave elaborate parties in his apartment in Rome, and as he told me in our interview, "Some mornings I feed the squirrels dates, just to see their reaction." Another important part of combating dailyness is to bring freshness to each moment, so that it *is* being lived for the first time. The person he was talking to *was* special and had every reason to think so.

The interview was a small success. People watched it and liked Eugene, of course, and he received a number of invitations to read around the state. Eugene then took to calling me his "benefactor." Well, I had read *Great Expectations* and knew what ironies were there, but I was never sure. He made me feel special, and it was only much later that I learned that many people tried to help Eugene in some way, almost all of them in ways far more useful and generous than mine. The temptation was to feel hurt, but this was a temptation to be resisted.

At the risk of seeming excessively literary, having begun with a quote from *Gatsby* (Eugene would not have minded—what was he if not a man of letters every moment?), I'd like to close with some fragments of Robert Browning's "My Last Duchess:"

1. *"She liked whate'er she looked on, and her looks went everywhere."*
2. *"She had a heart—how shall I say—too soon made glad."*
3. *"She thanked me... as if she ranked my gift of a nine-hundred-year-old name with anybody's gift."*

The Duke of Ferrara is so angry with his wife for bestowing her grace equally on all around her that he has her killed. The reader of the poem knows that in this egotistical action the duke has destroyed a treasure. Eugene strikes me sometimes as our Duchess and it would be sad and wasteful to indulge in any competition over whom Eugene liked best, or to allow one's feelings to be hurt because one was "fooled" into thinking one was special to Eugene, only to learn that he had lots of other buddies, too. Eugene's great gift was making people feel special because, in his one-in-a-million childlike eye, we all really were.

Dr. Sue Walker

Eugene Walter served as an Advisory Editor of *Negative Capabilities,* a literary journal which I publish quarterly, from Issue 2, 1981 until his death in March of 1998. I first knew him when I edited the city-regional magazine, *Alabama Sun.* He spoke at the University of South Alabama where I am a Professor of English and currently Chair of the English Department. Eugene's love of literature and language, his editing experiences, his knowledge of writers, and his associations with them, enriched the lives of many students and broadened our perspectives. It was Eugene who urged me to publish my first book of poems, *Traveling My Shadow.* In fact, the picture on the back of the book was made in Eugene's garden.

Lord, Love a Duck

MEMORY recalls beyond mere knowing, for who, indeed, knew Eugene Walter? I was walking from the parking lot to the humanities building on an early morning this past end-of-millennium spring when a voice that seemed to emanate from the highest branch of the tallest pine called my name. I looked up and heard clearly: "Lord, love a duck!" Was a parrot nearby? A crow who had learned speaking louder than cawing? Scrutiny revealed only a few students ambling along as if time had no connection with classes. I heard the voice again: "Lord, love a duck!"

"Well, Eugene," I answered. "What is it you want?" Pine needles fell as if in reply, and I remembered Eugene Walter saying on more than one occasion: "Lord, love a duck" when no other comment would suffice. I scanned the horizon, looked up into the trees again, and waved to the heavens. "You've got it, Eugene," I said. "You've got it just right," and I walked into the humanities building ready to change my lesson plans and teach twenty-five freshmen that *"down in Mobile, they're all crazy"* is more than a fact; it is a cause for celebration.

It seems only fitting that Eugene Walter should signal from the sky on an early May morning to alert me to the day, to measure, if you will, my place in it, and to remind me that I had something to recall. Later that evening, when the sun nestled its rays in the popcorn trees on his front lawn, I would toast him with a glass of port. "Ladies usually have port," Eugene insisted. "They have port, rather than sherry or madeira."

I think of Eugene serving port. I hear his lips linger over *apéritif* as if the word were as sweet as only white port could be. "Just a little *apéritif*," he would say. Eugene knew what to serve—before lunch, during lunch, and after—so that when a meal was over—following a soul-satisfying lagniappe of language, literary tales, and a complaint or two if the pepper were powdery, Eugene settled into his siesta. His lunch companion, especially if unused to imbibing in the middle of the day, left his Cat-Free sitting room with an extra swagger in the step and anxiously avoided attention via automotive acceleration.

My Eugene's exotic lunches featured marvelous capers—the kind you eat and especially the kind you don't. He spoke of Carson McCullers, of her various escapades with Reeves, and he told of an evening after a feud when her husband shoved her naked out of their apartment in Paris. She had to go outside, make her way up a fire escape, and crawl through a window in order to return to her flat. It was such literary lollapalooza that I loved: the production of Mardi Gras punch served at Princess Marguerite Caetani's party for her cousin T. S. Eliot in Rome. Eugene said that he unearthed a punch bowl that hadn't been used since World War I. "I brought it up from the cellar of the Palazio Caetani," he said. In it, he plopped a huge block of ice from which he had excavated an arena for sliced oranges, lemons, and apples. Next he added two cups of cognac, two bottles of good white rum, Peychaud bitters from New Orleans, and a glug glug glug of champagne. It tasted, Eugene said, "just like fresh fruit punch from the farm." It was so fine, in fact, that Mr. Eliot forgot himself and remembered football cheers he had heard in his youth. Imagine T. S. Eliot with a yellow rose in one hand and a punch cup in the other singing "Rah-ra-rah, sis-boom-bah, go to war, Holy Cross!"

I heard about Eugene's peanut butter party on the slopes of Mt. Olympus, a party in which the poet Jean Garrigue appeared in a black dress, a fringed cape—and festooned with ostrich plumes—helped Eugene hide kittens under the dinner table. In Mobile, especially in the sizzling heat of "subtropical" summers, Eugene engineered parties to combat "dailyness" and to protest commercialization. It was at the Triggs' marvelous Termite Hall, one just-before-Christmas evening when the "Black Holly Wreath Society," eschewing store-bought, on-sale items, were dining and making merry, that Eugene's headpiece, sporting fancy feathers, met with a candle flame as he bent to spread deviled crab on a cracker and caused a minor conflagration.

The Eugene Walter I recollect was a master of inventive events. A special photograph tucked away somewhere in Nell Burks's archives memorializes the founding of the Mobile Assembly of Sages and Savants, an organization of which Eugene was a strategic part and of which he was especially fond. He relished the evening at Sue Hawkins's house when Prieur Jay Higginbotham initiated a serious discussion regarding the name that would signify this August group. It would spell out the word MASS. A picture of the Assembly is featured in Eugene Walter's *"EWEW"* column in the February 27, 1986 edition of the *Azalea City News and Review*. Eugene is all smiles sitting by me who is next to Sue Hawkins, who is beside Jay Higginbotham. Standing behind these four sages are Nicholas McGowin, Nell Echols Burks, and Fred Baldwin. "Lord, love a duck," two of the seven are eating chicken salad with lots of dark meat in some park east of the Pearly Gates while the others are arranging another MASS performance to kick off the new Millennium.

My recollections of Eugene also relate to our mutual interest in editing and publishing. It was after the second issue of *Negative Capability* in 1981 that he took an interest in the journal and became an advisory editor. In this capacity, he pushed for translations, contributed stories and poems, and devised a rejection slip that urged writers to tend a garden, care for a pet, and get involved with the world according to their whim. He reminded those who were submitting manuscripts that they should "leave room for thumbs," always double space a submission, and above all else, send clean copy. Eugene urged me, as a new editor, never to say: "This is bad writing; throw it in the trash." Instead he would urge novices to "go into the woods once a week, stare into space, take seventeen breaths and ask, 'Where am I? When am I? Who am I?'"

When the Pulitzer-prize-winning poet W. D. Snodgrass visited prior to a reading at the University of South Alabama, we were at dinner when Snodgrass said to Eugene, "I sent you some work once when you were working with *Botteghe Oscure*. You rejected me." Eugene smiled, took a sip of wine, and commented on the veal scallopine. Later I said, "Eugene, when Snodgrass told you about your rejection, you didn't say a word." I learned from Eugene that lost manuscripts are never lost, they're simply "in a safe place," but sometimes its better to smile "Southernly" than to say anything.

Among my favorite memories of Eugene are his connections with students. He never said "no" when I invited him to visit my class and talk about writing. He would mosey into the classroom in that writerly way of his, look around to give ample time for consideration, and pick up a piece of chalk. He would write a word or two, or more than that, on the board and address the marvels of the language: *un peu, assez, beaucoup, passionnement, a la folie, pas de tout.* "Flirt comes from the verb, *fleuter*— and is the action of the butterfly. Learn French," he would say. "It helps you analyze and define emotions. Write. Read." Over and over he would urge writers to "go to the library, walk down the aisle, grab a book. Carry a pad and grab a word from the dictionary. Write down what your house says. Unzip your skin; write down ideas as they occur to you. Do you know that livid means ashen?"

The last time I saw Eugene was only a week before he died. I had invited my poetry class to my house for a meal and to read their poems. Eugene came and listened attentively. He commented on each student's work. He engaged them in conversation and urged them to tell about themselves. "What is your astrological sign?" he asked. But what I noticed was the fact that Eugene, a gourmand and a person who loved food, didn't eat a bite. "I think I'll take mine home with me," he said. "I've been having trouble with my teeth." I prepared a plate of food for Eugene before we drove him home. Each mile of the way he said again and again how much he enjoyed those young people.

In recollecting that last evening with Eugene, I think that I wanted to avoid reading the signs—noting that he was thinner than I had ever seen him before, noting that he had not touched a morsel on his plate, and failing to note the significance of a picture he brought me as a gift. It was, though I didn't realize it at the time, a last farewell. The picture now hangs on the wall in my dining room. When guests sit down to dine, Eugene is there too. I won't dare serve powdery pepper, and joy shall be served up with the "you'll never know it's cucumbers" dish Eugene once pressed upon me. It is a dish jazzed up with sweet cream and a dash of nutmeg that will, he said, fool them into thinking it's elegant fare. "Lord, love a duck, Eugene. Lord, love a duck."

The only known photograph of Dr. S. Willoughby, author of *A Concise Compendium of Herbs, Spices, and Flavors* which appeared in the *Azalea City News and Review* for one-hundred-fifty issues.
(Photo courtesy of the Willoughby Institute.)

Jay Higginbotham

Jay Higginbotham is director of the Mobile Municipal Archives. He is the author of fourteen books, and his works have been published in twenty-seven languages. He has written for the *Encyclopedia Britannica* and is listed in the *Dictionary of International Biography*. Jay is also a founding member of The Mobile Assembly of Sages and Savants.

Can Do!!

There were many facets to Eugene Walter's bubbly individuality, but the one I keep remembering was his "can-do" spirit, which was sometimes almost magian in the effect it had in realizing mad ideas.

One late June day in 1985, I received a call from the renowned Russian poet Yevgeny Yevtushenko, perhaps the world's best-known writer. I'd met Yevtushenko the previous autumn in Russia and we'd gone bouncing around Moscow from one literary gathering to another. Now Yevtushenko was in America to do some poetry readings in New York and remembering the wonders of the Gulf Coast described to him, decided he'd like to perform in Mobile. Could I set up a performance for July third and make all the arrangements by the end of next week?

"....why, sure," I said, somewhat dubiously, and promised to call him the next morning.

Frantically I began telephoning close friends, many of them patrons of the arts. After several hours, I was at wit's end. I was leaving for Mexico and California the next morning and wouldn't be back until the day before Yevtushenko's proposed concert. Responses to the proposal ranged from "Who's Yevtushenko?" to "Nobody could draw a Mobile crowd on a Fourth of July weekend."

Sadly, I was about to telephone Yevtushenko to tell him the timing was impossible, that it couldn't be worked out, when Eugene returned my call. I was pleasantly shocked when his immediate reaction was an effusive, "Ooh, let's do it!" This was the only positive response I'd received, and enough to encourage a few more phone calls, after which interest gradually heightened. Within a few late-night and early-morning hours, we managed to form a group initially called "The Mobile Committee on Fine Arts." In the project now were Dr. Sue Walker, Fred Baldwin, Nell Burks, Nick McGowin, and Sue Hawkins, all close friends of Eugene's.

Over the next ten days, numerous details were worked out. Yevtushenko put on a sterling performance at the Joe Jefferson Playhouse and was made an honorary citizen and given keys to the city by Mayor Arthur Outlaw. In all, it was not only a highly successful occasion, but it led to the formation of an ongoing performing poetry group known as the Mobile Assembly of Sages and Savants. In addition to our own performances of Russian, Chinese, English, and Hebrew readings, MASS also brought Yevtushenko back to Mobile three more times, and hosted Allen Ginsberg and other acclaimed American and Canadian poets.

In re-living some of these lively occasions I often think how none of them would ever have happened had we not heard those wonder-working words, "Ooh, let's do it," from the never-say-nay lips of Eugene Walter. For me, it was Eugene's most characteristic reaction and one that saw hosts of local art projects through to success.

Sure, I know that sugar ruins your
teeth... but everything you do ruins
something.

Laurel Wilson

When their first book, *Coasting: A Guide to the Northern Gulf Coast,* was so well received, they (Judy Barnes, Jolane Edwards, Carolyn Lee Goodloe, and Laurel Wilson) decided to focus on Mardi Gras. In 1995 they wrote *Coasting Through Mardi Gras: A Guide to Carnival Along the Gulf Coast.*

During their research they happily discovered some of Eugene Walter's sketches and, of course, he graciously allowed them to use some of them. In addition to reviewing their book on the radio, he enthusiastically supported their endeavor.

In Memory of Eugene Walter

One of our favorite memories was lunching with Mr. Eugene Walter, Mobile's own "Renaissance Man." Mr. Walter graciously allowed us, "the Coasting Belles," to use some of his whimsical sketches for our Mardi Gras book and after the book was published, we invited him to lunch. At noon we arrived at his eclectic, part Southern, part European house for a pre-luncheon drink—a fine port served in tiny crystal glasses.

After drinks and conversation, we piled into a car and headed out to a restaurant in Spring Hill. Parking was scarce so we let Mr. Walter and two of our group out while the other two parked the car about three blocks away. Before he looked over the menu, Mr. W. announced that he would like to order a bottle of wine. Just as the owner was explaining that he did not sell wine, the two car parkers appeared, flushed from walking up-hill in the sun.

"Dollinks!" cried out Mr. Walter. "Run quickly back to the car and hurry to the liquor store at the bottom of the hill and get us a respectable Beaujolais. This is to be a celebration!" And that is exactly what it was. Wine was finally procured, although the car parkers now had four blocks to walk. A fine lunch was enjoyed and the "Coasting Belles," as Mr. W. called us, were richer by far from having been in his company.

These memories along with some delightful correspondence from Mr. W. serve to remind us of that delightful man whenever "Stern Duty and Deadlines" get us down.

The following post card was postmarked May fifth and addressed to:

The Barnes, Edwards, Goodloe, Wilson Combo.
Whereupon he wrote:
Dollincks, the book is delightful! I'm reviewing it on WHIL on the 20th or 27th or whatever they decide—call WHIL in a week and ask them —
(380-4690)
Congrats; all best
Eugene Walter

And the following letter was written on September 6, 1995 on The Willoughby Institute, Inc. stationery:

Dear Bevy, Re caption of drawing and title on placard in drawing. Yes, of course change New Orleans to Gulf Coast. But I do wonder about that "Happy Mardi Gras!" After all, Mardi Gras is simply

one day and we're speaking of the whole forty days of Carnival.
Why not one of these:

> *Live and Let Live!*
> *Glee, Spree, Whoopee!*
> *Dance and Let Dance!*
> *Don't Stop Now!*
> *Point That Toe, Thumb That Nose!*
> *Have Fun, Come Undone!*
> *Live It Up, Live It Down!*

Let me know. When are we going to meet for lunch and yack-yack?
I'm chained to Stern Duty and Deadlines at this moment but only
for a few more days. Buzz me: 479-9829.

> *All best,*
> *Eugene*

Since this letter was addressed to the Coasting Belles and since none of us are named Bevy, we presumed that "Dear Bevy" meant Bevy of Belles! I personally loved *Point That Toe, Thumb That Nose!* but I was voted down. (I guess I liked it because I'm not a native Mobilian!)

I'm a Southern belle ... I like travel ...
and real estate ... and money and gin and
travel and skinny-dipping in the moonlight and ...
oh, you know ...

Mickey (Mary B.) Cleverdon

John, my husband, and I have recently completed a chapbook of poems and woodcuts entitled *Questions of Form*, published by Slow Loris Press of Fairhope.

Eugene was the great encourager of all who worked in the arts, warmly enthusiastic, supportive, and optimistic. He often inquired about the progress of our book: "Now send me an advance copy so I can promote it on the radio." He was referring, of course, to *Eugene at Large*, his bubbly Saturday morning show on WHIL featuring book reviews, recipes, and his own idylls of Southern life, past and present.

Sorry, Eugene, that we were too late to send you a copy before you left.

What made Eugene "Eugene" was his way of turning the ordinary into the extraordinary, his ability to seize the day, the hour, the minute, the moment, and whirl them into his own space-time continuum for as long as the extraordinary lasted.   It was *Eugene-time*, in which schedules disappeared, and somehow it was all right. Knowing Eugene, you accepted the givens—they came with the territory, and what a territory he could create!

John and I had met Eugene when he returned to Mobile from Italy that horrendous summer of 1979, the summer of Hurricane Frederick. But it was this day, several summers later that we got to be with him for an occasion, when Nell brought him across the bay to our house.

When I say *house* I mean an old Point Clear summer house with dark pine paneled interior, a large central hall, and wrap-around screened porches, with clothes lines and a sink on the back porch. The house had fallen into some disrepair at this point in its history (post-hurricane Frederick; we were concentrating on rebuilding the pier and bulkhead). I was a bit dismayed because of the way the white paint on the porches was peeling—not just in places, but all over—ceilings as well as walls. And not just little flakes—oh, no. Ribbons of paint hung down, curling and draping along the walls, miraculously not falling, but trailing down, suspended in frail feathery stalactites from the ceiling.

So, nothing to be done about the paint, I concentrated on what to fix for lunch—fresh shrimp from the bay, boiled, and served with garlic butter and a lemon/catsup/horseradish sauce, green salad, and French bread, with blueberry pie and ice cream for dessert. Knowing Eugene was an international expert of Southern cuisine made me a little nervous, so I tried not to think about that.

As soon as I saw Eugene, I realized I didn't have to be nervous at all. That beatific smile, those big blue eyes that encompassed, in one loving glance, John and me, the old house and furniture, the screened porch, the long linoleum-topped table and dark green painted benches.

He raised his hands in praise, oohed and aahed. He took it all in, how things looked and smelled and felt, the balmy air, the sound of the bay. "This is how I always think of 'across the bay,'" he said.

He gave us all hugs.

Then he stopped and gasped. He was looking up.

"Oh, no!" I thought. "He is looking at all that peeling paint."

"Look at that!" he said, his hand making a sweeping movement around the porch. "This is wonderful. I love it! Don't touch it; it's marvelous, just like it is." He couldn't look at the paint enough. "It's Gothic, Southern-Gothic elegance."

And so, we all believed that it was as elegant as he said, wonderful just as it was, *meant* to be, a creation of time, the forces of nature, and now, by Eugene's eye, a commonplace turned into a thing of beauty.

We decided to eat right away—we were all starving, so I went into the kitchen to tend the shrimp, which was almost ready. In fact, I was just about to empty the shrimp from the boiler into the strainer. My mother-in-law (who grew up in New Orleans, and knew everything about cooking seafood) had stressed to me the importance of never overcooking shrimp—the cardinal sin. In her book, shrimp must be simmered to the point of tenderness, but not beyond, should be taken from the stove, strained, and immediately plunged into ice water and cooled, to avoid disgrace and mushiness.

I was poised to do just this, out in the kitchen but within earshot of the back porch table, standing by the stove, pot-holder mitts on hands, when Eugene called out, "You let that shrimp sit in the water to cool, didn't your, darlin'?" I could hear him explaining to Nell and John and Kathleen (Nell's dear friend) how you should let shrimp stand in the seasoned water to cool—to absorb the flavors of the celery and lemon and bay leaf and whatever herbs and spices you put in.

I hesitated. Whose culinary advice should I follow, Eugene's or dear Mama's? Family honor won. "Yes, Eugene," I called back, plunging the shrimp into the icy water.

He probably knew I had lied, but the shrimp *was* delicious—it really was, and he said so.

After lunch we sat out on the wharf and Eugene took off his shoes, as we all did, and he read aloud to us *The Byzantine Riddle* and from *The Likes of Which*.

A day to remember, listening to Eugene's voice—the mellifluous pronunciations, melodious, but with a pleasant scratchiness, like bits of honeycomb lingering in the mouth, reading ...

"On Mobile Bay, the late October afternoons are golden and still, long and summery."

It wasn't Poetry or Philosophy that ruined me
as a Clown: it was a nouvelle Cuisine recipe
for a Quiche made of Liver, Artichokes, and Scuppernongs.

John Sledge

John Sledge is an architectural historian with the Mobile Historic Development Commission and Books Editor for the Mobile Register. Though he grew up in central Alabama, Sledge has deep roots on the Gulf Coast. His mother was born in New Orleans and lived in the Pontalba Building for a while, and his father, a Mobile native, grew up in Georgia Cottage on Springhill Avenue. Sledge is currently writing a book about Mobile's historic cemeteries to be published by the University of Alabama Press. "I got to know Eugene through his column in the *Azalea City News and Review*," recalls Sledge. "I admired the way he celebrated Mobile. He was a tireless champion of its historic buildings and never failed to speak out on preservation issues."

The Enchanted Rooms of Eugene Walter

In the hours after Eugene's death, things moved too fast for me to take stock of my emotions. There were people to inform and administrative details to handle to ensure that Eugene could be buried in Mobile's historic Church Street Graveyard, next to native luminaries Julian Rayford and Joe Cain. By the evening of the wake, I was running on pure adrenaline. A lot of hard work by scores of Eugene's devoted friends had paid off, and Mobile was giving her Renaissance Man a fitting farewell. I was proud of this, since one of the yardsticks of civilization is how a society treats its artists. Indeed, in the days following Eugene's passing I was overwhelmed by the spontaneous expressions of grief by citizens from all walks of life.

The full meaning of Eugene's death did not hit me, however, until I stood on the portico of the Cathedral, just before the funeral service. As mourners from far and wide gathered and conversed in hushed tones, it suddenly struck me that he was really gone. And with him a way of life had passed as well. Though I have many literary friends, I could think of no one else remotely like Eugene. So much history and lore were about to be buried with him in Mobile's sandy loam. How could he ever be replaced?

I initially got to know Eugene during the '80s through his column in the *Azalea City News and Review*, *"EWEW"*, and appreciated his love of Mobile and all that made the city unique. He was a great ally to the historic preservation community here, and on more than one occasion injected hope and energy into our cause. Over the years I would bump into him at various social events, but, incredibly, did not visit him at home until the spring of 1995.

It was an experience I shall never forget. The reason for the visit I do not recall, though it was probably as simple as Eugene wanting to be hospitable to someone who shared many of his views on the world. When we would chat on the telephone he always suggested that I come see him and confabulate over a bottle of Jim Beam. Not being a drinking man myself, I let these invitations lie, until one morning, again for reasons I cannot recall, I decided to darken his door.

The house presented a decidedly shabby appearance from the street. It was unpainted and shrubs grew in green riot all about the porch. I gingerly stepped over spilled cat food, pulled open the screen door, and tapped on the glass. Classical music poured under the door and I heard Eugene's cheery voice answer, "Come in!" I twisted the knob and beheld a magic realm.

Upon entering, my attention was distracted by the cats. Several of the creatures minced about the interior, over tables, and across Eugene's lap. A litter box odor pervaded the air. Then there was the room itself, a glorious jumble of art, books, and papers and ensconced amid it all, the great raconteur himself, glass of port in hand. Eugene bid me welcome and I sat opposite. While we conversed, I scanned the room in wonder, paying especial notice to the books which lined the room virtually from floor to ceiling. They ranged from a volume of Thomas Jefferson's correspondence to a book about Southern gardens to a leather-bound copy of Moliere's plays. But there was so much else besides. Pictures and paintings hung all over the walls. Some of these works displayed prodigious talent and made the room fairly throb with energy. There were a thousand knick-knacks scattered about. Mardi Gras beads hung over small figurines, little souvenirs were propped against the books, and German beer steins rested atop one shelf.

Here in Eugene's digs, I became fully aware of the impressive breadth and depth of his singular education. Before, when we had talked, there had often been a great deal of silliness and fun, but here, now, he was all intellect, and the range and agility of his mind staggered me. He had, in short, a beautiful mind, and spoke with an easy confidence, quoting favorite authors like Rabelais and Aristophanes as casually as one might speak of the weather. The old spontaneous Eugene was never far below the surface, however. Once, when the radio announced a test of the Emergency Broadcasting system, I was startled when he shouted, "Play music, damn you!"

After an hour's conversation, Eugene took me on a tour of his house, which consisted of only five or six rooms. "This is the Cat-Free room," he announced, shooing one of the felines and pushing open a door. I gasped at the sight of yet another room full of marvelous treasures: hundreds more books, a winged clock, a gilded mirror and most unusual, a stuffed monkey in a bell jar. Many of the books in the Cat-Free room were of higher quality and greater value than those in the room we had just left. Quite a few of them were leather-bound and a number were in French. I could have spent drawn-out, blissful days browsing among these venerable tomes.

There was far too much to take in, and Eugene was not about to let me absorb it at my own pace. He kept me moving, pointing out his famous Tallulah Bankhead reliquary, showing off his cardboard boxes full of works-in-progress, and then steering me into the kitchen for lunch. Though I knew of Eugene's reputation as a gourmet, I can only describe the thought of lunch as less than appetizing. The kitchen was in disarray and the cats had the run of it. Furthermore, there was an overall laxness in matters of hygiene which often afflicts the aged. I begged off, saying I was pressed and must depart. "One must not be pressed when one comes to this address," Eugene merrily chided. We shook hands and I returned to my car. I turned on the ignition, and was surprised to see by the clock that three hours had melted away.

Over the ensuing years, I visited Eugene often at his home (though never again to eat), and was always disappointed when the time came to leave. He was such a marvelous storyteller. Of his many tales, one has stayed in my mind as particularly exquisite. He described eating in a Paris restaurant with the great Southern novelists William Faulkner and Katherine Anne Porter. As the sights and aromas of Parisian life surrounded the trio, Eugene noticed that each of his companions seemed to be in a trance. Of a sudden Faulkner mumbled, "Blackberries." Porter dreamily replied, "Butterbeans." At this point in relating the story, Eugene threw up his hands and cried, "They were thinking about the South!" He was full of such charming anecdotes. After an idle hour in Eugene's magnificent rooms, listening to stories like this, my soul was always enriched and my spirit refreshed.

I last visited those enchanted rooms on the day Eugene Walter died. Ted Dial had gotten him to the hospital only hours before, and worried friends converged on the house for news. While a small knot of people stood sadly in the kitchen, I walked slowly into the Cat-Free room and closed the door. All around me were the silent books and objects. Their owner, the man who had so colorfully related the details of their acquisition and contents, was gone forever. I stretched out my arms, splayed my fingers, and deeply inhaled the musty rich smell of paper and leather. I wanted to absorb that atmosphere, feel intensely that environment, make its memory indelible in my mind. For here was the abode of a genuine man of letters and lover of life. I closed my eyes and imagined Eugene poring over these books in the small hours of the morning, when all his neighbors were yet abed. I pictured him shuffling back to his desk to jot down an obscure couplet, which he would likely repeat at some candlelit dinner party, to the delight of those at the table. In these fantastic rooms, all the world was within his grasp and he was surely never lonely. I sighed, opened my eyes, dropped my arms, turned on my heel, and went back into the kitchen, knowing that the coming months would see the dissolution of Eugene's household.

The legacies of Eugene's life are many. His published works speak for themselves and will outlive all of us who knew him personally. Mobile will greatly miss his unflagging advocacy of the arts. He never hesitated to affirm the worth of any artistic enterprise. When I would broach ideas with him, his stock response was, "Make it literary!" And so I have, in this tribute to a remarkable man. I will always count knowing Eugene Walter as one of the great blessings of my life. He enriched his beloved native city and all who were privileged to know him.

Eugene!
(Photo courtesy of Jason Thompson)

Julie Wilson

Julie Wilson is an artist and a feminist spiritualist who is owned by two cats. She dumpster dives for art supplies, is passionate about the earth, and is a researcher of feminist history. Her art has been both censored in Anniston, Alabama, and shown at Tiffany's in Atlanta. Her researches into almost forgotten techniques of marbleizing paper are what drew her and Eugene together for late night discussions of papers, ink, and magic.

One evening in a port haze
with sleeping cats in our arms
We sat like statues
No amount of elixir would
allow me to drop my guard
And you by now are tolerant
You took my hand and we gently
glided to the monkey case
There you told me a tale of
a woman bolder than myself
I absorbed the strength
I looked into your eyes
Even though I know I was
to be shy about you
Looking back was an impish boy
That I was not meant to see
We met there that night
and returned there occasionally
I was your baroque princess
with broccoli curls
And you were my Pan in
a far and distant grove.

Patricia McArthur

A former staff writer and editor for the *Azalea City News and Review*, Pat McArthur lives in Kennesaw, Georgia, with her two children, Mark and Katie, and the family cat. Three of Eugene's framed ink sketches hang in the dining room. They offer daily reminders to "Keep it flowery," to "Keep dancing," and that despite what the prune-faces would have us believe, "Mardi Gras is God's gift to Mobile and New Orleans."

Pat has not eaten iceberg lettuce or dead dust (pre-ground black pepper) since she met Eugene in 1981. ("Wow! My pepper mill is almost twenty years old!") She is never without unsalted butter and fresh lemons. And, she keeps a bottle of port in the liquor cabinet to toast his name whenever the mood strikes ... even if that happens to be Sunday morning.

I first met Eugene in 1981, when I signed on as sports editor (and staff) of the *Azalea City News and Review*. We worked out of a house on Government at Monterey (Bob Holberg's place now). Those were the days of Frank Daugherty's McCorquodale serial, Becky Paul's editorials and *EWEW*, Eugene Walter Every Week. My encounters with Eugene took place during his occasional visits to the office to deliver columns. These visits were heralded by the yapping of a dog on the front porch. It was Eugene, delivering sound effects that usually preceded him at any function—be it black tie or bayside.

Several years later, I became editor of the *ACNR*. I know Eugene must have been shocked. A sportswriter editing his work! Jocko and Jane Potts had sold the newspaper to a north Alabama owner and times were changing. The office, then on Dauphin Street in a turreted home renovated by Ted Dial, was packed and shipped west of the beltline. And to make matters worse, it was on Highway 90 all the way out at Demetropolis. Those were the waning days of the newspaper. There were no more visits from Eugene. But I began visiting him to pick up his columns. When he was napping or not at home, the sheets of typewritten paper were stuck in the mailbox outside the door of his white frame Grand Boulevard house. When he was home, I would spend a couple of hours with him, reminiscing over glasses of port about the "good old days" several years before.

The walls in the living room of his house were totally covered from floor to ceiling with framed paintings. The walls in the library were covered from floor to ceiling with shelves of books, sharing their perches with his many cats. The floor in the kitchen was made impassable by dozens of food bowls for those famous felines. Of course, they preferred the countertops. Sometimes we would venture to local restaurants for a late lunch, visiting the kitchen to chat with the culinary artists before sitting down to a bottle of wine and their house specialty.

Chris McFadyen, Charles McNair, Roger Dendinger, Mary Alma Durrett, and I went on to other things. We kept in touch, if not directly with each other, through each other. I had gotten married, had children, divorced, moved to Pennsylvania and back again before Eugene's death in 1998. My mother, Betty McArthur, is another *ACNR* alumna. The rainy day of the celebration of Eugene's life at the Cathedral of the Immaculate Conception, we went together and saw Becky, Jane and Jocko, Frank, and Charles with his wife and red-headed daughter. For an afternoon we were able to remember Eugene and his remarkable take on life. We were all in the fast lane and tied to deadlines. But that day we paused. I went home and pulled out the box of prints and old lithographs I bought from Eugene at one of his garage sales. I had already framed several, but I wanted to add his ink sketches as constant reminders to keep dancing, to not let the prunefaces get me down, and to avoid plainness by keeping it flowery. He wrote on one: *"Pat—heed the message."* I will, Eugene. Thank you for giving me a glimpse down your less-traveled road.

**Walls lined with art and an open door on a Spring morning –
"pure Eugene!"**
(Photo Courtesy of Walter Reinhaus)

Charles McNair

Charles McNair wrote for the *Azalea City News and Review* in 1984. Eugene Walter wrote several columns for the paper at that time. Eugene became friends with Charles and Patricia Wilson, his wife, also an author.

Mr. McNair is the author of *Land O'Goshen*.

Thirteen Ways of Looking at a Walter

One

Here's heresy.

I'm thinking the cats never really liked Eugene's visitors.

Once upon a Mobile time, Ruffo, majestic orange survivor of Rome, glared sullenly at me from across the room.

Tinkerbelle, young and spry, leaped onto the table and paraded down it, tail snaking a path among the wine glasses.

She came to my plate. She sniffed my fork. She gave a wheeze and coughed up a furball the size of Tillman's Corner.

"Tinkerbelle!" Eugene cried. "You are president of the Too Much Club!"

He brought Jim Beam and branch water to the rescue.

We drank to forget.

Two

Patricia and I drive down Dauphin Island Parkway, pass a sheltering grove of pecans and, like a Wordsworth poem, it appears.

A field of gold. Not daffodils, but coreopsis. Millions of nodding orange pilgrims with their faces turned up, drinking Alabama light.

We turn the car, speed toward Grand Boulevard.

Eugene is crabby, just up from his nap, eyes red.

"I don't LIKE surprises!" he protests, but we drag him to the car.

We pass the green grove.

The coreopsis field appears.

Eugene blinks.

Eugene climbs out of the car.

Eugene wades into a yellow fever-dream.

Three

Negative Capability has accepted one of my poems. It is a proud, fetching moment raw for a kid from Dothan who wants more than anything in this life to be a writer.

Eugene, an ever-helpful editor, decides my name will be Edmond McNair, for this poem.

He drops this casually into a dinner conversation. A month later, the poem appears.

My published poem.

Written by someone I've never met.

Four

My sweet wife, thrilled, breezes in one afternoon to our house on Bayfront Drive.

"Look!" Patricia cries.

She holds one of Eugene's whimsical and charming pen-and-ink drawings. Her own face smiles up from the paper, rendered so happily it pierces me.

"He gave it to us!" Patricia tells me, deeply touched.

All these miles and lives away, here in Atlanta, Eugene lives in those whimsical lines on white paper.

Five

This must be Mobile—I'm walking in cold rain behind a hearse.

Eugene's body lies in the coffin a few feet ahead, and just beyond the long black car the Excelsior Band soldiers on, burbling a sad hit from Dixieland. We are on our way to the grave, and the rain pours down like it won't stop for a thousand years, and the music washes into the streets and down the old buildings, off the leaves and eaves.

Fred Baldwin reads the most beautiful eulogy I've ever heard at a funeral—any of us would be proud to hear such fine words as our bones are lowered. And Fred's syllables wash off the gravestones in the rain and drip from the tent canopy and the lips of the umbrellas.

They lower Eugene, and that's it. We all head for home, wet to the bone.

Later, on the long drive back to Atlanta, I remember the story of old Joe Cain, the man who resurrected Mardi Gras, who made Mobile laugh again. He lies buried in Church Street Cemetery, a few feet from Eugene.

Once, those who loved him exhumed Joe Cain's body, the story goes, to move it to a better spot.

The gravediggers found an oak root piercing the eye of his mushroom-white skull.

Six

I was new to Mobile, 1983 or so, twenty-nine years old, unpublished and young in many ways.

In Eugene's living room, I held to the light my very first glass of Port.

A sweet, melted ruby.

Seven

Eugene is on stage. A crowd stares on, transfixed.

The performance: *Westchester County*.

The maestro tunes an invisible instrument — *plink! plink!*

He clears his throat.

"In Westchester Countyyyyyyyyy..." he begins. The words give way to a throat tromnet, an odd vocal sound like an entire second-grade class blowing combs and strips of paper, those primitive kazoos.

"... they let the apples fall to the ground," warbles the bard. And that's it. *Finis*.

The audience gets it, after a stunned silence. A blast of applause, whoops, catcalls, rebel yells. Feet stomp, chairs dance.

Eugene bows among the wows.

Eight

His backyard held the first and finest lizard condominium in North America.

Nine

It's after dinner, and the glow of fine food and spirits fills the room. Eugene says it's time for a surprise.

He totters to a cabinet that is spilling papers—every cabinet is spilling papers, except in the Cat-Free Zone called the Lucille Room.

He brings down a pill bottle. Inside it are three tiny stands of something that look like DNA, twisting coppery helixes.

We play a game—guess what this is?

You'd never guess either.

Tallulah Bankhead's pubic hairs.

Ten

I tossed and yearned for publication.

I worked hard writing, all the time, beavering down after the good stuff through all the bark and bio-mass of experience.

Two people spoke to me in those days of their belief in some little half-hidden light of ability in my work.

Terry Cline, over in Fairhope, repeatedly lifted me with his encouragement.

And Eugene Walter had the goodness to always say kind things about my most implausible dreams.

I'm passing that along, guys.

Thanks, for all.

Eleven

Brad Hutchinson, the craftsman who would one day print Barry Moser's Bible, is a senior at Spring Hill College. From a Jesuit father, he's commandeered a hand press—a piece of cantankerous machinery right out of Gutenberg's closet—and set it to clanking away in the basement of one of the buildings. Brad meets Eugene to discuss a project.

"My monkey poems," Eugene explains. "We have to do them just so."

Brad listens.

"They can't be too much this way or that way," Eugene explains. "They have to be just so."

Brad listens.

"They will enrage the Baptists," Eugene winks, then adds deliciously. "*Scandalize* them!"

Brad waits ten years before Eugene gets the monkey poems just so. They make a lovely edition, remarkable in their difference from anything else you see between covers these days.

Then, one day, Eugene is gone.

Somewhere on a barge floating down some fantastic river in the green hills of paradise, surrounded by millions of cats, Eugene holds a sheaf of monkey poems in the air and steadily fans himself.

Twelve

Eugene conquered Birmingham.

With the help of Ellen Sullivan, author and the publisher of Crane Hill Press, I wrangled an invitation for Eugene to appear at the Jefferson County Public Library as part of Birmingham-Southern's Writing Today literary conference.

Eugene read of giant 'possums with opaline eyes. He read of cockroach cotillions. He sang of the foolish residents of Westchester County.

He triumphed.

No one in Birmingham had ever heard anything like it. No one knew poetry could be just for fun, tra-la, with all Deep Hidden Meanings hidden and the mind left to glide on silver skates wherever it would go.

I was proudest of him that night.

Thirteen

Eugene is convinced that rocking in a rocking chair is an aerobic exercise. He sits on the porch of Termite Hall, the floorboards rumbling.

Man, oh man, what a workout.

The lawn shines. It's late summer. A mourning dove sounds too blue to fly.

Rumble. Rumble.

After a spell, Eugene stops.

"Dear Boy," he asks the nearest visitor, who happens to be about forty. "Would you mind?"

Off trundles Dear Boy. He returns with bourbon, nuggets of ice, water.

Eugene sips. He looks very happy, his porch overlooking the whole world.

Rumble. Rumble.

Eugene's in heaven.

Dale Foster

Dale Foster is currently Head of the Special Collections Department at Auburn University Libraries. He holds a master's and master's of library science from the University of Maryland and briefly studied screenwriting in the creative writing program at Harvard University's Summer School. With Christina Bowersox, Mr. Foster produced *Book Break*, a book-oriented radio news program in Mobile. Mr. Foster also produced *Bay Books* for Bay-TV and *Books This Week* for Alabama Public Television. It was during the production of *Book Break* that Mr. Foster first met Eugene. Ms. Bowersox and Mr. Foster visited Eugene at his home which Mr. Foster recalls as being a "living museum of art, literature, and just plain stuff."

Dancing Naked on Grand Pianos: Memories of Eugene Walter

Eugene was the spirit of the artist personified. While most of us labor in a world of job stress, unending bills, and social ills, his world was one of monkeys, pixies, clowns, frisky felines, and enchantment. He had the uncanny eye of the artist which looked upon us "human creatures" with somewhat of a detached, but intense, curiosity.

Eugene first entered my life in 1991 when I was producing an upstart book program on local radio. I knew immediately he was a remarkable person. His presence filled the studio and the airwaves. Eugene was there again for me in 1993 when I ventured into television production. As one of my first interviews, Eugene's insightfulness and warm, bubbly smile reinforced my earlier impressions. As my last question of the interview I asked, "You've done so much, what is next for Eugene Walter?" With an air of mischief and without hesitation he responded, "I've always wanted to dance naked on a grand piano before I die."

As different as Eugene was from anyone else I had known, he was also as generous. We all know of his bent toward inquisitive conversation, and upon learning I was a single parent with a small daughter, he whipped out a copy of *Jennie, the Watercress Girl* and scribbled a brief inscription. This was the first of many gifts Eugene would provide Cierra and me over the years.

Anyone who spent time with Eugene knew he could be a bit fastidious as well. Upon picking Eugene up for lunch to discuss one of our television projects, I wanted to take him to one of the best restaurants in town. When I mentioned the name of the restaurant, Eugene threw his hands in the air and shouted, "I'll never go to that place again." When I inquired as to why, he replied, "They don't heat their bread!" Needless to say, we chose another restaurant ... and I made sure there was no grand piano inside.

After I left Mobile, it was four years before I saw Eugene again. If he hadn't been standing in the doorway of his Grand Boulevard home, I don't think I would have recognized him. The glowing cheeks and the pudgy mid-section had dwindled. The bubbly smile had given way to time and illness. Eugene was half his former self. Yet a flicker of that mischievousness still remained in his eyes, but just a flicker.

At his request, I visited Eugene many times in the weeks before his passing. His wit and gift for conversation continued strong, but the decline in Eugene's physical condition was more noticeable each time. Once, I had to catch him as he teetered to the point of falling. During all this time, I never heard Eugene complain... at least not about himself. Of course he was never too ill to complain of bad food, bad music, and bad government.

Upon leaving one late-March morning in 1998, as I stepped down off his porch, I turned back and said, "Take care, Eugene." Hooking the latch on the screen door to keep the cats inside, he responded emphatically, "*You* take care!" I took this to mean, "Don't worry about me." Sitting in my car, I hesitated for some time staring at the unassuming white-frame house thinking, "Is this the last time I will ever see Eugene?" It was.

Anyone who met Eugene Walter will always remember it as "an experience." His kindness, wit, generosity, and agile intellect left a lasting impression on those fortunate enough to make his acquaintance. The same can be said of his writing. The memorable opening of *The Untidy Pilgrim* recounts,

Down in Mobile they're all crazy, because the Gulf Coast is the kingdom of monkeys, the land of clowns, ghosts and musicians, and Mobile is sweet lunacy's county seat.

As one of the kingdom's most gifted clowns, Eugene left an indelible mark on the lives of those he entertained with his writing, art, music, and intriguing conversation. We will never look at monkeys and grand pianos the same way again.

"WANTED
EUGENE
WALTER

CHILD AMUSE!
LECHERY!
TREACHERY!
COUNTERFEIT
APPLE PIE!
FOGGERY!
BOGGERY!
EUGENE
WALTER
CATTINESS!
BATTINESS!
RATTINESS!
CORPULENCY!
BURPULENCY!
DRUNKENESS!
SKUNKENESS!
BUNKUMNESS!
EUGENE
WALTER
MESS!
LITTERING!
SKITTERING!
FLITTERING!
GLITTERING!
FARTING
IN CHURCH!
SINGING
DIRTY SONGS
AT FUNERALS!
EUGENE
WALTER
ETC. ETC.
ETC.
ETC. YEAH!
CALL THE
DAUGHTERS
OF REVOLUTION
IF YOU SEE
THIS MAN!

WANTED! VAUNTED! HAUNTED!

WANTED! VAUNTED! HAUNTED!

HAVE YOU SEEN THIS MAN?!

Carmen Brown

(EXTREMELY INSPIRED, BUT LOOSELY BASED ON EW'S *THE POKEWEED ALPHABET* AND BECAUSE I HATE DOING BIOS ... EVERYONE WHO'S CROSSED MY MOLECULAR PATH HAS A SPECIFIC OPINION OF WHO I AM [WHICH IS OK WITH ME BECAUSE S/HE IS ENTITLED TO THAT], SO WHY SHOULD I HAVE TO QUANTIFY A BIO WITH IMPORTANT, BUT INANE DRIVEL ABOUT MYSELF THAT SEEMS ONLY VITAL WHEN APPLYING FOR A GIG? GO FIGURE! WHAT HAPPENED TO PERFORMANCE, IMAGE, AND COMMUNITY COMMITMENT? AND HOW MANY TIMES HAVE YOU BEEN ASKED FOR A COPY OF YOUR TRANSCRIPT? BET THAT NEVER HAPPENED TO EUGENE!)

My alphabet begins with the letter "M":

M-other (Most important role in my entire life! Thank you goddesses! I love you Greg—my wonderful, talented, destined-to-be-world-famous teen-age son.

N-egro (At one time in my life—colored at another, but the Census says I'm Afro-American now. As Steve Martin would say "Ex-c-u-u-u-se me!" I am American-born and raised in the USA and have not been and have no desire to ever go to Africa or anywhere else off this continent. You can't and won't niche me—I'm Carmen Brown!)

O-pinionated ('Nuff said—but people think and listen).

Q-uirky (see above).

P-isces (Sun, moon and rising signs! Go figure, plus I have the tattoos to prove it!)

R-eader (I love books! I love the library! Anyone who does not have a card and does not visit there regularly is living in a vacuum.)

S-ane (But sometimes I wonder!)

T-ruthful (Even though it's gotten me into trouble more than once. So what? If one can't learn and grow from mistakes—s/he must be dead!)

U-npretentious (*There's a reason why they call it show business—if you don't take care of business, you'll have nothing to show for it.*—Levi Stubbs, the Four Tops. This kind of r'n'r philosophy keeps one very grounded. After more than thirty-five years in the entertainment industry, will thankfully admit that my feet have been planted for years—and have to stay that way—for Greg and my Mom.)

V-oice (A special gift from my mother, my father, and the goddesses. Blessed be and thank you, all!)

W-illful (See above)

X-(See *The Pokeweed Alphabet*)

Z-ealous (Great word! Let's stop here! After all, it is EW's alphabet—and I am just a short-term pokeweeder. Why go anywhere else but *STRAIGHT AHEAD*?)

Memories of Eugene

My first encounter with Eugene Walter was in the pages of the *Azalea City News and Review*. (Boy howdy, do I miss that paper!) While working at a local radio station in the late '70s and early '80s, I found the newspaper a fabulous source of "what's happening"-type information—plus, it was free, so I picked it up at every opportunity.

Eugene was one of the regular contributors; I would read his incredible writings and wonder, "Who is this man?" I never met him face-to-face, but felt a creative connection. When he wrote about recipes, I found myself trying them; about authors and poets—reading them; when I read about his cats, I didn't get one, but I enjoyed reading about them. You catch my drift.

In March 1982, my friend, Sandy Jackson and I celebrated our birthdays together by hosting a party at the Palladium, a now-defunct, swank, black-owned club at the corner of Springhill Avenue and Broad Street. The theme was "Music, Muscles and Magic." I decided I'd send Eugene Walter an invitation—and what do you know—he came! And, of course, brought a friend (because he didn't drive, something I soon learned). It was a wonderful night—Darlene Hill and her band played, bodybuilders from Jason's Gym choreographed poses to music and a magician (I can't remember his name) performed slight-of-hand and table tricks.

Eugene was ensconced at a table on one of the second levels and, if I remember correctly, sent one of the waitresses to ask me to come to his table. That was our first of many face-to-face encounters. I was so thrilled that he came and that I had the opportunity to meet him, that when I got back to my hosting duties, I acknowledged his presence in the Club. Everyone applauded — loudly! The majority of the crowd was people of color. They knew him and he was right at home. (Very natural for Eugene, I came to know later.) It turned out that he was a fan of mine, too! Listened to me on the radio regularly.

The next edition of the *ACNR* came out, and lo and behold! there was a glowing review of our party! He didn't miss a nuance. Imagine my surprise! Of course, I called Eugene to thank him and our friendship began.

I went on to enjoy his performances in Tom Perez's South of the Saltline Regional Theatre productions (*Cockroach Hall, The Best Christmas Pageant Ever, Society Shell*, to name a few), to seek him out and sit with or by him at dinners and other social events, to occasionally call him just to chat, and once in a blue moon, give him a ride home.

One thing I'm really happy that happened is Auburn University's decision to recognize Eugene as Alabama's First Renaissance Man. I was so proud that he received this honor while he was still dazzling this planet with his illuminations.

In closing, here is a favorite poem of mine from Eugene's *The Pack Rat and Other Antics 1937-1987*:

Young Poet to the Old Anthologist

*When I tear the sun from his socket
and rearrange the stars in rows,
Cause the sea to blacken and churn
Casting up green goblins on prosaic shores —
When you behold me, on a moonless night,
Clad in ire and white fire,
Then O then indeed
You shall be very sorry
You were not listening when I spoke.*

Mme. Hecate takes her favorite bat for a midnight stroll in Washington, D.C. Hell is closed for the evening...

Walter Reinhaus

Walter Reinhaus is a Mobile native, Spring Hill College-educated, resident of Chicago. He spends his time running an artists' group space, learning about nature, and helping to develop cultural opportunities in his neighborhood. He is a cat person and also keeps a very nice human companion named Filtod.

On being asked to contribute a recollection of Eugene Walter, my immediate thought isn't Eugene speaking word for word. No, I was always having too much fun to be that studious. I hear his voice; a smooth slightly raspy up-and-down lyrical rhythm, with pauses drawing one to the visual, eyes off gently to one side, no-nonsense lips, head cocked any direction but down. Then the pause ends as he would breathe in, having figured out the next question or line or lament, only taking a second for breath to prepare for delivery. Content? Unpredictable as only a feline could appreciate fully (and they generally won't talk about it with me). But it always made a lot of sense at the time.

On one visit a few years back, Eugene allowed me to take a few black and white photos of him inside his house. If you look at them more than a moment, you can often hear WHIL in the background. Be sure and have an ample glass of port nearby.

Maria Xenia Wells

Maria Wells is the Curator of Italian Collections and adjunct professor of French and Italian at University of Texas at Austin. During the course of organizing an exhibit on *Botteghe Oscure* at the University in 1991, Ms. Wells "discovered Eugene Walter by chance, and what a chance that was! ... I was totally lost in the flow of warm appreciation by Princess Caetani for Eugene's work on the magazine, the requests for advice on several aspects of the magazine, [the] quick personal notes, 'I am sending over some hot broth, for your cold.'"

Dr. Wells has been at the University of Texas since 1962, coming from the University of Pisa, where she received a doctorate in comparative language and literatures, English, Italian, French, and Spanish. She has concentrated her work on Renaissance and modern authors.

In 1992 Dr. Wells received the title of "Cavalier in the Order of Merit of the Italian Republic," not only for her teaching and research, but also for being, for about twenty years, the representative of the Italian Embassy and the Italian Consulate in Houston. She has been a recipient of a Fulbright Research Fellowship to study in Rome, both at the Carlo Levi Foundation and the State Archives, and the Camillo Caetani Foundation.

Dr. Wells is married to an attorney (a Texan) and has two daughters, an artist and teacher and a psychologist. "Eugene met the latter and said she looked like a Greek goddess!!!! You know how he was!!"

A wonderful friendship developed between Eugene and myself, all thanks to a Princess... . Well, he had quite a few in his life, you know. In 1991 I was preparing an exhibit on *Bottteghe Oscure*. The main source of information came from some biographical notes written by Eugene Walter and dictated by Princess Marguerite Caetani. The Harry Ranson Center has a good part of Eugene Walter's archive and the most interesting part of this archive is the letters from the Princess to Eugene, which give a detailed history of the publication of *B.O.* (from 1948 to 1960). Her letters close with: "in haste, love, Marguerite." Sometimes she was "in great haste!" I "discovered" Eugene and told him about this exhibit I was preparing and asked him if he would provide a recollection of the Princess for our brochure. One thing led to another and an invitation was extended for Eugene to come and give a lecture at the Harry Ranson Center in December of 1991. Of course, he did more than that!

In the course of our preparations for this event, Eugene discovered that my middle initial stood for Xenia. He said, "Oh! You are my first 'Xenia.'" And from then on he called me, in all his letters, "Xeniabelle" and signed: "mille fleurs" as a greeting.

By far the most amusing and pleasant evening during his visit to Texas was at a dinner at my house, where he started on his memory trail about "La Caetani" and the period after, the collaboration with Federico Fellini. (The University has his translation of *Satyricon*, with all his doodles!!!) That evening he was telling this incredible story about the search for dwarfs for a Fellini movie. Eugene was riding around Rome in a limousine with the dwarfs who protested because they could not see out of the window, and that they were going too fast, anyway. Eugene had the limousine stop in front of a bar, went in, and returned triumphantly with a couple of old telephone directories which the dwarfs used as pillows: then they were happy because they could see out of the window. The driver slowed down, too.

It was impossible to be tired around Eugene, he was always so cheerful.

Fred Marchman

Eugene Walter wrote the following bio for Fred Marchman in 1988 when the artist exhibited in the Nine Wits Cartoon show:

Fred Marchman is a wandering artist and scholar born in Mobile, Alabama. He graduated from the University of Alabama and received his master's of fine arts from Tulane. He spent two years in the Peace Corps teaching in Ecuador. He has lived, worked, and exhibited in California, South Carolina, Connecticut, Pennsylvania, and Louisiana. He came back to Mobile in 1979 where he has taught, painted murals, exhibited paintings, drawings, and sculptures (including carved decoy ducks of great style), has published poetry, and has worked for years on his literary Magnum Opus, the *Dictionary of Nail*, as well as the chronicles of *Dr. Jo-Mo,* and *The Southern Belle*. Busy, Busy, Busy, they call him in Mobile.

When Eugene first began writing for the *Azalea City News and Review,* Mr. Marchman loaned him an old Underword typewriter that belonged to the artist's father. Later, Eugene returned the typewriter and also gave Mr. Marchman an electric typewriter.

"Eugene hated electric typewriters. He said, 'You're sitting there while the thing is humming, buzzing, demanding that you do something. It sounds like a machine gun—it's a Remington.'"

One of Mr. Marchman's sculptures contains Eugene's wrist watch in the composition.

I was enmeshed in a *tête à tête* with Kathy, my girl friend at that time, at a downtown restaurant. It was an unplanned casual meeting where Eugene, Tom Perez, who happened to be in town, and Frank Daugherty were at a nearby table. I went over and introduced my girl friend to Tom. That was one of the last occasions I remember talking to Eugene.

I enjoyed EW's company because he was a genuine person, wise, honest, witty, and an intellectual. Some of my moments with EW were sporadic, spontaneous. I had hoped that he might provide some leverage for my stymied literary aspirations and help me get published, but above all else, I was attracted to him as a bona fide member of the literati. In his thirty years in Europe and his fifteen plus years elsewhere, New York City, the Aleutian Islands, downtown Mobile, EW had met some celebrities. Lots of them. Tallulah Bankhead, Anais Nin, and many others. I don't recall if he said he knew Henry Miller or Lawrence Durrell, Picasso, and other stars of the Paris art scene who were some of my favorites. The stories of his rendevous with Tallulah in New York during World War II were well told by John Sledge at a remembrance at the downtown museum in the summer of 1998.

Within five years Fellini, Marcello Mastroiani, and EW were gone to that *dolce vita* on the other side. In the aftermath of Fellini's death, EW seemed to feel too upset to even talk about him. He would have to process the loss, I gathered, and return to it at a later date. I wonder if he ever did.

Eugene liked the direction in my artwork where I drew or painted or did prints of various kinds of belles, as he called them. He suggested that I do a sort of book of belles, which would be like a picture book with his introductory preface. As of this writing I'm planning material for this idea but it has yet to be compiled for publication.

During the '80s EW did a series of black-and-white ink drawings which he had reproduced by off-set printing, which he then hand-colored and shrink-wrapped and sold at various venues around town. I tried this idea with a reproduction print I called the Palmetto Queen. She was a Southern belle with a Moon Pie in one hand, an RC Cola in the other, and a Confederate flag pendant around her neck. I sold a few of these prints at a rather modest price. I would still like to follow through on Eugene's idea of a book of belles. It was a good idea.

Eugene was always one to inspire people and spur them on in their creativity. He will be greatly missed in the artistic and literary environment of Mobile. He dearly loved this city and did everything to promote it from the point of view of the fun-loving *bon vivant* with a deep understanding of his home town's culture.

Les Kerr

Les Kerr is a songwriter, entertainer, and recording artist who resides in Nashville, Tennessee. Originally from Mississippi, Kerr lived in Mobile, Alabama, from 1980 to 1987. During that time, he served as news director for two radio stations, WMOB and WKRG. He was also communications manager for the Mobile Area Chamber of Commerce for a short time.

A Nashvillian since 1987, Kerr's primary focus is music. He performs in Nashville and throughout the United States as a solo act and as leader of "Les Kerr and The Bayou Band." He records his own songs and has released several albums. *Southern Sound Sessions* was recorded while he was still in Mobile. *Below The Level of The Sea* is currently available, as is his latest album, *Red Blues*.

A graduate of the University of Mississippi, Kerr holds a degree in broadcast journalism and continues to write for various publications. His articles have appeared in *Voice*, the journal of the Tennessee Walking Horse industry, *ROCK*, a Norway-based music magazine, and various trade association publications.

Eugene Walter - Every*where*

In the '80s, his column for the *Azalea City News and Review* was called "Eugene Walter Every Week" but it could well have been named "Eugene Walter Every*where*." He was all over Mobile.

Because of the fact that he was Eugene Walter, he got around.

Between the time I moved to Mobile in 1980 and the time I left in 1987, Eugene seemed to be a fixture at all social events, theatrical affairs, and arts related hoo-hahs. It was my pleasure to know him during those years. Professionally, I split my time then between a full-time news director's job and a part-time entertainer. However, there was nobody in Mobile more entertaining than Eugene Walter.

If you go to enough "media receptions," even the best ones begin to seem repetitious. But we were lucky in the early '80s to have Eugene in the media, even if it was to write one column a week for a weekly newspaper. He made a lot of those functions fun. One occasion stands out in my mind as the definition of Mr. Walter's individuality.

When the chain steak restaurant Ruth's Chris Steakhouse opened in Mobile, an actual media dinner was held to generate publicity for it. All of us were thrilled to actually be invited to dinner at a restaurant that served good meat. You have to remember that when I was in radio news in Mobile, it was standard practice to cover certain civic clubs because they met at Constantine's and Korbet's and their members would graciously ask us to have lunch with them while we covered their speakers. A lot of non-newsworthy people got coverage that way. Radio did not pay well for newsmen and we took what we could get, even if we were at the end of the aluminum buffet. (By the way, I never saw Eugene at a civic club meeting.)

On the big night at Ruth's all of Mobile's media arrived. We were usually hungry for a story but that night, we were hungry for a really good steak. We were decked out in our finest suits and dresses with notepads, cameras, microphones, and tape recorders in hand. Local politicians, including then-mayor Lambert Mims, were on hand to greet the management of the New Orleans-based eatery. Even Ruth—the "Ruth" in Ruth's Chris Steakhouse—was on hand to personally open her new branch office.

Eugene arrived about the time everyone else was seated. I recall him wearing a white suit (yes, it was in the appropriate season) and that he was accompanied by a young man also dressed to the nines who appeared to be about twenty years old. It was an interesting entrance, an elderly but sparkling Eugene accompanied by a youngster whom nobody seemed to know. In fact, Eugene himself had to think about it pretty hard when making introductions later.

As Eugene and his companion were seated, our gapped-toothed Mayor Mims was welcoming Ruth and her entourage to town.

"W-e-l-l," the mayor characteristically drawled, "we ah proud t' have such a fine rest'runt in Mobeel, the h'aht of the Gulf Coast. Welcome t' th' Aza-alya City."

Ruth, having been duly introduced, then told everyone how happy she was to be here. She regaled us with stories of people who had had a few cocktails trying to say "Ruth's Chris Steakhouse." She added that New Orleans police officers often asked D.U.I. suspects to give the pronunciation a try.

While this was taking place, Eugene patiently listened. Then his feet got hot. I say that because he removed his slip-on shoes and revealed to everyone that he was not wearing socks. If it was hot enough for a white suit, it was too hot to wear socks.

Those of us close enough to see him wondered how long he would sit there in his bare feet. Because Ruth was attempting humor, she began to "play" to our table assuming we were laughing at her stories when we were really laughing at the silent comment Eugene was making on the evening.

As it turned out, Eugene did put his shoes back on.

After the event was over.

He spoke to the mayor and I don't think Mayor Mims realized he was talking to a barefoot man. (Lambert Mims and Eugene Walter together was quite a contrast in personalities, anyway.) He spoke to Ruth, of course, and he spoke to me.

"My dear boy," he called me, as usual, "somebody ought to teach these people (referring to the restaurant staff) what a salt shaker is."

In his next column, as I recall, Eugene mentioned the new restaurant and commented on the blandness of some of his dinner. But Eugene Walter was anything but bland.

Although I was not a close personal friend of Eugene's, our paths did cross a lot during my seven years in Mobile. I was in a play by local playwright Tom Perez and Eugene was always at rehearsals and may have even had a line or two in it. During rehearsals, Tom asked me not to bring any alcoholic beverages around because Eugene "loves his wine" and might make rehearsals last longer than usual if he got into it.

Among the last times I remember seeing Eugene was at a monthly meeting of the Press Club of Mobile. I had been president of the organization and it was my last official meeting in that capacity. Eugene was there and we both were at the cash bar (not unusual for either of us to have a "bloody" with lunch) and he told me he had great plans for me.

"My dear boy," he said, "I'm writing a play and I've got a perfect part for you. You're so jolly and fun, I think you would make a hilarious drunk."

I assured him that, indeed, I was a hilarious drunk in real life and would probably not need a lot of rehearsing. He laughed, sipped his drink and said, "I want you to promise me you'll be in my play when I get it done."

And I did.

If he had ever gotten around to writing that part for me, I would have been honored to act it. I'm happy that I knew him when he was Eugene Walter Every Week and Every*where*.

Renée Paul

I met Eugene more than twelve years ago when I was working as arts editor and part-time photographer for *The Vanguard*, the student newspaper at the University of South Alabama. One day I was told I was going to get the opportunity of a lifetime. Eugene Walter, "the Renaissance Man," had moved back to Mobile, and *The Vanguard* was doing a feature on him. My job was to photograph him for the piece. Of course, the chief photographer and I were told we would have to pick up the Renaissance Man and carry him on "a few personal errands" before the photo shoot. Now that I look back on that day, following Eugene on his errands couldn't have been more perfect for a photographer trying to capture his true personality.

The first photos I took of Eugene remain my favorite—a few candid shots of him in his parlor as he cuddled his cats before leaving home. After that, we took him to one of the old barbershops on Springhill Avenue where I photographed him as he had his "writer's curls" cut. From there, we moved on to a couple of places that were close to Eugene's heart—Three George's Candy Shop and the Haunted Book Shop. In these places, he was at home and in his element.

These early photographs grew to mean much more to me over the years as my relationship with Eugene became closer. I thank Carolyn Haines for reintroducing me to Eugene a couple of years after that first, brief encounter with him.

Eugene has forever changed the way I look at the world. And, now that he is gone, we must continue in his grand style and tradition, beginning each day with his credo in mind, "No matter what, keep dancing!"

Ms. Paul is a public relations specialist for the University of South Alabama.

Sundays were always special for Ted Dial and me because it was the only day of the week that we afforded ourselves the luxury of what we considered a "civilized dinner." This meant that it was time for family to gather around a candle-lit table in our home on South Catherine Street to enjoy the company of a few guests who were carefully chosen by Uncle Eugene.

Of course, family to Ted and me meant Eugene, Nell Burks, and Malcolm Steiner. Around the table, Uncle Eugene lovingly referred to Nell as Yoga Mae Pom Pom, Malcolm as The Bavarian Bunny, and Ted as Théodore, Maître Dial (pronounced Dee-ahl), or The Panther.

I, on the other hand, was given the more delicate title of Gazelle— named for the graceful, deer-like creature that gets so greedily snapped up by almost every predator known to roam the Earth. Although Eugene led me to believe I became Gazelle because of a certain gracefulness I possessed, I couldn't help but wonder what else he might have read into my character. Perhaps he also viewed me as a bit aloof or even vulnerable. Then again, maybe it was simply my long neck that brought a bounding gazelle to mind.

Although dinner was held in our home, Eugene was always placed in the role of "Papa Daddy," and we wouldn't have had it any other way. Only Eugene had the contacts, patience, and the imagination to pull together some wildly amusing dinner parties. I think he spent a great deal of his time each week silently interviewing potential dinner guests, carefully choreographing the play of different personalities in his head before extending an invitation. It didn't necessarily matter *who* was invited so much as it was the combination of individuals. And, of course, Eugene was on the side of variety. It was, after all, the way I met Ted.

Sunday dinners always began with an *apéritif* in the salon, where guests were instructed by Eugene to put their backs against the sofa and tell him the stories of their lives. Visitors had their choice of before-dinner drinks from "the medicine cabinet"—a glass of port, a *kir*, or a cocktail. But, Eugene's *apéritif* was always the same—Jim Beam and branch water. And whenever his Possum Piss, as he called it, would get low, he would either cue me with his trademark coughing fit or call out to me, G-A-Z-E-L-L-A! (This was his Italian pronunciation of my pet name.) If I didn't move fast enough from the kitchen to the salon to retrieve the empty glass, sometimes I could swear I heard, G-O-D-Z-I-L-L-A! But, when I questioned Eugene about it, he swore he could never call me such a thing and kissed my hand.

One of the most memorable dinner parties involved a ritual that was vintage Eugene. We roasted marshmallows over candles we'd placed inside small, dried beef jars—also Eugene's vessel of choice for the sacred *Porto*. He brought along an extra bag of marshmallows for me to stock in the cupboard. It was a dinner party staple and should be hoarded like hurricane supplies. He also kept us stocked with jars of capers, herbs, candied ginger, guava paste, Jim Beam, and a freezer full of candles. The candles were to be stored in the freezer because it kept them from dripping wax on the tablecloth. They were to be lit before the guest were called *à table*, but not before the wicks had been trimmed and a centerpiece was in place. He wasn't picky about the flora selected for the centerpiece, as long as it didn't block his view of the guests or Maître Dial, who held court at the end of the table opposite Papa Daddy. Most of the time, the centerpiece came from our backyard—blue hydrangea, pink hibiscus, and lantana (the ham and eggs variety). Sometimes Eugene would bring something exotic from his garden—orchids, narcissus, or Little Johnny Jump Ups (my favorite). But, the centerpiece I remember pleasing Eugene the most was a treat Ted brought into the house one summer Sunday evening. It was a banana tree leaf that reached from the table to the ceiling. When Eugene walked in and saw it, he was so surprised and delighted that he howled with laughter and applauded. It was one of those rare moments when Eugene was caught off guard and could find nothing to say. But his reaction said it all. The centerpiece was a success and, of course, it was the towering banana leaf's phallic quality that lent special appeal.

Although Eugene adopted a "devil-may-care" attitude about most things in life, he was serious when it came to dinner preparations. Once he hit our back door with his brown paper sack of delights from Grand Boulevard, he set to work like a fiend, preparing exotic dandelion and arugula salads picked fresh from his garden, putting the finishing touches on his famous patent leather pie, or heating one of his hominy and black-eyed pea casserole concoctions—courtesy of "Mr. Trappey," a canned food guru, according to Eugene (only salt and water added). Only when Eugene was satisfied that his dishes were heated, stirred, and garnished to perfection, would he settle into his favorite black vinyl chair in the salon to relax and sip a little Possum Piss before the guests arrived.

Evenings always ended back in the salon with a *digestif*. There was usually Grand Marnier, Galliano (which tasted like pine tops, according to Eugene and The Bavarian Bunny), "something from Mr. DeKuyper," and, of course, Possum Piss. To further aid digestion, we nibbled on candied ginger and dark chocolates from Three George's candy store—a divine institution. (The word "nibbled" may be too weak a term to describe the high-minded *dégustation* that took place while sampling the delicacies of Three George's.)

The fact that these late-night dinners were held on Sunday—the day before a sobering work week began—didn't seem to matter once our guests settled in and fell into the rhythm of good food and conversation. It never seemed the right time to break up the party. But, when the time came, Eugene instructed any new acquaintances to write down their names, addresses, telephone numbers, and signs of the zodiac.

I remember Eugene making the same request of me, more than twelve years ago, when we first met. Upon learning that I was a Libra, he said, "Oh, dear, the scales. One of the twin signs. The twins spend their lives looking at travel magazines but never going anywhere." He couldn't have been more right about a Libra's very neutral, sometimes debilitating approach to life. While fair-minded Libras have a gift for seeing both sides of any equation, they also suffer keenly from a kind of analysis paralysis.

About three weeks after Eugene's insightful evaluation of Libras—along with his assurance that they got along fabulously with Sagittarians—I anonymously received a subscription to *Travel & Leisure* magazine. And the next time I met up with him in public, he whispered into my ear and inquired as to whether or not I had received "the magazine" he sent me. When I assured him that I had, he chuckled and patted my hand. "Start packing your bags, Dahling," he said. And, like a mama bird urging one of its young to leave the nest and take flight, Eugene would continue over the years to nurture my creativity and sense of individuality, nudging me with words of encouragement until I felt confident enough to strike out on my own and take some chances in life.

I guess I'll always struggle under the shadow of the scales, but I'll also have memories of the many private, heart-to-heart talks with Eugene before Sunday dinner in our salon on South Catherine Street.

And, once again, with my back pressed firmly against the sofa, sipping port served in a dried beef jar, I'll tell Uncle Eugene the story of my life. He'll listen without interruption, and when I'm through, he'll say without hesitation. "You are S-O-M-E-B-O-D-Y, Gazelle." And the best part is, he'll mean it.

Frank Daugherty

As a staff writer for the *Azalea City News and Review*, 1979 to 1983, I worked on a daily basis with Eugene Walter, basked in the sunlight of his wit, and was swept along in the Gulf Stream of happenings he stirred up. Eugene had a moniker for everyone, and mine was most frequently "Professor Daugherty," presumably a wry reference to the aeons I had spent studying English and German literature at Duke, Tulane, Yale, Munich and Berlin—but maybe just because of my owlish glasses. Though we were separated by a generation, certain facts of our past and certain shared experiences made me see in him a kindred spirit: Murphy High School, a feeling of rootedness in Mobile, and paradoxically a taste for foreign languages and the experience of living abroad and trying to vanish into a foreign culture. I had lived in Germany, and later was to teach English in Saudi Arabia, Argentina, Japan, Bahrain, and Egypt. For me as a Mobile writer, Eugene was a predecessor, model, and mentor. He urged me to write my comic novel *Isle of Joy*, contributed ideas and details, and drew several illustrations for episodes in its original newspaper version. Currently, as director of the English Language Center at the University of South Alabama, I personify Eugene's nickname and sometimes indulge, in the sag of the afternoon, in the nostalgia of *et in Arcadia ego.*

Do What You Want for Best Results

Meeting Eugene Walter was preceded by a long wait for me. So long did I wait to meet Eugene that one morning after his death a year and a half ago, it was a shock to realize that our friendship had lasted longer than my vigil. He had seemed remote and legendary for so long that even now it surprises me that a time came when I knew him. Perhaps this feeling is abetted by certain long-standing doubts concerning just how much of his quicksilver image I ever beheld.

From the very first time I heard of him in 1965, I knew that he was someone unique, absorbing, central. "Nonpareil," perhaps, in Walterian parlance. It was my first year at Murphy High School and his herald was my French teacher, Annie Lou White. This is none other than the "Annie Lou and Anne Louise" to whom his *Monkey Poems* are dedicated and who had also taught Eugene at Murphy in the '30s. Miss White, as we called her, grew up in Mendenhall, Mississippi, a charming old town with a courthouse on a hill which still looks down Main Street at a famous old hotel. She studied at MSCW, which she spoke of often, before coming to Mobile in the late '20s to teach at the brand new Murphy High School. Murphy, with its grand Spanish colonial buildings and college-size campus, and Annie Lou both seemed to loom large in Eugene's reminiscences.

It is axiomatic that every small Mississippi town produces lone geniuses and isolated individuals of culture and verve, and such was Annie Lou. In 1965 she must have been around sixty and was a smallish woman with very erect carriage, nondescriptly blond hair, feminine gestures, glasses, and sensible walking shoes. She irradiated a subversive fey presence, did not care for rules, and would sigh as she told us about her run-ins with the football-coach-principal and other martinets who were constantly struggling with students going up the down staircase. She often laughed a girlish little laugh that combined helpless resignation and sly mockery. Most striking was her cultivated accent, with deliberate and drawn-out enunciation, odd pauses, and well-pondered lingering on certain words and syllables. Speech, like life, was art—very much the creation of Anne Louise, though if one listened very carefully one could distinguish faint vowel colorings of the Mississippi Annie Lou underneath.

Since foreign languages were compulsory, the classroom was crammed with forty or forty-five students, most of whom vegetated in the back and off to one side, but would start and stare in stupefaction if Annie Lou called on them once in a great while. When they got rowdy she would extend her hand and ineffectually snap her fingers. But on the whole she was content to let them mildew in peace and focused on the small enthusiastic group who sat up front near the South Street windows. On busy days we did ALM substitution drills, listened to dialogues as Annie Lou put on forty-fives, and memorized them. I still recall snippets of lines like "Come on, get up out of the snow" or "because the record player doesn't work": "*le pick-up ne marche pas.*"

What she liked much more was teaching French culture. We learned French songs of all sorts, looked at pictures and slides, heard many Edith Piaf records, and listened raptly as Annie Lou told us about Piaf's triumphs and her protégé Yves Montand, who became Piaf's young lover! There were many relaxing days when she held up picture after picture of Montmartre, the Left Bank, Les Invalides and other great monuments of Paris and scenes of Parisian life, especially famous sidewalk cafés where intellectuals gathered and the quais of the Seine lined with bookstalls and strolling crowds. She told us that after one emerges from the theater, the thing to do is go to Les Halles markets at one or two in the morning and have onion soup and wine, which I promptly did as soon as I got to Paris six years later. Slowly an indelible picture emerged of a kind of capital and homeland where people lived with passion, worried about ideas and art instead of business, and did not give a damn about football.

When Eugene was Annie Lou's student, she taught English, not French, and was sponsor of the *Murphy Hi-Times*, the student newspaper for which she encouraged him to draw and write. Still, I think she contributed deeply to his fundamental feeling that Europe was a second homeland and kind of paradise. She must have given Eugene many things his spirit needed in his teen-age years after his grandparents and then his father died, and he lived, for a time, a somewhat hand-to-mouth existence.

On days when Annie Lou had had enough of French, she simply let it slide and talked instead about her favorite books. Her life was intertwined with books. She read us poems and passages from William Alexander Percy, Stark Young's *So Red the Rose*, St.-Exupéry, particularly *Night Flight* and *The Little Prince*, Isak Dinesen tales, and the Irish writer James Stephens's *Crock of Gold*. Most of her authors were off the beaten track and many were from the intellectual world of the '20s and '30s. But the author that she read aloud more than any other was Eugene Walter. I can still see her standing up front with the marbled cover of the Éditions Finisterre edition of *Monkey Poems*, carefully showing us the strange, other-worldly collages of monkeys. Off the beaten track. The lines I could never forget were, "Oh I am monstrous proud, this life to live, this joy to laugh out loud."

Annie Lou was fascinated by Eugene and loved to talk about him. She was proud of the book's dedication to her. In later life I realized that Eugene also had a special affection for her and had given her an innermost place in the sanctums of the Willoughby Institute, his august, shadowy foundation of culture and learning, which is to say, a place in his heart. He wrote her long, chatty letters, and she sometimes read us passages from them. I particularly remember her reading letters about Isak Dinesen's arrival in Rome and how he welcomed her. He was leading what Annie Lou must have considered the perfect life.

We soaked up all of this, and in a mixture of teen-age rascality and fan club admiration, made up a somewhat bawdy song. Among the lore Annie Lou imparted was the tidbit that *poule* (chicken) meant streetwalker. So the lyrics went,

If you knew Annie Lou, like I know Annie Lou,
Oh, oh, oh what a *poule!*

They went on to have her with Edith Piaf, Yves Montand, and Eugene Walter on the Rock of Gibraltar. But now she was teaching, because *"le pick-up ne marche pas."*

We sang this at conclaves of our joke fraternity-sorority Nu Moon. Eugene, I later learned, had also formed a little group in high school called Les Flip Trois. All his life he adored little secret societies and in-groups, like the White Gloves Club of the '40s, (meaning people who had been in Mobile before the enormous lowbrow, rural influx of population during World War II) the Willoughby Institute, the Waifs and Strays Society, who met on Christmas Day, or a group called the Mobile Assembly of Sages and Savants. No doubt there were many others.

Late one afternoon about ten years ago after a winy lunch at his house, I confided the story of Nu Moon and sang the song to Eugene. It was the only time I ever saw him at a loss for words. In fact, the great free spirit, the *épateur,* blushed.

Dear Annie Lou, with her fading violet ways, her playful suggestions and faint whimsy, planted many seeds and shaped many lives. "The weak can overcome the strong," says the Tao Te Ching, "the supple can overcome the stiff."

For eleven years after graduating from Murphy I continued to think about Eugene Walter. My freshman year I told my best friend at Duke University all about him, and other friends from those years say I used to talk about him a lot. Sometimes my mother would send me newspaper clippings from Mobile about Eugene Walter. Some of them said that he would be coming back "to terrify the young." It was like the return of Arthur, always hoped for, never happening.

One of Eugene's many proverbs was, "People should do exactly what they want to do, for best results." How right he was. During much of the '70s, instead of traveling as I wanted, I attended graduate school. I have never felt so far removed from literature as when I was studying it at Yale, listening to arid discussions of theory and deconstruction. I felt so far adrift that finally in 1979, at the age of twenty-nine, I decided simply to stop, spend the summer in Europe, then return to home ground, see what would happen.

I came back two weeks after Hurricane Frederic, and many thousands of the trees that the squirrel in Eugene's *Jennie, the Watercress Girl* celebrated were lying in the streets. My parents had had extensive damage from huge fallen oaks and had to move to a rented house while they made repairs. I had no friends left in Mobile, and for several weeks was entirely busy helping my parents move things out of their old house. Then one day I heard the astonishing news that Eugene Walter had returned. It seemed simply incredible, an incongruous mixing of realities.

Our rented house had no phone yet, so I walked around the corner to a pay phone at Spring Hill Shopping Center that very afternoon and nervously called. I was not sure what kind of reception I would get from this celebrated person, but a warm, Coastal Southern-vaguely European accent reassured me. What would he look like? I imagined an intimidating, perhaps caustic intellectual type like Gore Vidal or Leonard Bernstein. That evening I pulled up on Palmetto Street before an archetypal white coastal Creole cottage surrounded by lush live oaks, ferns, and aspidistra. It was the 1850s Cox-Deasy House, where he stayed for the first few years after his return. After knocking on the door, I heard someone inside calling "Whoo-hoo! Whoo-hoo!" Eventually the door was opened by a very stout middle-aged man in a sports shirt and sandals. The face cried out to be interpreted by an eighteenth-century phrenologist or by a Goethe. There was an impression of wizardly whiteness augmented by a shock of white hair wet-combed back neatly; a kind expression spiced with picaresque eyes which were semi-veiled behind the lenses of his glasses; a corpulent bon vivant smile. Out of his face shone playfulness, sanguinity, deep intelligence, fulfillment, and inner balance.

Whenever Eugene met a new person, he launched a hurricane campaign of seduction and devoted his full attention to him or her until they were charmed and in his power. That night Eugene began a tour of his house and showed me the famous clock with wings ("time flies"), the statues of monkeys, the exquisite books bound in marble paper by Florentine binders, the paintings by de Chirico and other avant-garde artists. Every object exactly fit images that had reverberated in my imagination for many years. He dazzled me with inside stories of famous people, like the young actor from Georgia in *Satyricon*. I told him that one of the most profound film scenes that I had ever seen in my life was that in which the African slave girl speaks to the two profligates in a lost ancient language. Eugene told me that it was he who had made up the language and taught the actress how to say those lines!

But there was also the Mobile side of the conversation, the careful sifting for connections. My mother was Eugene's exact contemporary and classmate at Murphy, and he pleased me by exclaiming, "Oh you're Dorothea Rhodes's son!" He quickly established that we were "astro twins," since I was born on May thirtieth, six months after his birthday on November thirtieth.

Eugene's Italian cat Ruffo, who had also made the sea voyage, was there. A magnificent, unforgettable orange and white creature with a ruff around the neck and almost human presence, he listened to everything with a wise demeanor. There was also a rugged old striped cat, Deasy Bee, that Eugene said had been living under the house and was animated by the ghost of Mr. Deasy, the late occupant of the house.

Hours later, after many bourbons, I tottered out to my car and into the humid Mobile night with a gift from Eugene in hand (Hugh Fleetwood's *A Painter of Flowers*, in which a character is modeled on Eugene), feeling that by coming back home, I had found the right path again.

I became a regular on Palmetto Street and went several times a week to help Eugene sort through papers and file things in his treasure cave. It was a role that many other young people also played over the years. Shortly after Eugene had gotten settled in the house, Hurricane Frederic hit and damaged parts of the roof. Various stacks of books and papers and boxes had been rushed to other rooms. It seemed that from that day until the day he died, Eugene was locked in a losing struggle to reestablish a paradisaical lost order. Sometimes he would joke about a missing paper and say, "It's in a safe place." At other times he would snap mildly at me when I curiously picked up a book or magazine on top of a pile, "Don't touch anything! Every stack has a meaning." Later when he was on Grand Boulevard he would say, "I got up at dawn-thirty this morning and set out two garbage bags full of paper." And yet the rooms where he lived were always crammed with papers, which must have copulated and multiplied during the night like the dust curls in one of his poems.

I first experienced Eugene's dinner parties at the Deasy House: the long table elegantly set with gold-colored cutlery, the hors d'oeuvres, the copious wine and hours of conversation. The cooking was always finished before the guests arrived so that he could fully socialize with them. There was a stately rhythm of *aperitifs*, usually sherry, port, or bourbon, dining, and then *digestifs,* generally his beloved Triple Sec, Crème de Menthe, or myriad other treats, like Jägermeister bitters or Grappa. Absolutely no one ever dared to walk into the kitchen before dinner for a look at the food, stand around there, or ask what he was going to serve, which was always a surprise. Everyone sat in a parlor until the meal was ready, and then everyone sat at table, facing each other. "Put your back to the chair!" he would order young people who lounged too much or acted restless. Never did we serve ourselves from a buffet and eat with a plate in our laps. The meal always started with a first course of soup or *crudités.* In one meal I remember there were coquilles with crab and perch, ham in aspic, and cabbage and carrots soaked in ginger. A little folded, hand-lettered menu in French stood at the end of the table with the heading, *"Les délices de la cuisine chez Oncle Eugène."* Salad was strictly served *after* the main course, Italian style, and to this day many old members of Eugene's circles serve the salad this way. Often they were wonderful bitter salads from his garden. Dessert was frequently candied ginger. Delchamps burgundy flowed like Bayou Sara. No one worried about cholesterol or fashionable dietary restrictions. No one ate and ran. We babies had to be taught proper behavior, and so he educated us in dining.

Eugene drafted me to help him with his translation of *Undine*, a fairy tale by the German Romantic poet Friedrich de la Motte Fouqué. Eugene explained that he had been smitten by the tale when he saw a theatrical production of it as a child at the old Lyric Theater on Conti Street, and it was a lifelong dream to translate it into English. Late every afternoon we would meet, have a few sherries, then sit down at a table where he had several lavishly illustrated nineteenth-century versions spread out, and line by line he would read his translation and I would compare it with the original German. The book that eventually came out explained that he had translated Aloysius Bertrand's French version, yet he was characteristically mysterious about his sources with me and hinted that he had indeed used the German text. Once I had the effrontery to ask Eugene how he had translated a German book when he did not know German. He took a deep breath at such obtuseness and impertinence, fixed me coldly for a moment, and hissed, "By sense of smell."

My decision to settle in Mobile was made possible by the appearance of a new weekly newspaper in Mobile with the homespun-sounding name of the *Azalea City News and Review*. It was started in the late '70s by the intelligent and energetic Domingo Soto as an anti-establishment weekly of social and political criticism and hippie/countercultural sensibilities. The readership was mainly University of South Alabama students and scattered "radicals" around town. The spiritual successor of this paper was the *Harbinger*, which is still associated with university circles today. But when the *Azalea City News and Review* was bought by T.J. "Jocko" Potts in 1979, it underwent a complete metamorphosis. Jocko, just past the age of thirty, was a good-looking, dapper former college baseball and football star with a background in advertising and excellent business connections. He had grown up in Mobile and knew the lay of the land. An inveterate reader, he loved Faulkner, was a disciple of Walker Percy, and was conversant with the Southern literary scene. He had an unlimited repertoire of salty country expressions and could mingle affably with everyone from Old Mobile socialites to Eight Mile truck farmers.

This unexpected combination of traits was reflected in the newspaper. Jocko continued the strong arts coverage but added a sports page and some serious reporting. He aimed to attract the middle and upper middle class, yuppies, the educated, and the city's leadership, but he also maintained a sassy, nonconventional tone. The *ACNR* was frequently superior to the daily newspaper in its political and business reporting and dared to be controversial and satirical. The other part of the successful equation was Jane Potts, Jocko's wife, who led the advertising sales staff. Jane was a beautiful Mississipi brunette, a ball of fire with a ready wit and salty tongue but also a very Southern sense of tact. She could call up a business and charm them until they were positively dizzy. They had no *choice* but to advertise. The rest of the talented young staff included our editor Becky Paul, elegant Beth Meyer, wry Mary Alma Durrett, dubbed "Valeska" by Eugene, Jon Steele, Yvonne Williams, and others.

After the splash of Eugene's return to Mobile had subsided somewhat, he began to need something to do and some income. But in true diva style, he simply waited for something to turn up, and emanated celebrity vibrations until Jocko decided to approach him about writing for the *Azalea City News and Review*. Eugene's first visit to our office on Government Street was very grand. I remember him taking measured strides, smiling graciously, tossing off jokes, flattering the women ("Ah, the three graces"), and calling us all "babies" ("So you're the baby publisher?") while we all smiled ear to ear and congratulated ourselves on our good fortune. I had previously worked for Dom Soto the summer of 1978, had known Jocko in high school, and so was delighted to be able to join the staff. I felt that with Eugene on board, something special and historic was about to happen, and so it did.

Despite occasional grand airs, Eugene was totally accessible and threw himself into the newspaper with an enthusiasm that carried all before it. More sober people might have seen the paper as small potatoes, but Eugene sent copies to friends in New York, England, and Italy, and I believe he took it as seriously as his work with the *Paris Review* and *Botteghe Oscure*. Conversely, it is hard to imagine what Eugene's old age would have been like had not the Pottses given him that crucial mouthpiece. Eugene strove to bring to Mobile a publication of charm and wit, and an atmosphere of camaraderie like the café society of European Bohemians that he had known. For this reason it is impossible to speak of Eugene without including the halo of faces that surrounded him.

The inevitable seduction period ensued in which the whole *ACNR* staff fell unquestioningly under his spell. I was commissioned to write a long profile of Eugene and his advent to the newspaper which was run on the front page under the headline, "Chaos Is Come Again!" In another early issue Eugene had us running a banner headline and lead story about his chum the English flower painter Anne Sanders, with photos of some of her paintings in his possession. The fact that Anne Sanders lived in Rome and had no connection with Mobile whatsoever, not even an art show in town, shows how flexible our sense of the newsworthy still was and how persuasive Eugene could be. He also talked us into running long episodes of Kate Chopin's *The Awakening* until Jocko decided that serializing the entire novel was not a terribly desirable idea and discontinued it.

Eugene began writing three regular columns that showed his multiple talents and brought a large readership who never would have paid attention to the newspaper otherwise. The first was *EWEW*, "Eugene Walter Every Week," which continued a column by the same name that he had previously written for the *Rome Daily American*. It combined theater reviews, book reviews, lists of seed catalogues, random musings, and society reporting on the model of the famous Chandler sisters, the social arbiters and snobbish newspaper columnists of '30s Mobile. Eugene was not truly snobbish, but loved grand gestures and high tone. Frequently he reported on social gatherings with asides to the Chandler sisters' legendary "Babs," and among the guests at real parties and gleaming Old Mobile names he often reported favorite characters of his imagination, such as Miss Charlie Compton, Dr. S. Willoughby, Miss Lulie Hawkfoot, and so forth. After an Opera Guild luncheon, or a party to inaugurate the Christmas tree show at the art museum, Eugene might spend a whole morning making a glamorous collage of photos of the ladies attending that made the event seem positively jet set. Sometimes he would write new poems for his column, like *The Cockroach Cotillion*. Once, following a story tip from a caller, I drove him to a little house off Dauphin Island Parkway, where an old man very short of breath gasped and blew an enormous, magnificent soap bubble for us. The result was the sonnet *On the Late Dr. Vines*, the "architect of bubbles." We heard that the old gentleman was thrilled, and he died not long afterwards. In his column, Eugene often referred to European customs and refinements as though every Mobile reader would be conversant with them. By the same token, he would sometimes refer to vanished restaurants, stores, people, and buildings that had truly existed in the great tradition of the city, and that only he could have written about. Eugene often illustrated his many columns with what seemed to be an endless collection of humorous nineteenth-century drawings that gave the newspaper an elegant New Yorker look. He also had fabulous nineteenth-century Mobile Mardi Gras invitations and float designs which he would print in our Mardi Gras editions.

Eugene's food column, "Table Talk," would have done credit to a newspaper in a city vastly larger than Mobile. With his restaurant reviews, he introduced a sorely lacking element of food culture to '80s Mobile. Often the material he had to work with was, God knows, pedestrian enough, but he made much of the restaurants' strong points, and introduced his barbs among many blandishments. "When I complain," he wrote of one well-known restaurant, "it's as an old friend. And complain I do. When I ordered French fries, I was served huge sodden bits of something whitish which might have been kindling wood pickled in crocodile tears." Eugene, like all of us at the *Azalea City News and Review,* was a Southern patriot, insularly Mobilian and Gulf Coastal, and believed that the local was the root of civilization. Thus if a restaurant had really good hush puppies or an authentic gumbo, it could be praised as much as another restaurant for a good French or Italian dish. Going into a restaurant with Eugene was a very regal experience. Often the owners had been informed that the reviewer was coming, and they met us at the door and effusively ushered us to our tables. Generally Eugene would spot acquaintances and make a little tour of the tables, shaking hands and calling out "Darling!"— particularly if they had any social prominence. Occasionally he might kiss a lady's hand. One had a feeling of being out on the scene and at its epicenter, and Korbet's Greek restaurant with its tasty veal cutlets suddenly felt like a chic eatery on a Roman corso. In "Table Talk" Eugene led a fierce crusade against iceberg lettuce, pre-ground pepper ("dead dust"), the inevitable seafood fried in heavy batter ("mafia's revenge"), coffee whitener, crackers in cellophane, and other horrors. When we sat down, often he would pick up the pepper shaker, drop it on the floor, and demand a pepper mill while the waiter or waitress gaped in astonishment. Generally he contrived to think of *recherché* things to order that were not on the menu. In the many Mobile restaurants without a liquor license, we always brought a bottle of wine, but journalistic damnation awaited the redneck restaurant that did not allow any alcohol! Eugene loved Tommy's Terminal and praised Sophia Clikas's homemade horseradish to the sky. The Moongate, run by members of the family that owned Antoine's in New Orleans, was beautiful but with uneven food and imaginary French on their menu. The Casbah was a wonderful place for cocktails until the fabulous old Mediterranean mansion on Government Street was demolished for a Burger King. His favorite place was Roussos, not only because of the good seafood, but also because the genial Greek-American owners always made much of him, always opened a closed-off section at his behest, and catered to his every wish. By far the best restaurant in '80s Mobile was the Ivory Chopsticks, run by a volatile Corsican French army veteran, Jean Casanova, and his talented Vietnamese wife. Its cozy atmosphere in an old bungalow, the wonderfully subtle and satisfying French and Vietnamese food, the low prices and the witty conversation of the Casanovas and their children who visited from Paris, made it our chief gathering place.

Eugene's food columns projected a vision of European cuisine and vast cultural knowledge combined with Southern home cooking. He seemed to have files of thousands of recipes. One week it was homemade country pickles, crackling cookies, sweet potato pone, or persimmon corn bread. He projected a vision of Southern catchups and relishes that suggested Indian chutneys. He championed the idea of using traditional, local, fresh fruits and vegetables. The next week there was a pudding or a cake recipe from Ruth Huger or other legendary Old Mobile personages, or venison or bear recipes from Klotz's, a famous nineteenth century Mobile restaurant which kept live frogs in their show windows. Another week he would run a recipe from Leontyne Price or "Wally Windsor," or give tips on making Italian *gnocchis* or French *profiterolles*, or describe an ancient Roman sauce made of fish entrails and white wine left in the sun. He was, after all, a contributing editor for *Food and Wine* magazine at this time. His locally printed cookbook, *Delectable Dishes from Termite Hall*, gathered many of these recipes and concentrated his vision. Eugene never wrote merely about food, but also good times, Pickwickian conviviality, cornucopia, Old Mobile memories, grand tradition, conversation, and good cheer. All of this was symbolized by Walter Wade Welch's cartoon of a table laid out for a feast, which was run every week at the top of the "Table Talk" column.

As if "Table Talk" and *"EWEW"* were not enough, he also wrote a weekly column called "A Concise Compendium of Herbs, Spices and Flavorings." Every week the piece arrived typed on his shaky old portable typewriter and illustrated with charming botanical drawings or caricatures of personified plants, often drawn on a bit of cardboard or scrap paper with a ballpoint pen. These columns were a whole education of the palate and the imagination. We learned that one can make syrups from maidenhair fern, salads from dandelions and nasturtiums, gumbo thickeners from elephant ear bulbs. Soon we were all cooking with thyme, mace, and tarragon, and trying to grow rocket for salads and sorrel for soup. Many of these columns had recipes, and often gardening tips as well. Eugene could easily have written a separate gardening column, and possessed an encyclopedic knowledge of local garden plants and many wild ones. Gardening is a traditional passion in Mobile, and like so many people here Eugene would light up with pleasure over some old-fashioned rose, cerise phlox blooms, an old, surviving mulberry tree or palm downtown, a wall covered with coral vine, trumpet vine or morning glory, or a blazing lantana bush in a vacant lot. Among the reasons for modern neuroses, he always cited the fact that people don't make things with their hands, walk on the earth with their bare feet, swim in running water, or work their hands in the dirt. Sometimes his enthusiasm over certain weeds, like the intrusive corn flower, left us puzzled. "I celebrate all wayward things...bindweed no less than corn." One had the feeling that Eugene could perceive the life force in plants and animals, and that they shared some quiet secret, so attuned was he to them. "I saw the green man make a sign: / O he was holy, he was lewd, / Bright his ichor; green his blood."

The reportage in Eugene's columns often involved interviews, and when Eugene opined that these were not spicy enough, he felt no compunction about improving upon them. He loved to tell the story of how once he wanted to interview Fellini, but had trouble tracking him down and so simply made up an interview for publication. It was full of robust pronouncements along the lines of "What is art? Art is an old whore. The more you beat her, the more she loves you." So amused was Fellini by this interview, Eugene said, that he quoted from it later when he himself was interviewed by reporters in New York. Nevertheless, when the *ACNR* received heated complaints from several individuals about things they were reported to have said, our editor, Rebecca Paul, was charged with the unenviable task of calling Eugene up and checking out every quotation. Fiery, intelligent, tart-tongued, red-headed, and petite, Becky was the mainspring of the paper and Eugene's distant cousin on the Lewinburg side. I can still hear Becky's quiet, patient, twenty-five-year-old voice going over the quotations line by line with Eugene on the telephone. "Now this dry cleaner, this Wilmer Plunkett. Did he really say, 'I'm such a busy bee, just call me Mr. Dappertutto'?" There would be silence for a moment as Becky listened, then she would persist quietly. "But did he really say, 'Mr. Dappertutto'?" Eugene adored Becky and admired her greatly. He generally called her "Beckalina" or, in her professional capacity, "Madame Paul," but on the occasions when she was holding his feet to the fire, he called her "Lady Macbeth."

Since Eugene was one of the few human beings in Mobile who did not drive, often one of us would be assigned the lucky mission of picking up his copy. Woe to the hapless fool who showed up after three in the afternoon and woke him from his nap! Eugene would appear at the screen door growling like a Tasmanian devil. The proper time to come by was elevenish or noon. Naturally, this entailed a long, leisurely lunch, preceded by numerous bourbon-and-waters, with several courses and many glasses of wine. Generally there were a number of guests, and the flowing conversation went on for several hours until we felt constrained to return to work. At these lunches, it seemed that time stood still as soon as one passed through his door. Cares and anxieties faded, and pressing duties and work itself began to seem not so very important after all. Everyone joked, laughed, told bawdy jokes, argued, but the underlying tone was serenity and safe haven. One finds this luxury of abundant time, what he calls *dolce far niente*, in many of his poems. "I sometimes find I like much more / Doing nothing with a very quick spirit / Than doing something slower."

After he left the Deasy House, Eugene stayed on the third floor of Termite Hall, an imposing, sprawling old mansion that was once a halfway inn between Mobile and Spring Hill in the mid-nineteenth century, but was added onto and converted into a Creole/Victorian manor house. According to Eugene, the name derived from an incident in which the former lady of the manor, Mrs. John Marston, fell through the floor, and, spectrally suspended from the waist up, remonstrated with the onlookers in long-suffering tones, "I *told* y'all to call the termite man." Her daughters, Adelaide Trigg and Eleanor Benz, and Adelaide's husband, Edwin Trigg, resided there and gave Eugene help at a crucial moment. The home and its inhabitants had everything Eugene's heart could have desired, and I believe his time there fulfilled a kind of archetype he had of life in Mobile, just as he achieved an archetypal wish for *la vie bohème* when he was in Europe. By this I mean not some Old South cliché, but something coastal and remembered from childhood, the living quick of tradition. Adelaide and Eleanor dressed sensibly and had down-to-earth ways and playful Mobile irony, but were highly cultivated, read incessantly, displayed refined bearing and manners, and had (and still have!) the most resplendent old Mobile accents ("Would you care for another buibon?") They were descended from true blue, aristocratic, Old Mobile Catholic families, the Marstons and the Rapiers of *Mobile Register* fame, and Eleanor's late husband was a descendant of the illustrious German architect Rudolph Benz of Victorian Mobile. They ran Termite Hall with Tudor largesse and hospitality. Children, grandchildren, and guests were constantly coming and going. They threw the house open to Eugene's friends and visitors and welcomed them. There were numerous lunches and dinners where Eugene presided at a huge old table in a dining room whose walls were covered with dark old paneling. On at least one occasion Eugene decorated the tablecloth with glitter and sequins. Adelaide and Eleanor kept a table in a corner crowded with bottles of spirits and liqueurs of all description which they dispensed with a liberal hand. Guests were also received in a parlor after they passed through the wide old entrance hall. All the rooms were filled with splendid old antiques–inherited, not bought–and there was a slightly cobwebby patina of disrepair and grandeur which no amount of money could duplicate. Best of all was the deep front porch, looping around a corner of the house, on which we rocked in rocking chairs, sipped bourbon and water, glimpsed the faraway traffic and foolish commotion on Dauphin Street through trees and hedges, and cultivated the leisurely art of conversation.

It would not be too much to say that the house had a kind of presence. Besides Eugene's cookbook, there was a play written about the house in the '50s by Thomas Atkins, and another by Thomas Perez in the '80s. Many lives and fates had been lived out there, and not only Eugene but other guests as well spoke of seeing ghosts. Sometimes, sitting at the dining room table, Eugene and other people saw a woman with marcelled hair and in a beautiful gown, as for a Mardi Gras ball, passing down the entrance hall toward the front door. She would smile as she glanced into the dining room. Eugene also told me about having had a fitful sleep one night because he kept hearing two young men named James and Lacy walking back and forth and talking on the adjacent rear upper-floor gallery. They had soft, old-fashioned accents, and were excited because they were going to catch "the diligence" across the bay in the morning to meet a young woman. "When I woke up the next morning, I realized that they had been walking through a wall dividing the gallery," Eugene recounted. He said that ghosts are a kind of crystallization of lives at certain moments and emotions.

Eventually Eugene moved to 161 Grand Boulevard. The house was built in the nineteen teens, with just four rooms and a kitchen, much smaller than the "white elephant" he said he was looking for, but still a home of his own through the generosity of Betty McGowin and undoubtedly other anonymous patrons who helped him with living expenses. In the first few years there the house was fairly orderly, and he had fulfilled his oft-expressed wish of "getting the books on the shelves." The meals he served were tasty, the cats were not yet allowed to lick the butter on the dinner table, and there was an odd, charming fragrance, probably of the old-fashioned Florida Water cologne he was partial to. The walls crammed like the Louvre with paintings, established an Ali Baba ambience, and a sparkling stream of classical music wafted from the radio, which was permanently set on WHIL even when he left the house, because it kept the cats company. VIPs and friends who had been especially good were sometimes conducted into the sanctum of the "Cat-Free room," also called "the snuggery," where all was order and calm. Eugene was still plump and strong. Whenever Alabama Power Company crews showed up to hack the willow and tallow trees in front of his house, he screamed and cussed at them lustily from his front door at the top of his voice. He expended enormous effort on having topsoil hauled in and constructing raised beds in the back yard where he grew delicious salad greens and herbs. Up until the very last time I crossed his threshold, despite the disorder of his house in later years as he grew older and weaker, the feeling never left me that I was enormously fortunate to have been admitted to a privileged secret club.

The glowing halo of faces surrounding Eugene's after his return to Mobile in 1979 is vast. No one could name everyone he knew here. Practically everyone associated in some way with the arts in Mobile was touched by Eugene, and countless young people were influenced and championed by him. In thinking of these times and seeing these faces, some of them departed, I am reminded of our excitement and pride at the *Azalea City News and Review* when the twenty-fifth anniversary issue of the *Paris Review* came out in 1981. There for all the world to see were our Eugene's reminiscences of the review among those of other literati, plus affectionate descriptions of him by George Plimpton and others, and a glamorous group photo taken in 1954 in front of the Café de Tournon of Eugene with the likes of Jean Garrigue and Niccolo Tucci. It was something we could show to skeptics and out-of-town friends to prove who our friend Eugene really was. What did not occur to us was that in our remote corner of the Gulf of Mexico we were experiencing our own collective, youthful *vie de bohème* thanks to Eugene, and that one day we would be writing our own reminiscences about it.

Sometimes personalities from Eugene's European days would flash like meteors into Mobile to visit him. One of the brightest was the young photographer Guy Deacon of Toronto. Though only twenty-six or twenty-seven at the time, Guy had known Eugene in his Roman glory. His real name was William, but Eugene decided that was much too dull and gave him a French name which everybody who met him in Mobile used. Guy seemed to enjoy the transformation, and his four or five visits to Mobile were tornadoes of social events and photo shoots. He seemed to find the Gulf Coast extremely exotic, and, seeing ourselves in his eyes, everyone played the part and took him to ruined buildings and got him to photograph all the local color and eccentrics we could find. Handsome, energetic, aware and ambitious, with crisp Canadian intelligence, Guy was truly loved here. He was a great artist; his photographs wrought the most amazing metamorphoses, and he took the best pictures ever made of Mobile Mardi Gras. What is more, Guy was the only person who ever dared to throw the headstrong cat Tinkerbell out the front door after she started strolling on the dinner table. He and Eugene traveled the region in preparation for a book which was to be called *The Baroque South.* It is a mystery why Eugene never completed the text to the book despite pleading letters from Guy, just as Eugene never completed *The Blockade Runners* or his memoirs. The loss was compounded by the tragedy of Guy's untimely death a few years later.

"Old" and "downtown" were the two key words for my own activity at the *ACNR*, plus the word "revival." Many of the articles I wrote were concerned with historic preservation, and my soap opera serial *Blood of the Rochefoucaulds,* which after many rewritings became the novel *Isle of Joy,* was a spoof of destructive urban planning, an elegy for what was lost here, and an attempt to revive the old urban spirit of Mobile. The '70s and '80s were a bleak time for the city. During World War II a huge immigration took place of rural people who were largely hostile to city life and indifferent to Mobile traditions. Furthermore, the general American movement to the suburbs had hit the older parts of the city hard, and then the city government and downtown property owners administered the *coup de grace* by tearing down hundreds, indeed, thousands of nineteenth century houses and buildings. Eugene used to talk about his return to Mobile in

1970 when he stayed at the Battle House downtown. He decided to take a stroll through the ancient neighborhoods south of Government Street, but when he got to Church Street he was horrified to behold a vast plain of dirt and rubble as far as the eye could see. With money from the federal "Urban Renewal" program, the Mobile Housing Board had bulldozed the entire South Side and Down the Bay areas. Eugene staggered back to the hotel in shock and went to bed. No wonder he described downtown Mobile as looking like "a North African city after bombardment, with gaping spaces," and added, "Dauphin Street has that ineffable sadness of certain long vistas in de Chirico's early 'nostalgia of the infinite' paintings."

Eugene had predicted the destruction of Mobile—as well as the trajectory of his own life—in *Jennie, the Watercress Girl* in 1946. The perpetrators were "red-nosed do-nothings elected to responsible office" and "dollar-brained souls...confused about the idea of Progress." In the book, Jennie comes home after a scintillating artistic career, but her hair turns instantly gray when she sees that Bienville Square has been paved. In reality, what happened here was even worse than his predictions. In one aspect, *Isle of Joy* is a sequel to *Jennie,* happening after the orgy of bulldozing.

With my preservation articles, a special tabloid insert called "The Azalea City Preserver," and my serial, I attempted to evoke an almost lost identity of Mobile, what Eugene called "the spirit of slatternly arrogance and naiveté, the raffish and sunny character of the town—the studied *vif et gai."* Eugene contributed wonderful memory pieces about old downtown, Mardi Gras, houses, streets, and people. "Reader, give me your furry paw, and let's stroll down Dauphin Street that was." Eugene was a consummate writer, and could toss off lines in some of these casual pieces that more famous authors could never have produced. This is something that must always be remembered in assessing his work, and not just the number of books and how many copies were sold.

Even more precious to me than his articles were conversations in which he recalled Mobile in the '20s and '30s as a lazy, subtropical city full of quaint nooks, smells, street life, and great eccentrics. I was especially intrigued by his tales of going with his grandmother to visit a very old man named Mr. Willoughby and his sister in an ancient house on the north side, around St. Anthony or St. Michael streets, and listening to the conversations of these elders who were more of the nineteenth century than the twentieth. The Willoughbys still used an old chamber pot or "thunder mug," as Eugene called it, with a picture of Ulysses S. Grant on the bottom. This Mr. Willoughby, who gave his name to Eugene's Willoughby Institute, worked as a waiter at the Scottish Rite temple, and Eugene was also a waiter there shortly before the war.

Completing the picture of this lost Atlantis of old pre-suburban Mobile was the hidden Atlantis of Eugene's youth. He never liked to be asked direct questions, and so the occasions when he chose to talk about himself were all the more memorable. One day in the '30s, Eugene said, he was leaving the Mobile Public Library when he heard a woman calling, "Hey, you, come over here! How come your aura has two colors?" It turned out that it was a Mrs. Bixler, an astrologer who had learned Greek, Latin, and classical Arabic for her studies. She was so impressed by Eugene that she wanted to cast his horoscope. The day he arrived at her house, she excused herself for being nervous because the astrobody of her dead cat was tapping against the window. She told him he must always live close to the water, and that the things that were most difficult to do were the things that he would do best. She counseled him to avoid facility. When Eugene came back from Italy, he found her predictions and said that they had all come true.

Occasionally one heard tantalizing stories from other people about Eugene's youth. One day we ran into William Edward Davis at Three Georges' candy store. He said that he had known Eugene when they were four years old, and they gave puppet shows together at Eugene's garage on Old Shell near Broad Street. Eugene's grandmother gave Eugene an expensive erector set for intelligent children and "indulged him," he said. He also told about visiting Eugene in his apartment in New York, which was painted black with white footsteps going up the walls and across the ceiling. Then there was a basement apartment where Eugene hosted a party for Dylan Thomas. According to Eugene, Ed Davis was on the verge of making a breakthrough as an actor in New York when he came down with throat cancer and had to return to Mobile.

Another childhood friend of Eugene's recalled attending a lawn party in the '20s at St. Joseph's Catholic Church downtown when they were both six years old. Eugene's parents were there and were an attractive young couple, she said. His father was a young businessman and Mardi Gras mystic society type. Eugene wanted them to buy an enticing toy, and when they refused, he staged a fainting fit until they came around. Another lady remembered walking home from high school with Eugene. He was "a nice boy," she said, but he embarrassed her by declaiming soliloquies from Shakespeare and dying on the grass. Passing cars would slow down to see what was happening.

My friend Andrew Dacovich, a great Mobile personage in his own right and a model for one of the characters in Robert E. Bell's *The Butterfly Tree,* was nine years older than Eugene and grew up on St. Joseph Street just blocks from the waterfront when it was a fine old residential neighborhood. Andrew knew Eugene's wealthy, cosmopolitan friends and patrons, Hammond Gayfer and Aimée King, very well, and throughout the decade of the '30s Andrew was active in their Little Theater in the old Seaman's Bethel downtown. At the age of nineteen Andrew directed his first play there, and he took part in a production of *Peer Gynt* that was one of Eugene's lifelong enthusiasms. Eugene acted in these productions as well, and Andrew remembered first seeing him as a very young teen-ager curled up asleep on a table in the lobby. "Who is this blond elf?" Andrew wondered.

Their friendship took a literally fateful turn during World War II when Andrew was drafted and sent to Atlanta for processing. Waiting for his papers in an interminable line of soldiers, Andrew finally arrived up front at the table and was flabbergasted to find sitting there–Eugene Walter. Eugene read the orders sending him to the Pacific front. "Oh no, you don't want to go there!" he exclaimed brightly, and simply tore them to shreds. Then he wrote out a new set of orders sending him to a research lab outside New York City. All of this was highly illegal, and Andrew was sweating with fear, but as a result Andrew experienced two wonderful years in New York before being shipped out to India and China and thus fulfilling his lifelong dream of seeing those ancient cultures. Quite possibly Eugene saved Andrew's life.

To me, this story more than any other exemplified Eugene the magician, able to deflect lives and turn the ordinary into the extraordinary. "Only grab into abundant human life, and wherever you seize it, there it will be interesting," says Goethe. More than anyone else I have ever known, Eugene was able to work this spell.

Thank you, dear maestro, for teaching us.

What I say is, if you
have a big nose, be nosey;
if you have a flashy ankle,
learn to dance with a tambourine;
if you have no sense of humor,
then drop dead . . . anyway, that's
what I say . . .

Patricia Forest

Patricia Forest grew up with all the stories of Eugene and finally got to experience the man himself during her sojourn in Rome. She now resides at Termite Hall in the gracious home of Eugene's co-conspirators in merriment, Eleanor Benz and Adelaide Trigg.

In 1969 Mary Trigg Scully and I were in Rome spending our junior year abroad. The first weekend we arrived, Eugene invited us to his place for dinner. Mary and I did not drink; we were only twenty and had not yet had a chance to immerse ourselves in the Italian culture. We arrived at Eugene's and the first thing he did was give us before-dinner wine. Neither one of us had a taste for wine, but it was good.

He showed us around his delightful apartment with its seven-foot cat-house. He introduced us to all his cats. We had another guest join us for dinner. She was a writer who had on a see-through blouse (with no bra). If you remember, these became popular at that time. This was quite a shock to Mary and me.

When we were seated for dinner, Eugene poured us red wine. After we began to eat, his cat jumped up onto the table and confidently made his way to my plate, and began to sniff. I really did not know what to do. Fortunately, Eugene removed him from the table. I didn't like the taste of the wine but it became very clear to us that we were not going to leave the table until we drank all of it. So I picked up my glass and drank it down. So surprised was Eugene, he said, "Well, I have never seen anyone drink wine like that!" To my horror, he promptly filled my glass again.

I don't know how we made our way back to school but somehow we did. We went right to our apartment and fell into bed. Hence, everyone at school knew we had been to Eugene's when we came back drunk as ever on Sunday afternoons.

Betty Rossell McGowin

Betty Rossell McGowin was born in Carlisle, Kentucky, in 1917. She died in Chapman, Alabama, in September 1998. She was an enthusiastic friend and patron of the arts. When Eugene Walter moved from Rome to Mobile, he was a frequent guest at her dinner parties and lunches in Chapman and in Mobile. He called her "Zongalina," showering her with light verse and drawings, including the following invitation to her eightieth birthday party that drew three hundred fifty people from around the world to rural Alabama on a rainy February night:

> *Some people shiver when they hear 'birthday'*
> *(Another fated 'tick' toward the final 'tock')*
> > *But I wind a different clock:*
> *Instead of 'birthday' I hear 'mirthday':*
> *Something more tender, something more rash.*
> *Put on my best ribbon sash,*
> *So come join me for a .... bash.*
> *My* maitre d' *is St. Valentine*
> *Bubbly and sparkly suit me fine!*

Betty McGowin bought the house on Grand Boulevard for Eugene, which was given to The Nature Conservancy after his death to benefit land preservation in Alabama.

Eugene Walter

I met Eugene Walter when he invited us all up to his third floor apartment in Rome, near that wedding cake place, Vittorio Emanuele. I was in Italy with Sam and Lilly Betty and Midge Bennett from Greenville. Eugene cooked the supper by himself, with his own hands. I'll never forget it. He made a Patent Leather Pie from eggplant done in layers, the insides chopped and gooked up and the black skins on the top and sides, skin side out, all glorious and shiny! Just that, and salad, bread, and wine. We were sitting at dinner, our glasses raised to Roma and each other and old Mobile, when Eugene jumped up and got a vial of oil of rosemary and began rubbing it on our temples, one by one around the table—to keep the wine fumes down, he said. So anointed, we could drink glass after glass and never get drunk! I never met anyone like Eugene. That was when he was editing *Botteghe Oscure* and told wonderful stories about writers he knew like Isak Dinesen. He sang and trumpeted an invisible horn and carried on. I fell in love with him and his crazy talk.

Then, later in the '70s, he kept getting tear-gassed because clashes between radicals and police happened downstairs, under his windows. Italy was a scary place then, when airport crowds got machine-gunned, bombs went off no telling where or when. Even the Prime Minister, Aldo Moro, was kidnapped and murdered by the Red Brigades. Eugene decided it was time to come home.

First he lived in a little cottage until a hurricane blew the roof off, then at Termite Hall. He never had any money. I wanted to help him but at a remove, through the bank, so he wouldn't feel beholden. The bank found a house on Grand Boulevard for him, and the original idea was that he should pay two hundred and fifty dollars rent a month, but when months passed and no rent was paid, I told the bank never mind. At least he should pay for maintenance, the bank insisted. The following two letters from Eugene in high dudgeon show why the bank had to back down.

*   *   *   *   *

161 Grand Blvd
Mobile 36607 AL

First National Bank
Trust Department

Dear Trust Dept.,

    I am uncertain as to whom I should address directly so address you severally. Another disaster. No sooner had I managed to have the 16 broken pipes replaced, and cleaned up after the sewage backup following the Christmas Week freeze, when night before last (Sunday) here comes that storm and the middle room was inundated from leaks in the roof. This is the <u>*third*</u> *time. Thank God Almighty that on Saturday I had removed the valuable paintings I had assembled for an exhibition,* **TWENTIETH CENTURY FLOWER PAINTINGS,** *which I am organizing for the University, which went off to the campus. I think you should threaten to sue the roofing contractor. Sometimes a threatened suit is better than a suit. But I really do think you should insist that the contractor himself come to look over the situation rather than as on other occasions send cheerful blacks who obviously did only the most summary patch-up. I'll appreciate your goading the roofer, since I have valuable books and pictures here and begin to lose sleep over them.*

Sincerely,
   Eugene Walter

*   *   *   *   *

161 Grand Blvd.
Mobile 36607 AL

Trust Dept.
FIRST NATIONAL BANK
Attn: Mr. Joseph H. Baker

Dear Mr. Baker:

I have not had the pleasure of meeting you, but shall address myself to you just the same. I am dismayed, puzzled, appalled and finally angered by the fact that the Trust Dept. has not had the common courtesy (common decency!) to reply to a letter I wrote over three months ago, describing an emergency in this property administered by the Trust Dept. The roof, never properly repaired after the hurricane or after the several subsequent storms and minor tornados, continues to leak, ever more badly. I have had to remove everything from the attic, and must scurry around with buckets every time it rains. Everything is in total chaos, I have no place to work. What does the Trust Dept. plan to do? The longer the delay, the more augmented the damages, the greater the final expense. Now I know that the Bank has no interest in my personal welfare, and couldn't give a damn about the books and literary archives of which I am custodian. The Bank would certainly express total indifference to the fact that the New York Public Library is in an uproar because I cannot give them copies of letters from the late poet Jean Garrigue which they have requested for a memorial volume. I don't think the Bank would have the slightest concern over the fact that the Ministry of Fine Arts of the Italian nation is in an uproar because I cannot supply them with photographs and documents I have promised for an exhibition in Rome called Images of the South. *But since you are trusted with the administration of Mrs. Julian McGowin's property I do think a little more attention to this problem might be in order. My lawyer is bringing a photographer to record the puddles in my library and the chinks of light in the roof. I have re-roofed the damaged part of the garage, constructed screens for the back porch, replaced rotting floor boards, replaced malfunctioning parts of the jerry-patched air conditioning system, replaced ancient and defective stove and refrigerator, have built proper vents for the heater, replaced broken defective pipes under the house, evacuated rubble in the back yard, etc. etc but the roof is your responsibility. What do you plan to do? Have the simple decency to reply. I have asked the contractor Mr. Ted Dial to report to you on the nature of the damages.*

Yours,
Eugene Walter

Adelaide Trigg

Eugene's love of books brought him into the Haunted Book Shop in downtown Mobile, and it was there that we became good friends. Eugene had several jobs, among them an usher at the Saenger Theatre and at Paris Printing Company, but he spent a great deal of time in the bookstore. It was a place of lively conversation and strong opinions.

I had a classical education and was suited for nothing, but I wanted to open a bookshop. Cameron McRae Plummer and I formed a partnership. The city didn't know what to charge for a license because there hadn't been a bookstore for years. But we pressed forward. At last, the Haunted Book Shop on Conception Street was opened. The title came from Christopher Morley's book, and he gave me permission to use the name.

I managed the bookshop from the spring of 1941 until October 1943, when I left to get married. My husband's job required a lot of moving around, but I always remained interested in books. It was then that I got involved in book searches.

Today, I manage Far Corners Book Search at my home, which all of Eugene's friends call Termite Hall.

My sister, Eleanor Benz, and I were lucky enough to have Eugene as our extended guest for several years when he first came home from Italy. We all loved books and words, and we have wonderful memories of the adventures Eugene concocted with such energy and ease.

When Eugene Walter appeared at the Haunted Book Shop in 1941 and asked me to find Maurice Sand's *History of the Harlequinade*, I knew he'd be someone interesting to know. He was. Almost daily he came by, often brought his lunch, and naturally we discussed books to find how many favorites we shared.

The Marine Junk Company sold books by the pound, so periodically, we'd go there to see what treasures we might find. Books were piled to the ceiling on the second floor and were shoveled like coal, to be dumped into the bailing compressor. It was horrible to see such ill-treatment, and to climb on them, not knowing if we might be smashing some Rare Tome. Mice and spiders resented our intrusion, but we plowed ahead. One day, Eugene saw some leather-bound books pushed by shovels toward the elevator, and practically dove down the shaft to save them from untimely demise. Among the prized titles was *The Arctic Explorations of Dr. Elisha Kent Kane*. We'd never heard of him, but Eugene thereafter considered him a good omen when he found any books by or about him. He found *The Love Letters of Dr. Kane* in some small shop in Rome and several other titles here and there.

Eugene was working at Powers Printing Company in '41 and brought us a large scrapbook for customers to write or draw in. He was always sketching whimsical characters therein, imaginary or otherwise. We had a beautiful gold-framed "ancestor portrait" over the mantel in the front room, so I suggested he paint something to hang over the mantel in the adjoining room. One day he arrived at the shop with a captivating painting of the MAD TEA-PARTY, as large as the portrait in the front room. Fortunately I unearthed a gold frame in my attic which was a perfect fit. Many customers and friends wanted to buy it.

I believe it was the first time Eugene returned from Europe for a few weeks, that he said there were so many friends he'd not seen. And, really, only a party at Termite Hall could remedy this—so we agreed. Yearly, I sympathized with the Christmas trees relegated to oblivion on the streets so each day, after depositing the children at school, I'd stop to rescue as many trees as the station wagon could hold. These were ensconced in strategic places on the porch, in the hall, living room, and wherever they could stand. Then came the idea of the MOOSEHEAD TAVERN. I made a life-size head of brown paper painted with shoe polish and he was hung over the mantel in the dining room. Jean Fitzsimmons (Delaney) helped me festoon bamboo and ivy along the beams in the ceiling, which was quite effective. (Especially when leaves fell into the food.) The dining room table was de-leafed, pushed into a far corner to make room for card tables with the usual red-checked cloths. The bar was set up in the sun parlor off the dining room. A large sign tacked up near the front door read, in part:

> *The Moosehead Tavern*
> *Girls, Girls, Girls*
> *See Lottie Lou Goonjaw and*
> *The Heavenly Hags in Song and Dance*
> *Admission Free — or your money back.*

Conversation and laughter reached unknown decibels, when suddenly, a clock chimed demanding silence. It kept on chiming—two hundred times! It had been silent for years, no key to wind it. I'd moved it from the mantel to make room for the moose and put it on the floor. I can only suppose this displacement joggled its innards into activity—to join the party. And welcome home our old friend.

Concert in the snow – Aleutian Islands – 1947
(Photo courtesy of Adelaide Trigg and Eleanor Benz)

Vernon Raines

At the age of sixteen, Mr. Raines learned to conduct by listening to recordings played by Catherine Ann Middleton. Mr. Raines was the first conductor of the Mobile Chamber Orchestra, which later developed into the Mobile Symphony.

Mr. Raines was the conductor of the Meridian, Mississippi, symphony for many years.

He currently lives in Mobile, and among his numerous civic and artistic endeavors he continues to play the violin with the Mobile Symphony.

One of my early memories of Eugene, aside from my college days when a friend and I joined him for entertaining trips to the Bluebird Cafe near the waterfront, was the wonderful party he gave at Termite Hall after the publication of *Jennie, the Watercress Girl*. Eugene had decorated the walk all the way from Dauphin Street to the front steps with candles and filled the trees with Japanese lanterns. These cast an eerie glow which created the perfect atmosphere for meeting the effigy of Marie Reed, literary editor of the paper. She stood at the top of the front steps and greeted all comers young and old.

In reviewing *Jennie*, Marie had totally missed the point of the little satire and proceeded to write about it most unfavorably. In his inimitable way, Eugene had created a delightfully funny look-alike complete with large wide-brimmed hat and imposing pendant made from a coffee can lid with a picture of Robert Taylor pasted on it. What a beginning for a fun evening.

The party was a huge success and was kept lively by repeated playings on an old wind-up Victrola of a 78 RPM record of a country singer wailing away a song called *Atomic Power!* The humor of the serious subject combined with the simple, direct style of the singer (whose voice had an almost unbearably nasal quality) proved so compelling that many listenings were needed to fully appreciate the total effect. A tape of this recording today would be a great party booster. But back to Marie Reed.

I was told by a knowledgeable source (who might have been Eugene) that later in the season he appeared at a Mardi Gras ball dressed in a dog costume whereupon he immediately sought out Marie, lifted a rear paw, and shot her on the leg with a water pistol. I cannot attest to the veracity of this story. But I am quite sure of the next episode because I was present for every detail.

In 1951 I traveled to Europe to attend the Casals Music Festival in Perpignan, South France. Eugene had preceded me to Paris by several months so I stopped for a visit before going on to the Festival. I arrived in Paris two weeks before Bastille Day during the two thousandth anniversary of the city. It is impossible to describe the mood. There were decorations everywhere, streets roped off for dancing, dance bands every few blocks and fireworks displays almost every evening in the Place de la Concorde. I was told by one who attended Eugene's first fireworks experience with him in Paris, that Eugene became so excited he came down with a fever and had to be put to bed for several days to recover. The air was literally charged with the excitement of the time.

It was into this wild celebration that I injected myself after twelve days at sea on the SS Volendam. Arriving in Paris on the boat train from Le

Havre, I went directly to the Hotel Helvetia at 23 Rue de Tournon. This was Eugene's place of residence and it was just a few doors down from the Luxembourg Palace. After being greeted by M. Jordan, the concierge, and depositing my bags in the front room on the fourth floor, I located Eugene at the Cafe de Tournon across the street.

I soon learned that this cafe was one of Eugene's haunts and that cafe sitting was a daily ritual. I found myself slipping into this practice too easily and on one particular day, I went over for breakfast at nine in the morning and did not return to the hotel until two a.m. the next day. Except for lunch and dinner at a nearby restaurant, the entire time was spent at the cafe in conversation. I could easily understand why Eugene spent time in the cafe. It was frequented by fascinating individuals from around the globe. Poets, musicians, artists, and students from the Sorbonne were constantly in and out. Artistically this was one of the richest periods in post-World War II Paris, and Eugene made many friends here in the arts who later became international figures. The "cafe sitting" was not just an idle passage of time.

One evening when the conversation at the cafe was not too exciting, I decided to go to bed early. As I retired I could faintly hear the rat-tat-tat of Eugene's typewriter. In fact, that was the last thing I remember as I drifted off to sleep. I must have slept several hours before I was sharply awakened by a tremendous sound. Scrambling quickly out of bed, I pulled on some trousers and headed for the stairs. Immediately I spied Eugene running from his room dressed in a bathrobe and carrying his passport in one hand and a cantaloupe in the other. "What are you doing?" I yelled. "I'm heading for the Marie de Medici Fountain to hide," he retorted somewhat gleefully. I realized he could not be serious as the Luxembourg Gardens closed at sundown and I simply could not see Eugene clambering over a sixteen foot iron fence in a bathrobe while clutching his precious cantaloupe in one hand and his passport in the other. Furthermore, having seen the Marie de Medici Fountain, I could not imagine it providing protection from anything more dangerous than a mimosa blossom.

We had to go outside the hotel to discover the source of the noise, and we ventured forth with the fearlessness of youth. To our amazement we discovered that three blocks from the hotel a de Gaullist had bombed a communist bookshop. The windows were all broken out and the street was littered with communist literature. The most curious touch of all was the inhabitants of the area hanging out of their windows laughing hysterically.

# # #

Through the years Eugene and I corresponded. The following are some of those letters in inimitable Eugene style.

Dear Vernon:

'S a g-u-d thing you wrote me about La Rosita because I never read the papers and there's a chance I may have missed her. I save the Book theatre Music sections and read them several weeks late. Anyway, I got to the box office in time to get a ticket in the Dress Circle; and besides it's the first letter I've received from you, and I hope now that the ice is broken you'll write often.

Well, Rosita's concert turned out pure and simple the most exciting event of the entire musical season, and actually I can't remember any other concerts creating such a furor except some certain performances of Landowska and Tyete. First, some friend of Rosita's, I am told, bought ALL the boxes in Carnegie Hall, other South Americans in New York bought 100 seats or 250 seats or 50 seats, and had parties. Otherwise the audience was composed of many young musicians, and ME and all my friends I could muster (all of whom have thanked me with tears and protestations for telling them about the concert). Some woman flew from Switzerland for the concert, had a hell of a good time, and flew back after the encores. The whole town is talking, literally. Another concert has been arranged for Feb. 18 when Rosita will play a Bach concerto, AND a Mozart concerto, and a Beethoven concerto with the Philharmonic. Most of my <u>inside</u> information comes from the divine Blanca, though everyone has talked of nothing else since. Also, there's a <u>great</u> deal of agitation for Rosita and Blanca to give a two-piano recital. I'd sell my teeth to hear those girls step out with some Mozart. Well, Rosita has very formal stage manners, in fact she pretends the audience is not there. To hell with you, she says, God love you, but I'm busy with Bach and Mozart and can't cope with all you Mongolian idiots. She manages to do this charmingly though. But she doesn't have the divine Blanca's presence, however. She strolls out briskly (dressed in sleek black) and heads for the piano and before her fanny has touched the seat she is finished about four measures of the opening Bach. Velocity! why the girl is like something let loose! She plays everything at a tempo (such a tempo! how does she think that fast?) we are not accustomed to hear, but it's all truth and daylight. You know how I feel about the classic boys, I like them served straight with no gravy. Well, that's Rosita: she makes you feel that Mozart is an unexplored continent of poetry and that she is Miss Ponce de Leon of 1949 and has claimed Mozart for the King of Chile. I tell you the

God's truth, you couldn't tell it was a piano when she played the Mozart, only music, truth and daylight. She played my boys with great warmth, with radiance and joyousness, but no sentimentality and no slerping in the glerping. You know how people in movies about concerti always puff and strain (when they play the Rachmaninoff #2)—well Rosita is the opposite, in her most thunderous fortissimo she plays with the casual air of a child practicing scales when his mama is away.

You know, unconcerned. Absolutely relaxed.

YOU RELAX BEFORE YOU READ THIS NEXT PART:

I want you to come to New York for Rosita's concert on Feb. 18. Borrow the money from your uncle. Or anybody. Make Walter Russell come with you. I'll feed you and of course you'll stay with me, while you're here. There's a good inexpensive hotel which Russell must write for reservations. It is HOLLEY CHAMBERS HOTEL, WASHINGTON SQUARE, NEW YORK 14, NEW YORK.

That's in spitting distance of here. You must plan to arrive the afternoon of Friday the 18th and leave on the following Monday. I do not joke when I say this is to be the musical event of the decade. It will furthermore give us a chance to spend one whole day quietly discussing Chamber Orchestra all by ourselves, which we have needed to do for over a year. You and I alone can settle certain points.

Future plans, the premiering of scores, etc. Then we'll go to the theatre Sat night, the museum of Modern Art on Sunday, maybe have a soiree Sunday night. Oh and I have a clavichord here you must see. Write me an immediate answer so I can get Rosita tickets. If you don't want to come to NY its a sin and a shame. Thems my sennymints.

> *alons, mein enfant, this is the perfect*
> *Psychological moment for you to come.*
> *you need it.*

bye bye, nice to hear from you

answer immedjutlee.

> *Willoughby*

Please give gilt-edged regards to the Luna Moth, Mickey B. Papa O'Steen the charming Arlene, the delightful Christy, the darling Searcy and mad impetuous Ottokar.

# # #

Dear Vernon:
    The delay is occasioned by the fact that I've had trouble contacting Dr. Mendel, Senora Rosita's personal representative—it seems that the concert had hit a snag somewhere, and only today did I ascertain that it had been postponed. I'm terribly disappointed and know that you are, too. No date this season is in sight at all.
    So———. Alas!
    However, I still consider a New York trip somewhat important for you. Vernon, there are so many incentives to work, here, so many inspirations, so many sources of knowledge—every young person should have a trip to N.Y. You must plan now to make a future trip. Perhaps in early summer, if only for a week. Or perhaps next season. (The Music Library alone will give you nervous prostration.)
    I am involved in a fabulous project currently—a new group called Repertory Players Co., Inc., with an advisory board consisting of Stella Adler, Randy Echols, John Gielgud, Rex Harrison, and Joyce Redmon. I am designing five—count em!—five productions for them. You must come up during the run of the group.
    <u>Please write me your reaction</u> to all this. <u>Let me hear from you</u>.
    So upset—did so want to have a long talk with you.
            Write—
        Best
            Eugene

# # #

2 via Oreste Tiburzi
Tel: 504.436

Dear Baby Porcupine,
    I've been toying, but only toying, with the idea of coming up there. But it really is too hot for me to travel in the summer, now that I'm so old and fat and useless. I prefer to sit still like a monument and have everybody come to Rome and see me! Everybody on earth has been this season, especially the divine Leontyne Price, do you know her, a Laurel chile, sings like an angel having orgasm. But when yawl arrive there will have returned one of the most interesting musical creatures, Paul Wolfe, the last important pupil-friend of Landowska. (He's done five albums comprising complete

Handel clavier works, a Spanish album, early English, a Frescobaldi.) His harpsichord has flowers and bugs painted inside it, like a proper instrument should. We'll make him play for us, but only if you and Blanca Brighteyes will play for us, too. I never forget that one Scarlatti sonata she played for us in Tuscaloosa around 1948. I'll try and round up a decent piano. I have a baroque ruin of an upright next door to me in the apartment of Denis Vaughn, Beecham's assistant, who is off to Spain now. And you must save an hour with your fiddle for me, there are some Matheson duets I play that are delicious, and I want to hear the other line. I also have a kind of substitute Catherine Ann, a soprano named Anne English who sings Bach, Handel, and Traviata with a nice milk-chocolate covered tone. So we'll arrange a musical soiree. Try and arrive by sundown on Sunday the 13th and we'll go dine by a plashing fountain in my favorite piazza.

Telephone me at the above number—don't lose it, it's not in the tellyfun book.

> *see you, looking forward muchly, pretty pats*
> *and pinches for Blanca and Doublas,*

> *Eugene*

P.S. There's a little newish hotel called Hotel Condotti, why don't you have some Italian friend telephone from there and make reservations? It's modest, clean, hot water, not dear, near Spanish Stairs, etc. It's tel is 674769.

# # #

2 via Oreste Tiburzi
> *Dear Vernon,*
> > *(Why) (is)*
> > *(Who) (are) your party?*
> > *(When) (am)*
> *You give no details, and answer none of my questions, you bad thing. I am in-and-out of Rome but will rush to town to see you, if you let me know WHEN you plan to come. I'd like to do a party with musical creatures for yawl. <u>Who are yawl</u>???Pianists? Singers? Bead-weavers? First week of August would be nice. Or do you mean you are <u>there</u> until 13 August <u>then</u> wander? Write me instantly.*

> > *mille fleurs*
> > *Eugene*

# # #

2 via Oreste Tiburzi

Talk about bolt from the blue! I was so shocked to hear from you that I put two tablespoons (stead of one) of orange juice in my morning gin. Clears the blood. Well I can't tell whether you say you're coming in JAN OR JANE OR JUNE, the way you write it. But I'm delighted you're coming. And marvelous Blanca, how nice to see her—of course you'll come to Rome. I leave day after tomorrow for two months in Greece, tootling about, you know, all those islands and everything.

Then I'm in Paris a while preparing an exhibition (my poems all scrawled big, and huge collages by Roloff Beny) then lord knows where. A play I adapted from friends' translation of an Austrian original will be done about 1962 on Broadway and in London. I have books coming out. Of course I'll come right up there and give you all a spiritual goose. I have never visited Santa Margherita or Spezia. I urge you to take the house only for a month WITH AN OPTION for another. You might hate it, also you might find something far more charming in a smaller place.

If you have a car, all is possible. Piano might be a problem: urge you to bring three toy ones in car. Or one spinet type. I ENVY you being in Fairhope for summer: wish I were there. Hope you are making love with lots of beautiful boys and lots of beautiful girls under the pine trees. I am so busy packing and telephoning

I can't think any more . Bye for now.

All bes

Eugene

# # #

2 via Oreste Tiburzi

Dear Vernon,

It was so nice to see you but all too brief: might as well be twenty years ago now your apparition was so brief. Blanca is CUTE. So is Douglas. Don't forget to send me grits. Be sure mark package UNSOLICITED GIFT and REGALO.

Apply for all fellowships and come over and we'll write a boxful of television operas and get shitpots full of money. *Why not? Others have. Enclosed these MAD photos: suppose you didn't know anybody in the picture—how would you explain it?*

I am rushing over to sit for my state portrait (in an undershirt playing the recorder) which I thought I better have painted before the Great Sag sets in.

Chins up!
Eugene

Don't be afraid! I don't belong
to any gun club... this thing is
loaded with licorice drops...unless...
of course if I'm aiming at Newt or
Pat or Tesse or the Reed brat... then
I use goat droppings....

For Mme. Carolyn—the daughter of Hyppolyte - Eugene Gavell

Ann Gavell

I met Eugene through Nell Burks. She was attending Birmingham-Southern College with Rebecca Gray. Rebecca was a very good actress who went to Mobile to do summer theater. Eugene was involved in theater even then. When I visited Nell, we all sort of came together and I met Eugene. Nell gave a skating party and what a sight Eugene was! He had never skated before and he was slipping and falling all over the place. This was in about 1942, shortly before he went into the army.

We wrote letters back and forth while he was in Alaska. He mentions me in *Jennie, the Watercress Girl.* We wrote off and on over the years, often went years without seeing each other. Then he came through Washington, D.C., when he was writing the cookbook for Time-Life. Many think it was the best novel he ever wrote. You can imagine I was scared to death to entertain a cookbook author, but he did include one of my recipes in the book. He used a composite of the people he met and knew to form the characters in this cookbook. My mother is one of them, the character Mrs. Charlotte Winn.

I have always been in the newspaper or magazine business while in Washington. My favorite was writing for the *Philadelphia Bulletin.* For eighteen years I was a writer and researcher for the *Readers Digest.*

When I first met Eugene he asked me, "What do you do that's creative? Do you write; do you knit?" I remember thinking how unique that someone would include knitting with creativity.

Eugene Walter

Words fail me when I try to describe Eugene's way with words. His talent was remarkable and original, a source of delight over the years. His description of a troublesome friend: "She takes up too much oxygen;" a loquacious friend: "Parenthesis Queen of the Western World;" old Mobile: "Where a squirrel can travel from [the] heart of town to [the] farthest suburb entirely by limb and bough;" enjoyment of a concert: "Measured by my appetite afterwards. Upon hearing Beethoven's Ninth, I ate the hell out of three steak dinners;" a sunny afternoon in Rome: "Yesterday I was filming a scene in a low-ceiling room with a vast (hot) computer under dozens of (hot) lights and wearing a (hot) Einstein hair-do because I am playing a mad scientist in a crazy comic film. We finished the film at eight last night and today (hot) (Sunday) I am the only person at home in Rome, with Felix drowsing on the marble floor and eight foot yellow lilies (De Graaf hybrids from Oregon) filling the world with a heavy perfume like Christmas in a Turkish whore-house;" a serious person: "'Serious' in the Willoughbian sense—i.e., wider horizons, deeper mines, higher ozone."

One beautiful autumn day we were driving in Rock Creek Park in Washington, D.C. As we rounded a corner, a brilliant golden bush burst into view. "Look at that," Eugene said. "God sittin' in there, burnin'."

On that trip, my mother, a true Southern lady, was describing how she cooked turnip greens and cornbread. Eugene said, "Oh, Mrs. Blevins, sing me some more."

After we met in 1942, Eugene became an Army cryptologist in the Aleutian Islands. It was hard to imagine this *bon vivant* in that remote and desolate place. But he managed to help decorate the windows of a bookshop in Anchorage, and he found delight in the flowers of Alaska, especially the brilliant blue ones. They were the color of ink bottles held to the light, he wrote.

After the war, he headed for New York, landing a job at the Chaucerhead Bookshop, where the likes of Greta Garbo came to browse. When, for some reason, things became difficult, Eugene said he resigned with a simple, " 'Bye," to the proprietor. "And I went out on Fifth Avenue, and a winy wind was blowing, and I walked twenty blocks without knowing which direction I was going," Eugene said.

It seemed to me that all the past was vivid to him. The vast synthesis informed his inimitable writing, art, and conversation.

He wrote *Henry Howard, Earl of Surrey, on a White Horse*. Eugene *was* Henry Howard.

Delight is the cap
Fits square on my head.
Doff I it only
Where heroes have bled.

Delight is the shoe
Makes pointed my toe:
No shadow of motion,
No tracks on the snow.

Ineffable tinglings
Inhabit my spine.
Time wears my livery.
The world's triply mine.

The sorrel that sings
In a high yellow key
Shall my silent-sweet
Bright equerry be.

Delight's the white ferret
To match my white hand.
Delight is for Howard—
No clown's contraband.

When red blood is dancing
Then blue blood has frowned
Level the sugar-scales,
Globe must go round.

But while Henry Howard
Is clothed in delight
all day shall be noontide
and outlawed the night.

Yon, honey-bee death,
Sweet stinger, sweet Joe:
Walk behind, little usher
When Henry must go.

> *By: Dr. Sebastian Willoughby*
> *(1526-1926)*

Words! Eugene peruses a Mobile paper
(Photo courtesy of Renée Paul)

Gerald Plain

Gerald Plain studied composition at the University of Michigan with Ross Lee Finney and Leslie Bassett. He held teaching positions at DePaul and Roosevelt universities in Chicago before being awarded the Rome Prize Fellowship in composition in 1974. Returning to the United States from a two-year sojourn in Rome (where he first met Eugene), he held teaching positions at the University of Wisconsin (Stevens Point) and the Eastman School of Music. In 1980 his *Violin Concerto* was awarded the Prince Pierre of Monaco Musical Composition Prize. He was also the recipient of the Charles Ives Fellowship in composition from the American Academy of Arts and Letters in 1988.

Mr. Plain's music has been performed in Europe by the Radiotelevisione Italiana Orchestra in Rome, the Philharmonic Orchestra of Monte Carlo, and the Nash Ensemble in London. United States symphony orchestras performing his music include Cincinnati, Milwaukee, Brooklyn, Indianapolis, Louisville, and the Alabama Symphony Orchestra, as well as the Pro Arte Chamber Orchestra of Boston and the Cleveland Chamber Orchestra. His music strongly reflects his early exposure to folk music through his parents and his Grandfather Salmon. Also, his passionate interest in playing the pedal steel guitar during his adolescent years is very much in evidence in his music.

The Centipede's Song for vocal ensemble is available from Oxford University Press; *Antics* for soprano and piano is available from the composer.

"Uncle" Eugene was a real inspiration to me. He was a magical person. I collaborated with him on *The Centipede's Song* for SATB vocal ensemble, and *Antics,* for soprano and piano, settings of a collection of poems. It is a great loss that he was unable to complete the Southern opera libretto (the Kentucky opera) that we planned for many years. He mentioned his regret in our last phone conversation. Woe, Woe, Woe!

My wife and I recall the story he told about the hospital doctor who asked him to what did he attribute his good health. He replied, "It was the good Doctor Beam (Jim Beam)." Then Eugene realized that the doctor didn't get it!

We also remember the dinner parties at Eugene's flat in Rome. They would include six to eight people, mostly Southerners, who were scholars, artists, and professionals. He would sit at the head of the table and "hold court." He was very skilled at directing the conversation away from the more mundane topics and stated on one occasion, "We will not discuss money at this table!"

Of course, the food, often Southern specialities, was fantastic. Felix, his favorite and very special cat, had his permanent place on a high stool at the table next to Eugene. Between courses, when Eugene entered the kitchen to prepare the next course, Felix would extend his paw and jump onto the table. He would weave his way through the dishes past the diners as if to say, "Yes, Eugene, this dinner party and food meet your usual high standards."

Eugene told us the story of Felix. He had been walking down the stairs leading from the Gianicolo to the Trastevere sections of Rome. Behind the Spanish Embassy his eye caught a movement to his side. Looking more carefully, he saw a very dirty, bedraggled, little kitten. He quickly picked it up and took it home. After he bathed the kitten, it looked around as if to say, "This is a nice apartment, Eugene; I'm really going to like it here! What's for lunch?" (Probably in Italian, of course!)

Eleanor Benz

Eugene and I knew each other for over fifty years. Much of that time he was in Europe, but he came home on occasion, and he always stayed in touch with his Mobile friends. When he returned to Mobile in 1979, he stayed at my family home, Termite Hall.

Only God could predict what Eugene would do next. He had many wonderful traits, and the one I found most dear was his pleasure in the moment and his eternal hope for the future. Eugene found that giving pleasure in the moment often gave someone else hope for the future, and I think he did this every day he lived.

Throughout our friendship I always worked. During the war there were different jobs, but for the last forty-five years I've worked in the library at McGill-Toolen High School. Because of my jobs, Eugene and I fell into the habit of going grocery shopping every Saturday. It was a custom we continued until he died.

Another custom we shared was a saying based on a friend of Eugene's grandmother who was also a friend of my grandmother. Whenever Miss Minnie J. Cox would take her leave after a visit with either grandmother, she would say, "Say a little prayer for Miss Minnie J. Cox."

This became Eugene's and my parting words when either of us had a problem.

Mrs. Benz served as chairman of the McGill-Toolen Library until her semi-retirement. She now serves as co-chairman. Refer to: What's In A Name?, *an original work by Eugene Walter, printed in the section of original works in this volume.*

Eugene and Termite Hall

I don't remember exactly the first time I met Eugene. I know it was during the bookshop years when Adelaide had the Haunted Book Shop. The war was on and there was gas rationing. I was working for Pan-Am Oil at the foot of Cedar Street downtown, and my son John was about nine months old. After work I'd stop by the bookshop before I went home. A lot of times I'd get a ride, but if I didn't, I could catch the bus. Stopping by the shop was just a fun thing. There were always interesting people there, and Eugene was so full of life.

I always read everything, just as Eugene did. We'd read anything we could get our hands on. I was reading some psychology books which interested me at the time. But Eugene and I would both read all the bestsellers. We'd talk about books with people who stopped by the shop. Eugene didn't really talk about his writing, but I'm sure it was in his head that he was going to be a writer. He was very involved with the Mobile Symphony at the time, trying to get it going. He was involved with all the arts.

Even then, Eugene was always creating plays and dramas. He'd give people parts and get them to dress up and act out characters. I had a baby, so I didn't get to attend a lot of the parties, but Adelaide did. And Catherine Ann Middleton. And Nell Burks. There were a lot of people who participated in Eugene's entertainments. They had a lot of fun.

When Eugene left to go to New York and then Europe, no one realized how long it would be before he came home. He came back from Rome in January 1979. Eugene's return to Mobile was like spring had come again.

Adelaide and I had several names for 2000 Dauphin Street, which became Termite Hall. My grandmother bought it in 1919 and our family has been there since. When Adelaide and I were dating some of the boys at Spring Hill College, we called the house Mad Marston Manor. All our friends came over all the time.

Mother was always home and there was plenty of space for fun, so it was a gathering place for the young people. After Mad Marston Manor, we called it Beetle Lodge and Mosquito Manor, but it was Termite Hall that stuck.

In one of the books about Termite Hall there's a story about how it got the name, but actually we discovered termites in a wooden balustrade on the veranda off the parlor. Adelaide and I used to sit on the railing, but we weren't on it when we found the termites. It was a beautiful balustrade, but it was hollow. The damage was done and it had to go. Eugene liked the name Termite Hall and used it in one of his cookbooks.

And we did some cooking when Eugene was with us. Goodness, if I'd eaten everything Eugene wanted me to eat I would have been fat as a pig. The first time he stayed with us he was on the second floor. Then he lived at the Deasy House for a while, and then came back and lived on the third floor.

We had dinner parties all the time. Eugene was the master chef and he'd have everyone in the kitchen chopping and cutting at his direction. It was so much fun that it wasn't like work at all.

We had people from London and Rome. There were opera singers and Russian poets, people from all over the world. God knows where some of them came from. With Eugene, it was just always fun.

Eugene knew all kinds of people, and they would visit him in Mobile. He'd entertain them with stories about the saints. Somewhere he'd read about the lives of the saints—the edition that hadn't been cleaned up. And he would talk about Saint Rita and St. Somebody Else. I'm sure he embroidered on them considerably, but it was all very amusing. On Sunday afternoons, we'd all sit on the porch in our rocking chairs. Everyone made what he or she wanted to drink—no one served, everyone just helped themselves—and we'd talk. Sometimes Eugene would tell stories.

I guess it was when he was living at Termite Hall that I fell into the habit of taking him grocery shopping on Saturday mornings. Eugene never drove and I had to go for groceries, so I took him. When he moved to Grand Boulevard, I continued to take him grocery shopping on Saturdays. It was never any trouble. It was part of the routine, part of life.

Eugene could make anything an adventure. A task as ordinary as grocery shopping could be fun. We all miss him.

**Eugene adds a touch of color to his residence in the
Aleutian Islands - 1947**

(Photo courtesy of Adelaide Trigg and Eleanor Benz)

Rebecca Paul Florence

Rebecca Paul Florence is a native of Mobile, a graduate of The University of Alabama, and a cousin of Eugene Walter through Bavarian lineage. She was editor of the Mobile weekly newspaper *Azalea City News and Review* from 1979 to 1984, where she worked closely with Walter. Working with PMT Publishing Company, also in Mobile, she held editor and associate publisher positions from 1984 to 1990 with *Business Alabama* magazine, the political newsletter *Inside Alabama Politics*, and *Alabama Magazine*, where she again worked with Walter, who was a contributing writer. She now lives in Tuscaloosa, Alabama, with her husband, Michael Florence, and her horse, Oberon, and is employed as director of college relations for the College of Arts and Sciences at The University of Alabama. She has not purchased ground pepper in over twenty years, keeps a pepper mill on her table, and uses only vinaigrette on her salads, served after the main course. Her salads come from a kitchen garden that includes parsley, cilantro, sage, rosemary, garlic, basil, three kinds of chives, and fifteen different varieties of lettuce, none of which is iceberg. One of her favorite pastimes is working in her garden, where she often thinks of Eugene.

I Will Do You Something Very Amusing

On a sweltering Saturday morning in August of 1979, Jocko Potts and I set out to meet and have brunch with a man named Eugene Walter at Barnard's, then the restaurant *du jour*. Jocko had been told by friends that Walter, a novelist and highly accomplished in the arts, had recently returned to Mobile after living many years in Rome and was interested in writing for the *Azalea City News and Review*, a weekly newspaper that Jocko had purchased just a few months earlier and where I had worked for six weeks.

Mr. Walter met the car in front of the Deasey House on Palmetto Street where he was living as writer-in-residence and guest of the Mobile Historical Preservation Society. Introductions. "How are yoooooooooo," he crooned in a soft, lilted, Southern song. Small talk in the car. Mr. Walter, sitting in the back seat, hummed.

I would not have seen the blazing fuchsia coral vine blooming on a telephone pole guy wire if this humming man had not interrupted himself with a soft gasp and urged us with a curved finger to look, see, how marvelous it is, as we walked down Conti Street and into Barnard's.

Just sixty, he was medium-sized, with a slightly round girth in easy proportion to solid shoulders. Demi-portly. But he had the lithe, limber carriage of a long-time citizen of European cities where one walks all the time. He was wearing a beige guyabera over grey pants, sockless feet in loosely-fitting loafers.

As he strolled with us to our table, he dignified himself nonchalantly, pulling his chest up and flattening the front of his shirt over his waist with open palms, his loafers slapping on the wooden floor announcing his entrance.

"You can take *that* away," he said to the waiter as he picked up the pepper shaker, set it down again like a chess piece, and poked it further away as if it were something unclean. "Now tell me, do you have a pepper mill?"

As we opened our menus, Walter offered culinary advice.

"There is no reason to use the dead dust, sweepings from the herb shop floor sold as ground pepper, unless one is stranded on a deserted island, where a squeeze of lemon would be preferable, or one needs volcanic dust for a mural of the destruction of Pompeii. The wonderful volatile oil in peppercorns, that which brings out the salad's flavor and wakes up our palate and nostrils to other flavors, dry out quickly. A pepper mill at table is one of the Joys. Of. Living," he said, emphasizing the last words with dead stops.

What is your sign?" he asked abruptly, almost touching me on the back of my hand. Virgo.

"I dare say your linen closets are tidy and you'll make a proper editress because Virgos like things *just so*, but tell me: Do you roller skate? Virgos really must roller skate, dance the Charleston, thumb their noses at policemen once a day so that they don't become too se-re-ous

As was his habit, he got business out of the way quickly. He laid stout fingers on the table, brushing away imaginary crumbs with a backwards stroke of his wide thumb. He liked what we were doing and said that Mobile needed a newspaper that told about the fascinating things—you would not believe—that people were doing in Mobile and Mobilians were doing elsewhere in the Big. Wide. World.

Art. Books. Photography. Theatre. Medicine. Bidnes. But no one hears of it. Wonderful eateries, nurseries in Semmes, Grand Bay, Baldwin County, and Old Shell Road growing things you can't find anywhere else. The *Mess Register* was boring. Why publish macaroni and cheese recipes mailed out by the thousands from Cincinnati when Mobile is a treasure trove of generations of cookbooks, has hundreds of its own variations on the gumbo, greens, hominy, summer ices, and ketchup?

"Mo-be-uhl has its own kult-chur," he said, then spelled it out: "k-u-l-t-c-h-u-r." And it's fu-un." A two syllable fun. " We must spread our net wide and write it all up. Write. It. All. Up," he insisted, his thick eyebrows and forehead rising in unison. "Just give me a page and I will do you something very amusing."

As we visited that morning it was obvious that this was a man of many gifts—a remarkable intellect, vast knowledge and creativity, wild humor, generosity and affection, capable of sweet formality as well as disarming warmth. A higher gift than these, however, was his imaginative and happy conception of the people and the world around him, which he bestowed on all but the meanest of souls, as if he were casting a charm.

Eugene's debut in the *ACNR* was delayed when Hurricane Frederic hit Mobile in September, throwing his household of cats, books, Southern icons, and papers at the Deasey House into disarray and flooding our newspaper's offices on Government Street.

He appeared on the cover in the first week in November. He had been back in Mobile only a few months with little public notice. How could we convey this highly individual man better than he? So we proposed that he interview himself. He thought this was "a grand idea." Photographer Alan

Whitman took a series of photographs of Eugene in the Deasey house on opposite sides of a table and in different clothes. Eugene then amended the photos to create the cover image of Eugene the probing, note-taking reporter, interviewing Eugene, the flabbergasted subject.

"Interviewer: How do you feel about being back in Mobile?

"Walter: Well, culture shock is a very real thing....and Mobile is unrecognizable, except around Washington Square and parts of Dauphin and the side streets...especially Downtown, a disaster area, look like Tunisia after the war, with all those hot, glaring walls of the parking lots. The city has been vandalized....

"Interviewer: How vandalized?

"Walter: Ride over town in a helicopter. Mobile was unique in the world for its trees, which existed Downtown up until only recent memory. The worse is the Mall-sprawls: hideous hot deserts with no public facilities. The vandals might have left a belt of greenery. I dream of seeing it all sink into primeval Wragg Swamp, which only has a thin layer of inferior cement over it and still churns and yearns below. I dream of alligators strolling arm-in-arm through Sears and Holmes. I was talking to God the other night and you know what He said? He said, 'I looked down there and I thought, well, you want the trees down? I'll show you how to get them down. So I sent my tree specialist, Freddie.'

"Interviewer: You're kinda rabid about it, aren't you?

"Walter: Always have been. I love Mobile so much I hate it. And I reserve the right to protest out loud, rather than mumble in my beard.

"Interviewer: But your reputation is for frivolity...

"Walter: A little dose of frivolity never hurt anyone. And I'm for gin, sin, and destiny. I do not believe in saving virtue and lofty thoughts, like so many old shopping bags, for the afterlife. Better to plant trees in vacant lots, never offend ghosts, rouse a few smiles every day, never drink cheap spirits, and get on with the show."

By pulling back the curtain and inviting Eugene to take the stage, the newspaper showed to both our new writer and our readers its readiness to suspend reality for fun, now and then, as only an upstart, alternative newspaper had the liberty to do. Eugene was in comfortable territory.

Some readers were puzzled, others elated by this new spirit on the scene. In this brief short interview, Eugene established an attitude that would change the way many readers looked at their city, and themselves.

Keep 'Em Guessin

Eugene's weekly column, *EWEW* (*Eugene Walter Every Week*), was popular as much for Eugene's humor and perceptive eye as for the wide range of Mobile doings he covered. It was also, by design, unpredictable.

"Got to keep em guessing and surprise em," Eugene would say as he handed to me for that week's *EWEW* illustration a quirky 1932 photograph of a jazz combo playing in a den of polar bears in Central Park Zoo. Eugene's caption: "Scientist measure the effect of jazz on polar bears."

There were over-the-top chatty wedding and party write-ups with lots of name dropping in which he often addressed his imaginary party-line pal, Babs.

On the 1979 wedding reception of Amanda Hunter and Herndon Inge III: "Shame on old Jupiter Pluvis for trying to ruin things with a drizzle and chill. But everybody turned out anyway, some darling creatures came toddling out who'd not been seen publicly in centuries...."

At a Vintage Fashion Show put on by the City Museum and the Historic Mobile Preservation Society: "All of old Mobile's notable names were there and then some: Van Antwerp, Aldridge, Cleverdon, Festorazzi, Snevelly. All nicely turned out and not a blue rinse in the whole shooting match."

The mailing of new seed catalogs in January marked the start of a season for Eugene: spring garden planning and seed ordering. Each January Eugene reserved at least one column to review some of the dozens of seed catalogs he received. An avid gardener and self-taught botanist, Eugene identified for readers old plant varieties come back again, new additions to well-proved strains, and warned them away from floral and culinary duds. He placed a botanists sense of importance on true representations of plants, and didn't mind judging seed catalogs by their cover.

"It is my deepest conviction that our seed catalogs are the result of a demented collaboration between MGM Studios, the Day-Glo Company, The Neon-Institute, the Optimist Club, and the sun-and-color-starved forced laborers in Siberia.

"I have a handful of them before me: roses in fluorescent hues that never were and never shall be open their shameless hearts next to asters as blue as a two-hundred-watt bulb seen through a bottle of True Blue ink. The charming, old-fashioned shaggy, yellow, Centaurea actually appears in one catalog as Lemon Fluff. But I reckon as how the seedmen feel they must cheer us up after the Christmas flurry and before Carnival. Still, the excesses of color printing, renaming some flowers each year, and the Madison Avenue tones of what is claimed for some of these plants causes the eyes to glaze and some catalogs slip quietly to the carpet."

Mobile's most dominant season, hot, was regularly the subject of Eugene's commentary in July and August when he both suffered and celebrated the sub-tropic summer.

The opening to a July 1981 *EWEW*: "In air thick as a souffle we move like cement-weighted cadavers on a river-bottom. Our brains melt. Activity is unwelcome, unlikely. We must work at something commonplace, repetitious. Thought is impossible...An older lady in Spring Hill goes through desk drawers and makes lists, lists of books to read, lists of household repairs—the handle on the coffee pot, the key that needs to be recopied, a list of buttons to replace belt loops to repair—at least in some small way to triumph over the dazy heat."

Interspersed between goings-on columns and light-hearted slices-of-life, Eugene would sometimes shift gears and offer readers a serious, well argued, and always strongly opinioned commentary on issues of the day—humanism, the Moral Majority, conservation of Mobile's trees canopy, the importance of reading anything and everything.

One might disagree with Eugene on an issue, but not for Eugene's lack of disarming common sense. He invariably brought issues to a least complicated and most obvious conclusion, however debatable. In an *EWEW* review of the book *Why Johnny Still Can't Read* by Rudolf Flesch, Eugene commented: "In all this roo-ra over the importance of education, it strikes me that nobody says something important that needs saying—that is that it is such FUN to know another language, to plunge into a whole world of ideas and concepts which can give one great perspective, jolt the liver, tickle the unused part of the intellect, rev up conversation power, offer delight on many levels."

By the first anniversary of *EWEW*, it was one of the most requested pages by advertisers and never missed by readers. The *ACNR* had gained an entertaining and highly original observer of Mobile life, and Eugene had an audience.

Anything That Sparkled, Spangled, Jingled, or Screamed

On a Friday in December, the phone rang in the office. Badly disguised voice. Deep, slow, and mysterious. "Maaaadame Paul? Thiiiiis is your Uncle You-Gene. I've got a big caper for you." Out of character. "Listen

Dah-link, come to supper tonight and bring your friend and your little sewing box."

The Hysterical Ladies, his hostesses at the Deasey House and at the nearby Oakleigh Antebellum Mansion, had asked him to play Santa Claus the next morning at the Oakleigh Candlelight Christmas Open House, one of the Historic Preservation Society's big annual events. His job: arrive in the Oakleigh carriage Saturday morning as part of opening ceremonies and take wishes from the children for a couple of hours. The ladies had delivered the Santa suit. It was plain, boring, not fun.

The drama instructor was speaking: "A good actor must make himself part of the character and the character part of him. The same with the costume. I wanna jazz it up."

My job was to swing by the five and dime and grab up any Christmas trim that sparkled, spangled, jingled, or screamed and bring my friend JoAnn Breland, whom Eugene called "That One With The Eyes" for seamstress duty.

We arrived with a card of forty-eight brass bells, twenty-four red velvet bows, ten feet of tinsel garland, various holiday sequins, and one artificial poinsetta blossom. While Eugene cooked supper, we sewed at his very particular direction. Well past midnight, every item was somewhere on the costume except for the poinsettia blossom, which I stuffed back into a sack as we prepared to leave. Eugene let out a long coo of alarm and snatched the poinsettia out of the bag. He was wearing the Santa cap. "I've got plans for *that*," he said. "It goes right here." With a flourish, he planted the big red blossom square on his forehead.

For the cold drizzly Christmas of 1979, Saint Nicholas arrived by carriage at the Oakleigh Candlelight Christmas Open House twinkling and jingling loudly with brass bells running every inch along and around each pant leg, tinsel trim at cuff and coat edge, a white beard festooned with a flock of red velvet bows, sequins on the collar, and a poinsettia blossom pinwheeling from his head like blades on a windmill. He was playing a kazoo.

Saturday afternoon the phone rang. Eugene was cold and exhausted and was closing the shutters for a long afternoon nap but he wanted to thank me and JoAnn for sewing duty. Once the kiddies recovered from the shock, he said, they were intrigued and delighted by this different Southern Claus. They, and he, had great fun. But I don't think the Hysterical Ladies ever asked Eugene to do Santa duty again.

Dressing It Up

For Eugene, journalistic integrity required that the reader be amused. If a photo for Eugene's articles seemed to him static and uninteresting, he would "dress it up a bit." Over the years a handful of images made their way into the paper that snuck up on the reader's eye.

Eugene would return photos to me with touches of ink added, and bits of paper skillfully cut and pasted on. Most often the enhancements were made to town-and-gown photos or to local actors and performers, but no dull image was safe. A woman sported a wide-brimmed hat with one long feather that she was not wearing when the photo was taken. A Roman bust and a row of classy library books materialized on a room's bookshelf, the additions having been sketched on paper, cut, delicately mounted, and edged in black ink to blend into the objects in the black and white photo.

"That arm was naked, she needed a little bracelet," he would tell me as he pointed to a photo where, indeed, a small baroque bracelet had been inked in with just a few strokes. "This one looks much better after I added those teardrops to her earrings."

Mobile native and opera singer Shannon Williams, at least her head and shoulders from a publicity still, appeared for a March, 1980 *EWEW* review of *LaTraviata* overlaid on a pen and ink drawing of a standing lace ruff and jewel encrusted Elizabethan gown complete with train. A pen and ink print of a lace mantle, cut to fit around the contours of her hair, fanned out around her head.

Eugene's photo "enhancements" were never done with the intent to deceive (the second glance was enough to give them away) but to make reality more fun. Knowing Eugene, his subjects did not seem to mind the embellishments, although I suspect they came as a surprise to more than a few. The inked in scepters, added tiaras, and pasted on ascots usually had the intended effect of making readers smile, if not puzzle a bit.

The Child Prodigy

Eugene frequently interviewed and wrote about artists, writers, and movers and shakers in his column, from his point of view, intertwining his observations with theirs. But the straight-on profile, in which Eugene reported the subject's point of view with the subject's quotes and opinions, did not interest him. From time to-time, however, he would set aside his role as a commentator and reviewer and pick up a reporter's notebook, usually when a friend of a friend pressed a request on him for a story.

The phone rang at the office one Thursday. An upset father. Mr. Walter, had interviewed his daughter for a story and it had just come out in the *ACNR*. She had won an award in French at her high school. The family was real proud of her. Eugene had interviewed her during a visit to his house. Problem was, she didn't say the things she was quoted as saying in the paper. Not much of it at all. Not that what was printed was bad, she just isn't doing, and doesn't know, some of the things she was quoted as saying. Very embarrassing. Family is upset.

Diplomatic phone call to Eugene.

"My dear," he protested, "I assure you I wrote down every world that poor child said. I am very careful to keep a pen and notebook."

I explored a bit. "Eugene, her father said she never said she was going to study at the Sorbonne in Paris but might like to visit France sometime."

"Oh, I'm quite positive she said she intended to study. Because I was asking her about French literature and..."

I pressed further. "Well, her father said she's only read one of the four French novels she's quoted as saying are her favorites. And she's never heard of two of them. So how can she say here that..."

Eugene, most irritated: "Papa must be mistaken. I suggest he consult that girl again. I am assiduous about keeping pen and notebook and writing every word down. Lord love a duck. That child."

I kept going. "Eugene, this paragraph, where she's quoting Voltaire. Her father said she couldn't have said that. Because he says they don't know a Mr. Voltaire."

Long silence on the phone.

Eugene, in angry stevedore character, growled in rapid-fire, "Wellthelittleshit. Sheoughtabegrateful. Imadehersound-a-hell-of-a-lot-moreintelligent thansheis."

Airplane Hangers, Black Raincoats, and a Turban in the Orchestra

In his theatre, opera, and symphony reviews, Eugene was deft at bringing theatre alive with his encyclopedic knowledge of it, at making it fun for the reader, at capturing the moment in prose.

The place and the people who attended performances were as a much a part of Eugene's commentary as the performance on stage. When "Airplane Hanger" Baryshnikov appeared with the New York City Ballet at Biloxi's Mississippi Coliseum in 1979, he noted, "Young ladies in the audience screamed and clutched each other at Baryshnikov's leaps and turns and I thought of Sinatra concerts in the '40s...Many of the local swain, strangling on their seldom worn neckties, were not inhibited in proclaiming the athletic springiness and male exuberance of this dance number."

Attending the Mobile Municipal Theatre for a performance of the Jackson, Mississippi Ballet, he complained, "the sad unpainted foyer of the municipal always makes me feel as if I were in an East African airport waiting for a flight that's been canceled. Why should we have the Last Gasp of North German 1920s architecture here in the South?"

All performances, books, and exhibits were worthy of praise by virtue of the attempt at artistic expression, if nothing more. Art, above all, was to be encouraged. Eugene held special contempt for reviewers who did not adjust their big-city expectations to the earnest attempts of local productions or who failed to celebrate that major road shows had at least come to Mobile, however disappointing the performance. He doled out genuine praise by the bucketful. But when something preventable marred the production, even in the most modest of performances, he didn't shy away from criticism that was an artful blend of sledge hammer and sweetness.

On a Bethel Theatre production of *Twelfth Night*: "What was lost in poetry was gained in broad comedy and the actors and audience both enjoyed themselves....I like my Shakespeare straight and did not care for the time shift to First World War Italy. Since most of the accents were strongly cotton-blossom, it might as well have taken place in Moss Point in 1865."

After seeing this performance of *The Nutcracker*, he recommended that the play be put on ice for several decades and replaced with new ballets on Southern themes, "Alligator Christmas" or "Hoe-down at Possum Hollow." "The corp de ballet was less precise this year, some arms were flailing and toes not pointed, and at least one minor traffic jam which shouldn't have, but the only glaring fault was the total disappearance of The Nutcracker in the second act...."

For Mobile Opera Guild's spring, 1981, *Tales of Hoffman*: "Arnold Voketaitis was just right as the evil spirit...but WHO gave him that nasty skinny black raincoat? It is classic, inescapable, required that the four-evil-characters-in-one wear a BLACK CAPE which can be swung, swooshed, and flapped. Mr. Voketaitis, get one! The cast was uniformly good. Wigs first rate throughout."

That fall, Eugene returned for the production of *The Barber of Seville.* "Carol Weber has exquisite phrasing and charm, but it bothered me that she didn't take some of the high notes. She was hindered by an unflattering costume....I had one awful moment in the second act. I hated the black raincoat foisted off on the villain in "Hoffman" and here it reappeared again, I swear it, as Bartolo's dressing gown."

Eugene said that political correctness was an oxymoron, and he usually dismissed its necessity as an absence of proper manners, which was the issue when he attended a performance of the New Orleans Symphony at the Municipal Theatre, at a time when American hostages were being held in Iran.

After offering much praise for individual musicians and the symphony's "clear and moving performance" of Aaron Copland, Eugene turned his attention to a distraction in the orchestra.

"Now then, the problem of that black turban. Black turban's make me nervous just now, and I get an ayatollah itch. If that young man has a real reason to wear his turban, religious or baldness, I'm the first to respect his right. But surely we could have another concert where each musician could wear his own fantasy bit. The Orientals could wear native costumes, the Cajuns wear boating or hunting costumes, etc. My eye kept roving to that black turban in spite of myself; and I lost part of the largo in the Dvorak.

"As a trained paradoxograph, I found myself ever more dizzily contemplating the possibilities of what he might be carrying in it. I ruled out grenades at once, but in turn thought maybe a pot of yoghurt, a plug-in Espresso machine, a toy violin, dirty comic books, shaving equipment, a change of linen, a bust of Shirley Temple carved from a ham bone, Tarot cards, a hamster or...or...but then I blinked hard and concentrated on Dvorak."

Works of Fiction:

A Speech, a Brochure, and Two Original Short Stories

by Eugene Walter

and

A Fictional Tale about the Grand Raconteur, Eugene

What's in a Name?

By Eugene Walter

As read by the author in the presence of the Honoree, Archbishop Lipscomb, and a Grand Mixed Bag of Types and Personalities, on the Occasion of the re-dedication of the Bishop-Toolen School Library [currently McGill-Toolen] as the Eleanor Marston Benz Library, 17 May 1989.

Once upon a time there was a very charming lady who was a public figure but pretended to be simply a modest mother and grandmother. Some people secretly referred to her as Princess Paradox.

Well, one day this lady was hurrying to a convention of librarians at Creola. (This all takes place in the future, just after the moment in which Creola seceded from the Union and set up barbed wire fences around its borders.) The only way to get in was over a Troll Bridge. If you remember your troll bridges you know that one is not allowed to pass until one guesses the name of the troll in charge of the bridge. But since everything about Creola is different...as, one might add, [is] everything about the heroine of this story...this process in this case had been reversed and one couldn't cross the bridge until the troll guessed the name of the passing voyager. Our heroine stepped briskly onto the bridge...she was anxious to be prompt for the meeting... and the Troll said: "Stop right there! I get three hundred guesses for your name..."

"I hope you make it in less," said the Lady.

"Let's see," muttered the Troll, rubbing his forehead and gazing into space. "I think...I see something taking shape...I get a B...is that right?... yeah, B...Beans?...Bentwood?...no...Oh, I know: Benz!"

"You are indeed one clever Troll," said the Lady. "May I go on now?"

"No!" he said hastily. "I have to guess *all* your name...names."

"Do hurry!"

"Benz is Bavarian and aristocratic and First Crusade...is your first name by any chance Geltruda?"

"I should hope not!" exclaimed the heroine.

He put on his mumbo-jumbo look again and said: "Let's see...I think I'm getting an M or an N...."

"Now you're cooking with kerosene," said the Lady, impatiently.

"Ah!" he cried. "What about Elfine Maypole Benz?"

"Could be... fairy tales... and I always observe May 1... but that's not it."

"Hmmm, is it Liliburlero Marching Benz?"

"Oh," she said mildly. "I like an Elizabethan ballad as well as anyone... and I'll carry a banner if I have to...Try again!"

"What about Liveitup Midnight Benz?"

"Aah," said she, smiling in recollection. "I, too, have dwelt in... the New Spic...but I attended convent school and I'm very tidy about curfews..."

"I know! It's *O livre, mon amour!* Benz."

"That's not fair. You know I'm on my way to a librarians' convention. Go on!"

"Lightfoot Maypop Benz?"

"I do stay on my toes," she rejoined. "Physically and mentally. And I can pop a may or may a pop or weed a bed as well as anyone."

"Hmmm... Leaveitalone Maybe Benz?"

"I don't believe in meddling," said our Heroine. "But then...curiosity is finally a Christian virtue...God helps those who help themselves!...without curiosity we'd never have had the steam engine...and somebody had to eat the first oyster..."

The Troll jumped up and down on one leg. "I got it! It's Everchic Modish Benz."

She smiled. "True, I do have a sense of style. Elegance at my fingertips. Always understated, never underrated...But, look, this could go on forever. Are you going to guess my name and let me be on my way or shall I summon the McGill-Toolen football team and let them pitch you over the line."

"Oh, maybe three more guesses and I'll have it," growled the Troll. "What about Everloving Marsupial Benz?"

"You're getting close," she said. "I am very fond of the New World's marsupial. In fact, some of my best friends are 'possums."

Now the Troll jumped up and down. "I've got it! I've found your name!"

"Shoot it to me, Troll-baby," said the Lady.

He smiled triumphantly. "It's Ronale Notsram Zneb! Funny, it sounds Turkish..."

At this our Heroine burst out laughing. "The closest to Turkey I've ever been is Naman's down on Broad Street, where I go to buy my Turkish Delight...but you're real warm this time...Actually, Ronale Notsram Zneb is my name just plain spelled backwards."

He thought for a moment. "WOW!...yeah...sure...then you're Eleanor Gertrude Peanut Butter Chicken Broth Beethoven Jitterbug Oporto Benz! That means Termite Hall and McGill-Toolen Library."

"Of course," said the Lady loftily. "And we have long dealt successfully with troll minorities in both establishments. May I pass now, please?"

"Pass? Oh, Lady, you can pass...and underpass...and over-pass...and pass the buck...and pass it up...and bypass...and more than that you can gas and you can sass! Upwards and onwards!"

"Troll, you're a doll," she smiled and went on at full sail.

Recollections of Princess Caetani

by Eugene Walter

(First published for an exhibit on Botteghe Oscure *by the University of Texas at Austin, 1991. Provided for this publication by Ms. Maria Xenia Wells, Curator of Italian Collections and Adjunct Professor of French and Italian, University of Texas at Austin.)*

"She is a bundle of complications," is how Alice B. Toklas described the Princess Caetani. The two ladies were members of quite different circles in the Paris of the late '20s and most of the '30s. If required to sum up the Princess in one sentence, I would revert to my native Gulf Coast style and employ a delightful Elizabethan word used to indicate a small hand-bouquet of many-colored scented flowers:
She is a tuzzy-muzzy of interesting complexities.
If one is to understand something of the variety and scope of the publication *Botteghe Oscure*, one must understand the background of the Princess. Marguerite Chapin was from New London, Connecticut, of a family of French origin. She always remembered not so much a youthful sadness as a sense of estrangement resulting from her mother's death and her father's second marriage. On Sunday, her Protestant friends gathered at church while she attended Mass with the Irish servants in a private chapel on the family estate. Endowed with a charming natural singing voice and musical taste, she went to Paris to study with renowned tenor Jean de Reszke, even performing in his *salon-théâtre*. Yet she was naturally shy, too, and, like great ladies of her epoch, shunned publicity.
The young Prince Roffredo Caetani first saw her at the Paris Opéra and had difficulties getting past a female attendant ("the Dragon" he called her) to encounter the young lady. Romance flourished and they married in 1911; they had a daughter and a son.
Upon the death of an older brother, Prince Roffredo inherited the title of Prince of Bassiano and during the period of the '20s and '30s in which the Princess's first literary review *Commerce* ("commerce des idées") was taking shape she was known as *la Princesse de Bassiano*. Later Roffredo inherited the patriarchal family title of Duke of Sermoneta and this led to many confusions about the lady from Connecticut.
Even worse is the total fog of error darkened by contradictory and erroneous clarifications over the name *Botteghe Oscure*, which Princess

Marguerite chose for her multi-language literary review. Via delle Botteghe Oscure ("street of the shadowy shops") takes its name from shops existing from the late Middle Ages in the street-level arcades of a ruined Roman amphitheatre. Friends and relations raised their eyebrows very high indeed over the Princess's choice of title since the Jesuit Order and the Communist party both had headquarters on the street. All over the world the name *Botteghe Oscure* meant "headquarters" in Rome, Jesuit, or Communist, according to the circles in which one moved.

The Princess stood firm. "The Caetani have been here since the 1500s," she smiled. "Those others are newcomers." So *Botteghe Oscure* it was. I still laugh at the endless confusions generated when Adlai Stevenson was staying at Palazzo Caetani. I received a letter from a friend in the Associated Press in Washington asking politely if I was aware of the danger of associating with certain types in Rome!

One myth would have that the Princess had little or no literary taste or knowledge, and depended on a circle of literary acquaintances for the choice of material for her review. No, sirree! The lady was interested in reactions of various friends to manuscripts by known and unknown, but the final choice was hers. She came from an educated circle which respected writers and painters and where, most of all, *ideas* were common coinage. The Princess didn't like professorial literary conversation; she would have nothing to do with criticism, commentaries, reviews. She wanted texts, texts, texts—some Olympians, some from gifted unknowns in the backwoods. Oh, the lady could be autocratic, couldn't she just! Wouldn't you be if you were rich, titled, international, energetic? What many failed to point out is that she had a healthy American disrespect for authority, and the lady was genuinely kind and most of all had a great sense of humor.

In the end, however, it is not as Miss Chapin, or Princess Caetani, or Princess di Brassiano, or Duchess of Sermoneta that we shall remember this lady. It is as the self-contained, slightly self-effacing editor Marguerite, always with a gardening basket full of manuscripts close at hand, always taking time to write both famous and unknown, always impatient with "literary" discussions, always eager for new works. Nobody yet, I felt, had perceived the extraordinary range of interest revealed in *Commerce* and *Botteghe Oscure* or the high accomplishment of regularly offering these rich periodicals almost without fanfare. The editor Marguerite, it seems, was perfectly aware of what she was up to (must have been so, if one studies the tables of contents of her periodicals and sees how many then unknowns are now knowns), and assumed her eventual recognition and applause would come at a later date. Perhaps her authentic title is "Princess of Paradoxes."

Rooted to the Spot

by Eugene Walter

The ladies are marching on City Hall this morning. They've chosen such a nice day for their march, I almost said protest march. But it's not a protest march, it's a matter of simply lady-like bullying, which they do so well. That's how they've gotten things done for years. Some speculator has bought the old Perrochet house on Augusta Street and plans to raze it. That has brought on their ire, but then Mrs. McCommer, who's not really from Mobile, but from upcountry, demolished the dog fountain at her corner without a permit and without offering it to anyone to preserve. And it had been photographed for *National Geographic*. I was at the meeting when it all came up. Mrs. Sibling was white and shaking when she read her report, especially about the dog fountain. She mentioned Miss Lulie Meadows, who has difficulty walking, and reported how when Miss Lulie took Spot for a stroll, she in her wheel-walker, he tethered to an upright, and with a tin cup on a little chain hanging from the armrest, she'd stop and give him a drink and often took one herself, if no one were watching. The image of Miss Lulie and Spot pushing along dry-throated under the oaks was too much, so they decided on a march to City Hall. I remember some of the discussion.

"... and he wants to raze the Perrochet house!"

"Why?"

"Cause he bought it, hon, and wants to do something on the lot."

"Why would he raise it, that height from the ground is standard for coast cottages, just ring the Architectural Commission and they'll tell you."

"Coast cottage or not, he's going to raze it, unless we do something about it."

"How high does he want to raise it?"

"He's going to...tear...it...down!"

"In order to raise it? There must be a structural flaw."

But now another lady pipes up in a sweet treble. "It has lovely structural flow; one room leads into another. Mattie Mae did her paper on it."

"Well, if he likes the house so much he'll take it down and put it up again, why are we complaining?"

Now the first speaker tries again, eyes fixed on a mote in the middle distance.

"He is going to *raze* the house!"

"And we're supposed to raise Cain because he's raising the house? Leave all that to Betty and Arch, I say. We'll march on the dog fountain question..."

"Mitzy Bahrfeld says she thinks she saw *part* of it at Virginia Wrecking Company, the stone with the bronze plaque about Man's Best Friend..."

Now comes a deep sigh from the first speaker...

So on this fine crispy clear October day they are marching on City Hall, clotting lower Government Street with traffic wheeled, footed, and some might say hooved.

Miss Charlie Compton, over from Baldwin County, thinks it's best occasion to show off her old goat-cart, so there she is, sun-hat and cotton work gloves, with Rob Roy bearded and sullen as he lowers his horns and pulls her toward the City commissioners waiting with some trepidation in their offices, wondering if they should 'phone for the State Militia.

"Onward!" cries Miss Charlie gleefully to others in various vehicles, including Miss Minxy carried bodily by her three stalwart grandsons who've driven her downtown in her old grey Plymouth, down off its blocks for the first time since the moon landing.

"On we go!" sings out Miss Charlie, in highest good spirits. "By wheel and by foot, by goat-cart and broomstick, two if by land and three if by sea, shoulder to the wheel, plough to the furrow, the hillside's dew-pearled, and Devil take the hindmost!"

All this activity, apart from the teas and rummage-sales! And it all started in the most paradoxical fashion...

#   #   #

What happened happened a few years back, when skirts were long, and the streetcars clanged, and bloomers came to the knees, at least in chill weather. On just such a morning, with a fine sun and the first chill in the air and everybody thinking soon we must all get to the woods and beat the 'possums to the wild persimmons, clever Miss Faber, wit and traveler, got up early, sniffed the air, could just make out coffee roasting down in Water Street, and knew that Autumn had arrived. She decided she'd walk down Government Street and cross over to Bienville Square and have herself a little private picnic luncheon. The Square then was a well-manicured public garden, where the iron benches were painted every spring and goldfish caught the light in the shadowy waters of the fountain basin.

Lia Faber had been unpacking winter garments early that morning, removing bloomers and pullovers and tweed skirts from tissue and peppercorns, so Angel, her maid, could hang them in the October sunlight. She set aside one pair of grey wool bloomers for repair: the elastic waistband had snapped. Angel came and went, she dressed, went down to the kitchen for her basket and thermos, put on her hat at the hall mirror, and set off down Government Street. She nodded to Miss Minnie Cox at the Broad Street corner, ditto to Miss Jessamina Ebeltoft at the Bayou Street corner, to the impressive Rev. Haginas talking with friends at the Dearborn Street corner, waved to Miss Emma Harris in the distance, caught a glimpse of Miss Hallie Triplett at a window.

It was just when she reached the Russell house that she had an intimation that something was wrong.

She felt a constriction of the knees, quite odd. Her knees were strangely bound, or hobbled. When she essayed another step, the binding grew tighter. She paused, reasoned, and realized what had happened. Angel had simply taken all the bloomers, including the one she'd put aside to wear, and left her the one with the broken elastic.

"Double damnation!" she muttered, and felt the side of her skirt, trying to pat the wadded cloth upwards.

"Hey, Miss Lia," cried a freckle-faced boy passing on a bicycle not two yards from her.

"Hello, Tunstall!" she called faintly, her hand fluttering to her hat. She felt her bloomers drop an inch.

She tried again, with little indefinite gestures, as if brushing something off her skirt, while actually tugging upwards at the sagging wool under her skirt. In panic, she stepped quickly into the unmown grass before the vacated Russell house, near the mounting steps where little Miss Eoline once skipped up into the carriage. The wishing grass and jimson weed would hide her ankles and...whatever.

Then she looked up and turned scarlet: here came handsome Neville Jemison (didn't he know it, too!) and his sidekick, the bony Jarvis Barnes. Laughing and gesticulating, they approached. Miss Faber looked upward, staring at the roof of the Goldsby house, rapt in a silent prayer they'd pass on without noticing her.

But life is not like that. The cloak of invisibility is not often granted. They both came close, although not stepping into the grass, since, albeit October, they were prolonging the season and both were attired in seersucker and both wore fresh-whitened shoes. They tipped their hats simultaneously.

"Miss Lia!" smiled Neville. "What are you doing waist-deep in *hay*?"

Miss Faber was tiny and endured with stony smiles jokes about her stature. Smart-ass Neville, she thought, go to hell, but she replied sweetly in her most lilting tones. "Have you ever studied—I mean really studied—the architrave on the Goldsby house?"

"Huh?" asked Jarvis, blank.

"Why, now that you mention it, I don't think..." began Neville, and pulled off his hat, shaded an eye with one hand, and followed her gaze.

"The detail is so fine," purred Miss Faber. "Just as nice as anything on a Roman palace."

"Very fine," said Neville.

"Of course the relation of the pitch of the central roof section to the roofs of the side sections...is something to consider as well...a perfect example of dynamic symmetry... *oooh!*"

Her tiny strangulated cry was taken as ecstatic appreciation by the two young men, but it had been drawn from her by the sensation that her bloomers were sliding irresistibly to the ground, effectively fixing her ankles, making all movement impossible. They darted looks at her after that part coo, part gasp, but she stared resolutely upward, so they looked back at the top of the Goldsby house, too.

"As for that chimney..." she said faintly. "Why, that chimney! Look at it! Doesn't it put you in mind of the Lee plantation at Stratford, Virginia?" Surreptitiously yanking a leg upward, she went on vehemently: "And as for those gates!" (Tug!) "Those gates!" (A harder tug, with the other leg; fixed to the ground by the iron grasp of fallen bloomers.) "Those gates...oh, you know, we *must* have a study club to consider all this...perhaps publish some monographs..."

Now Neville, forgetting white shoes, alarmed her by stepping forward into the grass, ruining his white shoes. Jarvis, unenthusiastic, remained on the sidewalk, said, "Oh, we've got some fine old houses in Mobile, but you think anybody'd want to *read* about them?"

"Some people *do* read!" twittered Miss Faber lightly, glancing straight at him for the first time.

"You're right," said Neville, thoughtfully. "They've torn down so many of our grand old houses. Grandma's is still standing, but empty, out on Dauphin. We could have a meeting there and have punch. Ollie keeps it cleaned up, and there's still chairs and tables and kitchen stuff."

Miss Faber kept her eyes on the roof of the Goldsby house, and wriggled her left foot forcefully. "Why, look at those gutter pipes... and aren't those ornamental braces treasures? Just treasures!"

"Yes," said Neville, still contemplative. "They really ought to keep these places in order..."

"Yawl are right, hon!" put in a new voice and they saw that Alice Babbs had joined them and was behind Jarvis who stared at the roof. He stood aside, tipping his hat. Neville nodded, replaced his hat.

"I love that house, the details and all," cried Alice. "I hope they'll never tear it down. Look at those odd red and blue panes here and there in the bow windows. Know what they mean? Well, when the Yankee beasts were billeted there in the War, people busted out those panes. The Goldsbys replaced them with the colors of the Confederate flag, red and blue, as a souvenir of all that happened."

"I swan!" said Neville. "I never heard that!"

"Gospel!" said Alice. "People have just plumb forgot their heritage."

"Just what I was saying," crowed Miss Faber. "We should study our architecture and our history. Neville agrees."

"Yeah, these old houses," Jarvis suddenly found his voice. "They's more than just wood and bricks. Remember Buddy Maystone? He lived in Paris all that time...his Papa died and his brother and sisters sold the house... said he didn't answer his letters...so they sold it...years later he came home, went to St. Michael Street to get his books that were in the attic... and the house was gone... Nothing left but the front steps leading up to air. He took his belt and got busy hanging himself in a chinaberry tree. Miss Henry saw from her porch and ran to stop him, but he was hanging already and kicked out one of her teeth. Watch her smile at All Saints next Sunday; it's the gold tooth on the left hand side."

"Houses!" said Alice. "They're not shells, they're repositories. Remember Betty Underdown who was so mean to her Mama? Her Mama lived alone on St. Louis Street for nigh-on forty years. She died and was buried before Betty came home and she just came to grab the jewelry and sell the house and she got out of the taxi and went up with the lawyer and he opened the door for her then went to pay the taxi, he'd come in his car, she's like royalty and doesn't carry money, and Lord, the way he tells it, he heard her scream in the front hall, 'No, Mama, no, no!' and when he got there she was lying on the stairs, blue in the face, dying in a fit. He said she was frothing at the mouth, just frothing at the mouth." Alice lowered her voice for the thrilling moment of her impromptu recital. "She was strangled by invisible hands! He said she was just blue in the face! Blue! Strangled by invisible hands!"

And I, thought Lia Faber to herself, must spend the rest of my mortal life rooted here with these morons, gripped by this pair of invisible hands which grasp my ankle. She tugged slightly with one foot.

"We'll get up a society," said Neville, taking charge as always. "We'll put Jarvis in charge. He'll arrange about the rum punch. And he'll get Bidgoods' to donate some tablets. If we're going to have a meeting, I reckon as how we'll want tablets, won't we?"

"And Number Two pencils," smiled Miss Faber. "I'd rather have two dozen sharpened Number Two pencils than all the long-stemmed red roses on earth."

"Well, and Sis and Bubba Beckerstall will want to join us. After all, he is an architect..."

"All the architects have to join," said Jarvis. "They know all about architraves, maybe they'll teach us."

"Some people can't be taught," muttered Miss Faber, then chirped, "I think that's a grand idea; when shall we begin?" Very cautiously she attempted to lift one foot from the wadded wool.

"Chiggers bothering you?" enquired Neville politely, sensing her secret treading in the high grass.

"But just look at that architrave!" cried Miss Faber in alarm, glancing at Alice.

"I have, often," said Alice, puzzled.

"How it changes when the light changes!" cried Miss Faber.

"Sure," said Neville, winking at Jarvis.

"Hey, Nev," said Jarvis. "We gotta get to the Bank in ten minutes."

"Sure," said Neville.

Miss Faber seized her opportunity. "Leave me here," she said to no one in particular. "I want to collect my thoughts. We'll organize the meeting for next week, any night you like. I'll wait for your call, Jarvis. But leave me now, I want to collect my thoughts...I want to *absorb* this building..."

Her gesture was superb, and did, indeed, send them all off. Palm outward, hand near her chin, her arm reached out to its full length in mid-air. From across the street it might have seemed Renunciation, Last Words, or Hailing a Cab.

Neville stepped back onto the sidewalk, stamping his feet. Lia knew that Alice would toddle along after Neville. She was as good as rid of them. But she trembled during their last exchanges, their leave-taking chatter in Southern style, as if leisurely sunny centuries stretched before them. Sunny and clear and calm, like this day. Finally Neville said, "Well, we'll call it the *Save the Architrave and Rum Punch Society*, Miss Lia, huh?"

"As you wish," she replied, almost faint with anxiety.

"Miss Lia," said Jarvis, with more hat-tipping.

"Toodle-oo," said Alice and finally they all went off.

Following their progress from the corner of her eye, Miss Faber stood still and breathed a deep sigh of relief, then waited for a street car to pass, and a truck. There came a lull in traffic. She put her basket on the carriage mount, bent over, and extricated her feet from the grappling bloomers, grabbed her things and scuttled across Government Street, tottering into a side street taking her toward Phillips' Pharmacy in Dauphin Street.

"Dr. Phillips," she begged. "I've been taken poorly, I feel as if I might faint. Could I just sit a moment in your back room and sip a brandy?"

He led the way without a word, so she collapsed into an old bentwood chair amidst a bracing redolence of iodine, cardamon, quinine, lavender, and rubbing alcohol. She sipped her brandy.

"*Save the Architecture and Rum Punch Society*, indeed," she muttered. "Better the *Shed a Skin and Save a Face with Cognac Society*. Whew! Mine was indeed an historical preservation...Why, double damnation, that's what we'll call it...O Elijah, Vishnu, Buddha and Louisa May Alcott, that's it!"

"Ma'am?" asked the pharmacist, parting the curtains in the door to the shop. "Feeling better?"

"You bet!"she said lightly. "How much, please?"

He told her, she paid, then [smiled] brightly at him.

"Historical preservation," she chimed, straightened her hat and sailed conqueringly down Dauphin for her picnic in the square.

#   #   #

So that's how it started. Through the years the ranks have swelled and now there they go, marching down Government Street.

"Forward!" shouts Miss Charlie.

"My God, where's the Chairman of the Fountain Committee? Where is she?" comes a voice.

"She got stuck in Conception!" roars Miss Charlie, then shakes her reins and cries, "Storm the citadel!" and Rob Roy lowers his horns and turns into Royal Street with a clatter. The petition-bearers enter City Hall, the City Commissioners stir uneasily in their chairs. Somewhere a train hoots as the ladies begin their club song, *Burning Issues*, the pigeons take flight, and the protest march enters into history.

Excuse Me, Ma'am

by Eugene Walter

Mrs. Mountjoy was not truly a mean lady; just nervous. Like take the time she spent all morning fuming with not the best results.

She had just moved into the grand new mansion her husband had built for her. She was striding about the elegant parlor, changing positions of ashtrays—she smoked ferociously; there were ashtrays everywhere. She lit a cigarette, snapped her lighter lid closed with a bang and strode to a window. Now, she paused to study her new blonde wig in the Venetian mirror. Impulsively she picked up the phone by the mirror. She dialed the beauty parlor.

"This is Mrs. Mountjoy," she croaked. "Give me Miss Maybelle."

Maybelle came quickly, slightly shaken. She had barely gotten out the "Hell—" in hello before the other end attacked.

"Maybelle, this way you did the wig is all wrong...I mean it's too flat over the ears and the bangs are too fluffy...now, I'm paying you to get things right so why didn't you? I mean—"

"Oh, Mrs. Mountjoy, I'm real sorry...look, honey, Alice is going to the hospital like she does every Saturday to do old Miss Muncie and I'll tell her to come by your place first. She'll be there right away."

"Good!" snapped the châtelaine and hung up. Puffing energetically, sending out little nervous clouds, she went to the window and lifted the lace curtain to gaze at a tall young man who was raking leaves.

"Oh, God!" she said, and rang a little enamel push-button on the desk. She had only puffed twice before a nervous middle-aged black lady rushed into the room.

"Yes, ma'am?"

"Beulah, run out there and tell that idiot Jenkins to come in here to me right away!"

"Yes'm," said Beulah and hurried out, crossing herself in the hall.

Mrs. Mountjoy dialed a number.

"Happy Day Nurseries," came a jovial middle-aged male voice over the phone.

"Mr. Waggett," growled the lady. "I've just been standing at my window looking out at the things you planted yesterday. I was in town, you know, checking on that fool cabinet-maker, so I didn't see how you placed these dogwoods and crêpe myrtles...all wrong! All wrong! When they've grown some, in about three years from now, I won't be able to see the fountain at all. I want you out here tomorrow morning early to move them all about six yards toward the east, you hear me?"

"Well, I planted where Mr. Mountjoy showed me he wanted'em," replied the nurseryman quietly.

"Bill doesn't have any idea about where to place a tree!" she howled. "You get out here tomorrow morning!"

"Yes, ma'am," said the nurseryman as he thought of how he'd pad the bill.

She dialed another number. She puffed and puffed until someone replied at the other end.

"Grace," she stormed, eyeing the lace curtains, "one of these curtains is at least six inches shorter than the others. I want you to come take it down and do it right and get it back here for my party on Tuesday. You hear me?"

"Sure," said Grace and hung up. Mrs. Mountjoy looked out the window and rapped on the glass. The room was full of smoke. She stubbed out and lit another.

She saw the gardener had not heard her and banged harder on the pane, then screamed. He looked up calmly, tipped his hat, looked puzzled, then put down his rake and started toward the house. Smoke everywhere. She opened a window a bit. The gardener cracked the door and smiled.

"Come in here, Jenkins," she said. "I want you to..."

"Oh, Mrs. Mountjoy!" he said nervously but she broke in.

"Look out of this window! Those perennials! How come they're in groups of six and eight at this end of the bed and all spaced out, two or three to a foot, at the other end..."

"Oh, listen, ma'am," he said with a nervous gesture.

"Don't interrupt me! Where are your manners? Now, I want you to—"

He shouted. "Please, Mrs. Mountjoy, listen to me!" He started toward her.

"Why should I? We pay you to do a good job. I can't stand sloppiness. I insist that—"

The young man asserted himself, with a scowl. "Goddamn it, you listen to me!"

She interrupted with a gasp, coughing, but he stopped her.

"Shit, lady, I'm trying to tell you that your wig is on fire!"

And it was, too. He grabbed it off her just as she began to feel the tickle on her scalp. But the lace curtains were on fire, too. Then the wooden window frames. He ran for help, for water. She collapsed.

Well, of course, the house burned down. Mr. Mountjoy, nagged by her, was in the cellar with the plumber where he had been for several days. They called the fire department, but the lady from the beauty parlor had stalled in the drive and the fire engine couldn't make it in time. Mr. Mountjoy had been so busy with her last minute instructions that the new insurance contract was still on his desk, unsigned.

Later, the Mountjoys moved to Idaho.

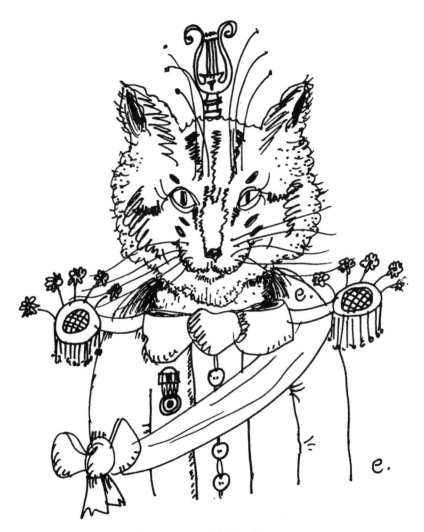

I was born CAT. lived last time
in Paris; long before, in Egypt... I'm
studying how to do the other six.

Stephen J. Zietz

Stephen J. Zietz is a librarian like his father before him. To Eugene Walter's annoyance, Zietz was then and still is a Leo, not an Aquarian. Eugene could never remember Zietz's name—first or last—and called him "the waterer," which was a paradox, considering that Zietz managed to water to their deaths all sorts of supposedly indestructible plants on Eugene's terrace in Rome.

Born in the Mobile Eugene knew as a youth, Zietz never adjusted well to the radical changes in Mobile's social structure brought about by the influx and ascendency of materialistic religion; he left in the '70s but returns yearly to have his taxes done.

Zietz was educated at St. Ignatius School when it was still Jesuit and had Sisters of Mercy (lots of them) and before it became "society" and secular. High school in Mobile meant McGill Institute for boys and the Convent of Mercy for girls: Zietz went to McGill. After high school there was no alternative but to attend Spring Hill College where his father was librarian. Zietz did, graduating top in his class. He moved to Italy to earn a Masters degree in art history. While in Rome he used his Mobile contacts and became acquainted with Eugene Walter. After a two-year stay in Italy, Zietz returned to the United States and received his Masters degree in librarianship from Emory University in Atlanta. He has also lived in Germany for a number of years and has worked for practically every library in America. In his spare time, he paints, writes, and drinks high octane coffee.

A Fictional Encyclopedia
(Excerpt from a Fictional Work-in-Progress)

For Southern boys with wanderlust, cats represent the independent spirit, good grace, high-strung passion, and sensual life style that is both desirable and unobtainable. They are a necessary part of the Southern household.

When I went to Rome to work for a summer in the big Jesuit library that is part of the Gregorian Institute, I was surprised to see just how Eugene Walter was possessed by cats. I was puzzled not by how much but in what way his possession manifested itself. Oddly, Eugene was obsessed with the *idea* of cats, making them conform to his fantasies about them. The names he gave them, for example, were suggested by the human characteristics he bestowed on them. I, on the other hand, let the cats call the punches.

I had arrived in Rome with references. Certainly more references from Mobile than anyone else who had been referred to Eugene's care. Adelaide and Ned Trigg and their daughters Mary and Eleanor; Nell Burks, of course; Eleanor Benz; the Bettys; and others "from home" whom Eugene had known at various times. He was not at all surprised when the *gettone* I dropped into the telephone connected me to him. He gave me specific instructions how to find him—too specific, too slowly drawn out, too pointed. After a few false starts, I found his building. He occupied the top floors in a Palazzo on the Corso Vittorio Emmanuele. Being quite young, not speaking the language, and terrified of the sheer size and confusion of Rome, I dared not take the rickety old elevator to Eugene's floor. I climbed the steps of the grand *scalone*—it was grand, but like the entire palazzo, run down. The top-most landing had a door to Eugene's apartment and a small set of stairs half a story up to another door in the back of the palazzo. Eugene's apartment was actually two apartments combined, the one in the front of the building with the large balcony was lower than the newer one in the back of the building with the small balcony. Eugene had not occupied the back apartment for as long as he had the front one. He had a complicated, dangerous (and no doubt illegal) stair contraption built in the interior to connect the two apartments. Following his instructions, I rang the bell on the upper apartment door. No answer. Fearing I had misunderstood his crystal-clear instructions, I tried the lower door. No answer. Eventually, a white and puffy face, very unlike the one in the photographs I had seen of Eugene in his youth in Mobile and not at all like that of the lithe sprite in the *Thrice-Patched Bustle*, stuck out of the upper door and said in a very girlish door and said in a very girlish drawl, "I clearly told you to come to the upper-most door in the building." I had arrived much too early, and Eugene was still in bed taking his afternoon nap. As I was to learn, he hardly ever arose before four p.m.

Feeling responsible for yet another wanderer from Mobile, Eugene was very annoyed that I had already found living accommodations. I had told him on the telephone that I was living in a monastery in *via del Mascherone* right off Piazza Farnese. He invited me to enter his apartment, and once we were inside, he proceeded to bolt the door with a bank-vault lock that sent steel bars into the wall, floor, and ceiling. I was relieved to think that *my* references were *his* references, and I had nothing to fear from him in his tightly-bolted aerie.

"You must be exhausted. Now, tell me about this monastery. How ever did you find it? Are you sure you want to be there? I mean, after all, this is Rome. You should immediately find yourself something more suitable."

I sat down on his beautiful yellow linen-covered sofa. "Father Navona arranged the room for me. He works at the Gregorian Institute. He says he knows you."

"That busy-body! He says he knows everyone. He's a social climber and would do anything to have me introduce him to all the right people. Now tell me all about yourself."

I got in few words about myself that day or any other. Eugene always did most of the talking. I didn't mind because the stories he told were fascinating; the people he knew were names I recognized despite my provincial upbringing.

In the months ahead, I spent many wonderful hours in Eugene's apartment. In fact, I spent more time with Eugene than I did with my fellow inmates in the monastery. Eugene commissioned me to do odd jobs; water his plants in his absence (he called me the "Waterer"), work on a bibliography of his writings, be present at lunches and dinners (that was the easy part), and paint over pictures he found, at least in part, objectionable. When not working for Eugene or at the Gregorian, or wandering for hours through the streets of Rome, when not being entertained by Eugene, I was to be found—at Eugene's suggestion—taking Italian lessons at the International House. There I met Dolly and John, two Americans on a lark in Rome. They were "up to something," but I never found out what. They were subletting the apartment of an American artist whom Eugene knew (of course). The apartment had a real full-sized American refrigerator—its only distinguishing feature—that Eugene coveted.... .

Padre Rossi, would not carry messages to me. In the monastery, I was cut off from everyone in the entire world except Elvira Echols Burks, "Nell." Nell and her husband Bill were in Frankfurt where Bill was doing a project for the Corps of Engineers. An especially close friend of mine and a dear, old friend of Eugene's from their years in Mobile, Nell chose my sojourn in Rome as an ideal time to visit the two of us. Eugene told me that Nell was due any day in Rome to visit us. "It's just like her to say she's coming but not say when or where she'll stay, or how long. Yoga Mae Pom Pom is just not reliable."

Imagine my surprise to be beckoned one afternoon by the monastery's porter. I could never quite understand what he said; his dentures didn't fit well, and he spoke a Roman dialect. He had never been to my room before. He babbled something about the "senora," and I followed him, thinking that Dolly and John had finally scaled the walls. In the entrance stood little Nell Burks in her modest but tasteful black linen dress with round neckline, the hem cut to just below the knees; immaculate white cotton gloves; gold circle pin over her left shoulder; small, black, pill-box hat with a mere whiff of net veil; lips pursed; feet and knees together; perfectly perched with equal weight on both tiny feet wrapped in black, low-heeled, satin pumps; a small, square, black silk handbag held gently in both hands at waist level. Nell had simply asked the porter to find Frederick Klash and deliver him to her. She asked him in her very best English, always extraordinarily correct and precise, with an unshakable Georgian accent. He knew that she was important, a real lady, and that she must have come to see me, the American.

#   #   #

Eugene announced to me and the world that his fiftieth birthday was upon us. He was having a dinner party to celebrate. Nobody famous was in town, so it would just be a few of his best friends. He had hoped that Muriel Spark would be there—she was traveling. The film-making wit "ini" was not to be had. Paul Wolfe, the brilliant harpsichord player and one of Eugene's friends who had rescued him from certain death in a Roman hospital, would be there. As would Theodora, a young American woman whom I called "Veronica," much to Eugene's annoyance. "Theodora, Frederick," he pointedly said. "Wherever do you get this 'Veronica'?"

"I just can't remember the name, Eugene. 'Veronica' comes more readily to mind."

"Just remember, 'Gift of God,' that's what 'Theodora' means. Gift of God. Forget Veronica."

"Just remember, 'Gift of God,' that's what 'Theodora' means. Gift of God. Forget Veronica."

For two weeks before the grand birthday celebration, I fretted over what I would give Eugene as a gift. I had little or no money, I ate dinner in the monastery each evening as part of my pension, and the only other food I had was what Eugene provided. I decided to write a poem for him and enclose it in a painting I would do for him. I gave him both on the morning of the dinner party. The verse began,

> *Up four flights of steps I ran,*
> *When waking up to find,*
> *A curious sort of monkey man*
> *Hanging from my blind...*

For the painting, I would do a watercolor of a cat and a figure holding up a drape with a birthday cake behind it. I had always worked from models or photographs, and I simply could not get the likeness of a cat down on paper. The figure was easy—I worked from a risqué photograph in one of the seemingly millions of Italian popular magazines. I roamed the newsstands looking for a suitable picture of a cat but couldn't find one. The owner of one of the stands in Piazza Campo dei Fiori was astonished with my request. In his sixty years of business, he chattered, he had never been asked for a picture of a cat in the city where there are at least twenty of the beasts per block.

I had been "repainting" some of Eugene's art work for him. One *gouache* on board that purported to be a portrait of him with two of his cats was my first victim. Eugene was particularly fond of the portraits of the cats, but he detested the likeness of himself wedged between them. He wanted flowers in place of his face. I agreed to paint a vase of flowers on brown paper and paste the paper over his portrait, queasy about painting over another artist's work no matter how bad the painting was. Eugene had this large wardrobe in the front apartment packed full of artist's supplies. I selected what I needed... .

For his birthday dinner, Eugene rearranged the furniture. I helped. Instead of eating in the lower, more formal apartment, we were to dine in the smaller, more intimate upper rooms. The table had to be extended out of the small dining room into the living room in order to seat the twenty-five or so people invited. We were careful not to bump the book cases Eugene had especially built to house elephant folios and a collection of monkeys in the media. He himself had decorated the cases with contact-paper, fabric, and all manner of cut-outs. They were truly fine pieces of furniture.

Eugene had restocked his day-glow liqueurs. These potent concoctions were lined up along the shelves of a dining room cabinet. They sported a wide variety of bright Mannerist hues and tints. He loved serving them for their colors, not their tastes which ran from bad to foul. The liqueurs made Eugene happy. After a long draw on a tall, thin glass of the multi-hued syrup, he would let out a long pleased sigh, his eyes closed; bring his two chubby fists together up to his breast still clutching the glass; open his twinkling eyes, eyelids aflutter, and coo with great drama, "Mamma, is it *real?*" In those instances, his puffy face looked childlike; he looked devilish and innocent at the same time. I was tempted to slap him or to comfort him with a, "No chile, t'aint nothing *real.*" I never did; either way, he would have understood.

There was also an abundance of wine. Eugene always experimented with new recipes, never cooking the same thing twice, oblivious to the ancient house rule that untested meals should never be served to guests. As usual, the dinner itself was not memorable. The company certainly was.

Theodora was seated next to me: "She's the daughter of someone important, so treat her nicely. I am sure you can find *something* to talk about. After all, she was educated at good schools, so she must know *something.*" This from a man who had never been to college and had no use for formal education. He was wrong. Theodora really had nothing to say to me or anyone else. She quickly ascertained that I, Frederick J. Klash, was a nobody, hardly worth her attention. She was interested—at least a little—in Paul Wolfe who sat across the table from us, but he had other more interesting conversations going on on either side of him. Periodically, Eugene would scowl at me from his position at the head of the table past the two unlucky guests who sat between us. He heard me calling Theodora "Veronica." He was not amused, and I couldn't help it. I hope Eugene's business transactions with Theodora's father were not impeded by my rudeness.

Paul Wolfe was a very interesting man. A harpsichord player who was in residence at the American Academy, his was a many-year friendship with Eugene. Paul was charming and handsome, but seemed to suffer the moody highs and lows associated with so many of the artists Eugene knew. That night he was particularly charming. He talked softly in Italian with the elderly woman on his right. She was the "clock-lady" who had the watch store on the ground floor of the palazzo. She was a "regular" at Eugene's parties. Unlike the dreary dinner parties I suffered many years later in

Newport, Eugene's parties never had an even number of anything: an odd number of guests, never an equal amount of men and women; uneven mixtures of young and old, high, mighty, and lowly, and the languages...his parties were true towers of Babel. In Newport, I was often called the "extra man." There was a law of physics or nature, or perhaps it was a local ordinance dictating all dinner parties in Newport be evenly divided between men and women, old and young, etc.

The guest of honor in his own house, our host and the celebrated host of Roman art society expounded on any number of topics. He spat great venom—cleverly colored, to be sure—on Richard Nixon. Eugene had a rather simplistic view of politics and the whole world: there were good guys and bad guys. Republicans were definitely bad guys, and Republican antics never failed but to reinforce Eugene's opinion. He followed the political scene in Italy, the United States, and France. Like so many of us from the old South, he didn't have much use for the English. *They* had betrayed us in "the War." Eugene was more at home narrating local gossip. That evening, he bowed to one of his guests, a young good-looking Italian male, and told us how there had been for some time in Rome a rash of cat burglaries. The thieves stole valuable pieces of furniture from heavily guarded palazzi. Not just any furniture, but the choice pieces, the very best there was. The new owners of the exquisite chair or the perfect table then set about making perfect reproductions. Five, six, or even as many as ten copies would issue from their workshop, aged and indistinguishable from the original. Much to everyone's surprise, the stolen furniture would then resurface at a police station to be returned to the owner. Or was it the original? No one seemed to know.

Eugene spoke foreign languages in exactly the same manner he gave directions, deliberately, slowly, and with exaggerated precision and pronunciation. Clearly not a linguist, he was nonetheless extraordinarily sensitive to the sounds and grammars of language, and senses, meanings, and nuances of words in general. His ear for languages was apparent when he strenuously objected to Nino Rota revising the tune to the theme song for the Zefferelli film, *Romeo and Juliet*. Eugene had written the lyrics to an early draft in which there had been a melisma over the first occurrence of the word "does" in the line, "A rose will bloom, it then will fade, so does a youth, so does the fairest maid." Without that embellishment, in the final version of the tune the word stuck out sorely and unattractively to Eugene. When Eugene's friend and sometime-employer, Pier Paolo Pasolini wrote his screenplay for *The Canterbury Tales*, he asked Eugene to translate the Italian version back into English *not* referring to Chaucer's original, but

On several occasions, I helped Eugene tidy up after one of his parties. I stayed on after his birthday dinner, but he didn't really want to clean house. He had imbibed too much of the bright purple (he said it tasted just like plums..."sort of") liqueur, followed by too much of the excellent wine always to be found around him. He wasn't sloppy drunk or maudlin, he never slurred his words, he just wanted to talk, and I was the last person left to talk to.

We were out on the large front balcony with all the plants, the avocado tree grown from a seed, the fuschia-arbor at one end, gardenias, and the pots and pots of unrecognizable plants that never seemed to thrive; they just hung on year after year, looking bedraggled. We sat in comfortable chairs, a cat in Eugene's lap. Eugene talked about his life in Rome; his life in Paris before; his editorship of *Botteghe Oscure*; his friendships with writers and artists; the correspondence with Dylan Thomas he'd been forced to sell to the University of Texas; Wanda Landowska, his friend; Karen Blixen and the puppet shows he staged for her; Muriel Spark, and the Black Holly Christmas parties; and, of course, his long friendship with the Princess Caetani, an American woman who bankrolled *Botteghe Oscure*, a lady who could never get over her noble Italian husband's dalliances with young women. They weren't all pleasant memories, but they were all good stories. He told me about his friendship with Leontyne Price. She had a ground-floor apartment in his building when she sang with Rome Opera. The little fountain in the courtyard kept her awake at night, she told him. However, after a few weeks she became so accustomed to hearing water splash, she was unable to sleep in New York hotel rooms without leaving the shower running. Eugene sighed, "For some reason she no longer speaks to me." I had no doubt that he had gotten too close to her, that his innate sense of Southern history...had reared its ugly head, and he had offended her with a careless comment.

Stretching—unusual, as he never stretched in public—Eugene got up out of his chair, picked up his drowsy cat, and moved a few feet closer to the balcony wall that separated his struggling rooftop garden from a sheer drop to the *Corso Vittorio Emmanuele*. The view was spectacular. Holding the cat to his chest with one hand, Eugene gestured with the other, "To the right the Gesù. Over there," Eugene turned with a look of great loathing to the left and pointed, "Gore Vidal. Poodles." They—Eugene and Vidal—had been feuding for some years; Eugene clearly resented Vidal's success. The *Chiesa del Gesù* was lit up at night, and its magnificent Baroque facade seemed but a few feet distant from where we stood. Gore Vidal also lit up at night, Eugene assured me.

303 MOMENTS / Zeitz

seemed but a few feet distant from where we stood. Gore Vidal also lit up at night, Eugene assured me.

I was exhausted despite my youth. Several times I suggested that I leave, but Eugene kept talking. I knew that if I listened carefully to what he was saying, I could live vicariously off his adventures, his tales, associations, and friendships for a long time to come. He sat back down, the cat happily sleeping in his lap. He talked.

"You know, I was so sorry when Judy [Garland] died. She was such a troubled soul. Small wonder, though, after all she'd been through. You know, she sat here on this very balcony while a party I gave was raging on in the living room. I don't give raucous parties anymore; this must have been some years back. There were just the two of us on the terrace. I hadn't even invited her; someone else brought her. I had never met her before and haven't seen her since. Oh, now that she's gone...In any case, she felt like talking. She said that she was happy to be out here with just the two of us, the air was fresh, the view inspiring, and it was so nice of me to have invited her to the party. But she didn't really like parties anyway, but so-in-so had insisted. She rambled on in her own nervous way. It was quite charming. I didn't tell her I hadn't invited her. I did tell her that I was happy she could make it. And I was! We talked a little, very little, about why she was in Rome. Some sort of show. She wasn't at her prime, and I couldn't imagine the kind of draw she would have in Rome, after all.

"Anyway, we talked about our youth. We had almost identical childhoods, but they were totally different at the same time. She was never loved. That was clear. I have always endeavored to be at the center of attention, and have usually succeeded. She didn't remember much about making the *Wizard of Oz*, she was so young, but she did remember that right afterwards, the studio boss, who wasn't expecting the movie to be a hit and wasn't prepared for another child star, packed Judy up and sent her to New York. Alone. To get a little culture, he said.

"So whose care does he send her to? Joan Crawford. Crawford was so sophisticated in those days (My, she's changed, hasn't she?), and Judy was, well, a very young star with little experience in the ways of the world. She's given enough money to take a taxi from the airport to Joan Crawford's apartment. Clutched in her tiny little hands is her one cardboard suitcase with all her clothes. We-ell, she arrives at the front door, the porter doesn't want to let her in. After much to-ing and fro-ing, she's admitted to the elevator up to Crawford's apartment. Meekly, she knocks on the door. Now, who should answer but Stevie. You know who Stevie is? No, of course not. I had heard of her, but, then again...Stevie was this dyke in a man's suit. She smoked cigars and had one in her hand when she answered the door. Stevie was Crawford's companion, bodyguard, and a whole host of other things. Let your imagination wander. You're young.

"Judy stood before the door in her cloth coat, her straw hat, her cardboard suitcase on the floor next to her feet. Stevie looks down at her, smirks, turns, and yells back into the farthest abyss of the apartment, 'Hey, Joan, it's the little hunchback.' Judy was called the little hunchback by all the studio bosses. She was, as you remember, a little stoop-shouldered. Stevie took the suitcase into the apartment, told the nervous and fidgeting little Judy to wait there in the hall. Then both Stevie and Crawford come out of the apartment; Crawford dressed in white sequined sheath, with a white fur coat draped over her shoulders.

"They ignored poor Judy, but her instincts told her to follow them— especially since they had locked the apartment door, and her poor little suitcase was inside. The three of them piled into a white limousine that sped through the dark streets of New York before arriving at a theater where one of Crawford's movies was premiering.

"There was this large crush of Crawford's fans waiting in front of the theater. This was, no doubt, all orchestrated like they did in the American film industry. The limousine pulls up to the entrance and waits a little while. With its dark windows, it makes the passengers invisible to the fans, but the three women can clearly view the cheering crowd. Stevie helps Crawford out of the fur coat she is wearing and helps her slip into another white fur that was waiting in the limousine. Stevie exits from the street side and goes around to the other side of the limousine to open the door for Crawford. Miss Crawford's bejeweled hand waves at her adoring fans as she exits the limousine, Judy fast on her heels. The fans go wild. They pull at Crawford's fur coat, snatching pieces of the fur. Judy's terrified and indignant. Judy turns on the crowd, slapping hands, and entreating, 'Don't hurt Miss Crawford's coat. Oh, my!' Crawford continues walking, smiling, and waving. Whey they get to the theater entrance, Crawford turns abruptly, a look of blood-chilling anger and rage on her face, grabs Judy by the throat, and shrieks, 'Keep your fucking hands off my fans!' Welcome, to New York, Miss Garland, and so much for class. As it turns out, Crawford kept a supply of rabbit-fur coats for her fans to tear up. The *real* furs were never sullied by hoi polloi."

When Eugene finished his story, it was clearly time for me to leave. I walked back to the monastery, rang the bell, hoping against hope that the porter was still in attendance and would open the *portone* for me. He was; he did. I slept very late the next morning.

Some weeks later, it became clear how Eugene supported himself in Rome. Yes, I knew about the glamorous projects, the work for the "ini's." He was in Fellini's *La Dolce Vita*, he had written and translated for Pasolini and Zefferelli, he was all over the Italian film world. These high points were few and far between, so there was also the bread-and-butter work.

Eugene was frantic. "She's left," he screamed at me in his very best diva voice. "She's no longer in her apartment. She left with that fast-talking Frenchman." "She" was Eugene's secretary—he always had one in his employ. Unfortunately, the secretaries were usually English, not American. Despite Eugene's dislike for things English, he was a sucker for the high-toned accents. English women, even at that time, were notorious in Italy for seeking out locals for sex. Their longevity in any one spot was determined by the quality and quantity of sex. I knew this even in my advanced state of obliviousness. Why Eugene didn't understand he could rely on no English female in Italy was beyond comprehension. "She left all my records in disorder." "Records" meant to me phonograph records, and Eugene had only a few hundred of those.

"I'll put them in order. There're not that many."

"No, you dolt, my scripts, my papers, and those South African bastards are on my ass to deliver." Eugene was clearly upset; no twinkle in his eyes now.

As it turned out, South African film companies would send him novels from which he was to write bang-em-up film scripts. Eugene never read the novels. He read the titles, the jacket summary, and combed through the text for all the proper nouns. He made his plots up. His secretary was supposed to type these scripts and mail them off to South Africa. The film script writing business was lucrative, but he had never seen one of the resulting movies. His real name was to be found in none of the credits.

Ann Dear came to visit for a few days. I wasn't expecting her, but she too came with references. She had attended Birmingham-Southern with Nell and so was "connected." Ann had a traveling companion, a young lady from her office at *Reader's Digest*, where Ann was an editor. She wasn't proud of it—*Reader's Digest*—but she kept up a brave front... .

When I arrived at Eugene's apartment one morning, he announced Ann's arrival and said we would be having dinner with her, her companion, and a set designer from the Washington Opera. The designer was there to do film work for the premier production of *Beatrice Cenci*. He had been to see *Palazzo Cenci* and now needed to talk "business" with Eugene.

That evening we all traipsed off to *Il Pompiere*, a restaurant in the Jewish ghetto very close to *Palazzo Cenci*. The name was the butt of jokes because in addition to meaning "the fireman," it also had an obscene meaning. It was near *Palazzo Cenci* and Eugene's apartment, and was well-known to Eugene. Upstairs on the *piano nobile* of an ancient palazzo it was exquisite and expensive. Eugene paid, and charged the tab, no doubt, to the Washington Opera. We were seated at a too-small table near the entrance, of course. Eugene could see all who came and went. The table chatter was interesting, as usual. Ann was talkative, Southern, and ever so bright and chic. Eugene was slightly guarded. The designer was clearly an asshole, and Ann's traveling companion could not be made to say anything, *anything*, even under penalty of spending the rest of her life having to listen to the designer make an idiot of himself. Eugene and I pitied Ann. Years later, Ann admitted she had made a poor choice from the office of someone to accompany her to Europe. Because Eugene had started the meal off by ordering wine and directing the formally-clad waiter to serve it liberally, I was woozy. I babbled. Eugene was annoyed, as usual, with me.

The designer stared at me uncomfortably—his looks did not go unobserved by Eugene. After the waiter took our orders, the manager sidled up to Eugene and asked him if he might bring the cook out for Eugene to instruct in a particularly complicated matter of food preparation. He had Eugene's number. The cook did, indeed, come out and listen to another of Eugene's painfully precise lists of instructions. He squealed in Italian sentence fragments with a stage whisper easily heard all over the ghetto. The cook made a great show of gratitude and bowed his way back into the kitchen. We were all just as impressed as we were supposed to be.

Hiram Keller came into the restaurant with his entourage of other beautiful boys and young men. He—they—brought two whippets on leashes with them. Keller made a beeline to Eugene, kissed him on both cheeks, and gushed enthusiasm. He was introduced to the assembly while his own party was seated in a back room. Hiram Keller had been one of the stars of Fellini's *Satyricon*. He couldn't act, but with his classical, homoerotic good looks, he didn't have to. Eugene had been coaching him for free in line delivery. Keller had been asked to read for a new film, and Eugene hoped to give him a shot at landing the part. Keller didn't get the part, and his star soon fizzled.

It was late when we all walked back to *Corso Vittorio Emmanuele*. Ann and her companion got a taxi to their hotel, and Eugene, the designer, and I went back to Eugene's apartment "to do business." That's the first time I saw it: Eugene's black book. Worth a fortune, the black book was stuffed not only with its original blank text block but also a host of ragged cards and papers protruding from all three edges. The book literally bulged at the binding. In it were the names, addresses, and descriptions of everything and everyone anyone needed to know about in Rome, Paris, and New York. The designer would say, I need costumes, or I need a location, or I need a really good photographer, and Eugene would page through his book and give him names and numbers. This amazing display went on for two hours. Eugene would tell the designer who to ask for, describe their English-language proficiency, and watch with disdain as the designer scribbled it all down. The book was held very close to Eugene's breast; he never put it down; it never was out of his sight. "This book," said Eugene, "will someday make me a rich man. And Daddy'll bring home greaseless chittlins for all his kittens."

# # #

That summer seemed so long—well, actually it was: four months instead of just three. I moved to Florence late in autumn. But I trained back to Rome whenever I could. More dinners with Eugene. I even played the "waterer" one more time. I thought of Rome in terms of Eugene. To this day, as I write this, Rome is still my favorite place on earth. Eugene left Rome to "go home."

Eugene Walter died many years later in a foreign Mobile, different from the place of his youth, different from the cities of his triumphs and successes. In Rome, Paris, and New York, Eugene had tried so hard to re-create the excitement of pre-War Mobile: imported stone-ground grits ("Now, they *must* be stone-ground. Those other mushy things just won't do.") covered with slices of imported Velveeta ("No *real* cheese has that plastic quality and that *orange* color that just can't be killed."); light verse and snippets of linguistic acrobatics; outrageous Victorian furniture whenever he could find it ("Those two cabinets in the formal living room I call 'White Elephants' 'cause they're black as the ace of spades. Ain't they the bee's knees, and I still haven't paid for them."); the conversation always riveting and never seemed to end; and the undying energy to go out to the barn and put on a play...or a puppet show for Isak Dinesen. He sacrificed great accomplishment in order to be *able* to live a grand life as he envisioned it: the life of a Southern boy and artist, the last embodiment of a lost, more advanced civilization. He directed his surroundings—people, events, history, and art—to support his vital habits, his view of the world.

In Rome, Eugene had been a relatively important person in a colossally important town. In Mobile he became a caricature of himself. He grotesquely aped the boy he remembered being and the artist he had invented. Just as the Mobile he and I knew had died and desiccated, the

Rome he knew was changing, moving forward without him. He was homeless. There *were* the cats, though. They lazily straddled the two existences, their backs arched over two continents and three-quarters of a century. Paws turned up pointing to the stars. Toward the end, they had their way with him. The cats did. From the beginning, he had directed their lives, putting words in their mouths, thoughts in their heads, comic human faces on their faces; he had bestowed *his* idea of their essence on them. He was wrong, and in Mobile, they had their way with him. That's what it was all about, after all, having one's way.

REBECCA PAUL FLORENCE
1913 8TH STREET
TUSCALOOSA, AL 35401
Sunday, April 2, 1998

Mr. Ted Dial
Ms. Renee Paul
153 S. Catherine Street
Mobile, AL 36604

Dear Ted and Renee,

I'm a little late in sending this, but I wanted to drop you a note to tell you how much Mike and I appreciated spending Thursday evening with you. After Eugene's funeral and a long, sad day that was what we needed most, easy conversation with friends "at table." Thanks for having us over. I know you must have been exhausted too, so I thank you twice again for cooking. The salmon was delicious.

Before we headed back Friday morning we stopped by Grand Boulevard to say goodbye to Don Goodman and to Eugene's house. That was difficult.

I always enjoy taking the back roads from Mobile to Tuscaloosa, especially in the spring when the pastures are green and the countryside is blooming. But this time it looked colorless to me. We drove back in silence. When we arrived home, Mike went to the grocery store to get supper things, and I went out on the deck and had a good cry.

And the most extraordinary thing happened. Miss Mattie Mae Harrison, a mature gray Persian who lives with our neighbor, appeared on the deck. In the four years that we have lived in this house Mattie Mae has never condescended to give me the time of day. Even during the many Saturdays when I work in the lettuce bed, she will not permit one pat. She reclines at the edge of the bed staring at me with cool indifference. If I try to be friends, she leaps away as if I am foul and beneath her society.

But Friday night she circled my flower pots and came to the base of my chair, where I was allowed to actually touch her highness's head. Then she jumped up in my lap and crawled directly up to my face, sphinx like. For a minute I thought she was going to give me a new hairdo with her claws, but instead she settled down, kneading my shirt with her paws. The original Miss Stuck-Up purred and rubbed her head under my chin, doling out lavish affection like we were old pals. We sat like that for some time—quietly chest-to-chest, breathing together, black velvet lips and little cat breaths in my face. And for the first time since the Sunday before, a tight knot just under my heart eased.

It was a celestial night. The sky was a clear blue-black, filled with a white half moon and constellations of stars. Maddie alternated between raising her head to scout the night and rubbing her face against mine. Then, without overtures, she jumped and disappeared into the darkness of the backyard.

I think it was Eugene, or at least an emissary.

Take care. Stay in touch.

Love, Becky

The Excelsior Band and mourners accompany Eugene to Church Street Cemetery in 1998
(Photo courtesy of Stephen Savage)